Navigating the English Language Classroom

Navigating the
English Language Classroom

Effective Practices for Novice Teachers

Lía D. Kamhi-Stein, Bahiyyih Hardacre,
and Jeremy Kelley

University of Michigan Press
Ann Arbor

Copyright © 2024 by the University of Michigan
All rights reserved

Published in the United States of America by the
University of Michigan Press
Manufactured in the United States of America
Printed on acid-free paper

ISBN 978-0-472-03911-1 (print)
ISBN 978-0-472-22077-9 (e-book)

First published July 2024

No part of this publication may be reproduced, stored in a retrieval system, or
transmitted in any form or by any means, electronic, mechanical, or otherwise,
without the written permission of the publisher.

This book is dedicated to
the many students who have inspired and taught us about teaching
—Lía, Bahiyyih, and Jeremy

We also dedicate this book to
Hannah Malena Stein (Lía's daughter)
Todd and Donna Meyrath (Bahiyyih's husband and daughter)
Stuart Evan Morse (Jeremy's husband)

Contents

List of Tables   ix

List of Figures   xi

List of Appendices   xiii

Foreword   xiv

Authors   xvii

Acknowledgments   xviii

Introduction   1

Section I: The Classroom as a Whole   5

Chapter 1: Building a Social Context   7

Chapter 2: Navigating Classroom and Institutional Policy   27

Chapter 3: Working with and without Set Curricula and Textbooks   45

Section II: The Teaching Situation   63

Chapter 4: Planning Lessons   65

Chapter 5: Delivering Lessons   83

Chapter 6: Fostering Motivation and Participation   102

viii   Contents

Section III: The Role of Assessment in the Language Classroom   123

Chapter 7: Understanding Classroom Assessment   125

Chapter 8: Implementing Assessment Expectations and Outcomes   142

Chapter 9: Managing Feedback   162

Section IV: The Integration of Technology in the Language Classroom   187

Chapter 10: Using Corpora as a Resource   189

Chapter 11: Using Digital Tools in the Language Classroom   214

Chapter 12: Integrating Learning Management Systems   236

Chapter 13: Teaching beyond the Face-to-Face Classroom   250

Section V: The Professionalization Process   265

Chapter 14: Building a Professional Identity   267

Chapter 15: Balancing Responsibilities with Life   284

Chapter 16: Additional Resources for Professionalization and Teaching   298

Epilogue: End as Beginning   312

Index   313

List of Tables

Table 1.1. Our Classroom Contract 13

Table 2.1. Overview of Institutional Policy Level Characteristics 31

Table 2.2. Overview of Programmatic Policy Level Characteristics 32

Table 2.3. Overview of Classroom Policy Level Characteristics 33

Table 2.4. Possible Syllabus/Calendar Components with Typical Corresponding Policy Levels 35

Table 3.1. Pros and Cons of Adopting a Textbook 55

Table 4.1. Sample Deductive Lesson Plan Activities 69

Table 4.2. Sample Inductive Lesson Plan Activities 70

Table 6.1. Summary of Terms 106

Table 6.2. Sample Activities for Visual, Auditory, and Kinesthetic Language Learners 111

Table 7.1. Assessment Instrument Evaluation Checklist 134

Table 7.2. Examples of Formative Assessment Strategies 137

Table 7.3. Examples of Summative Assessment Strategies 138

Table 9.1. Examples of Rubric-Centric versus Student-Centric Feedback Benchmarks 167

Table 9.2. Key Feedback Terms and Dichotomies to Consider 169

Table 9.3. Examples of Feedback Burden in Relation to Time 173

Table 10.1. Some Well-Known English Corpora with Their Size and Text Sources   193

Table 11.1. Digital Tools for Lesson/Activity Content Planning and Delivery   225

Table 11.2. Digital Tools for Project-Based Learning   227

Table 11.3. Digital Tools for Meaningful Communication (Video, Audio, Written)   227

Table 15.1. Tips for Relieving New Teacher Anxiety   296

Table 16.1. Strategies Designed to Identify a Mentor   305

Table 16.2. Web and Social Media Professional Development Sources   307

List of Figures

Figure 1.1. Sample student profile form.   19

Figure 1.2. Find someone who . . .   21

Figure 1.3. Teacher self-assessment on weekly multiple intelligences
use in the language classroom.   22

Figure 4.1. Reverse engineering a task to understand timing
and necessary steps.   73

Figure 8.1. Advantages of using a rubric.   146

Figure 9.1. Examples of direct, indirect, and semi-direct feedback.   177

Figure 9.2. Examples of marginal and holistic feedback.   178

Figure 10.1. Getting familiar with the iWeb corpus.   197

Figure 10.2. Find WordAndPhrase's icon on the COCA page.   198

Figure 10.3. Practice using iWeb with the word "researching."   199

Figure 10.4. Narrowing down results for the word "researching"
to verbs only.   200

Figure 10.5. Searching for verbs that frequently follow
the word "researching."   202

Figure 10.6. A sample activity with the word "suggest" using
the iWeb corpus.   205

Figure 10.7. Two useful search parameters for Google: "the exact match"
and the "wild card."   210

xii   List of Figures

Figure 11.1. Checklist: Tools under consideration v. principles guiding their use in the language classroom.   221

Figure 11.2. Digital tool evaluation form.   222

Figure 11.3. Food waste HyperDoc lesson.   229

Figure 11.4. Sample prompt engineered using ChatGPT.   230

Figure 11.5. Scratch project: About me.   233

Figure 12.1. Padlet activity embedded in a Canvas course.   240

Figure 12.2. Aligning student learning outcomes with weekly activities and assignments.   244

Figure 14.1. Suggestions of strategies for online self-promotion.   277

Figure 14.2. Reasons to market oneself online and/or create an online presence.   277

List of Appendices

Appendix 5.1. First-Aid Kit—Lesson Plan   98

Appendix 8.1. Graduate-Level Final Research Paper Analytic Rubric   155

Appendix 8.2. Upper Intermediate Composition Holistic Rubric   157

Appendix 8.3. Rubric for a Final Oral Presentation of a Film Class   161

Appendix 16.1. Professional Associations, Websites, and Social
    Media Sites   310

Foreword

Audience

This innovative text, *Navigating the English Language Classroom: Effective Practices for Novice Teachers*, provides a bridge from teacher education programs, such as an MA in TESOL, to the actual classroom for novice teachers. Based on the real life experiences of the authors and other case studies, this text effectively addresses the concerns of new teachers beginning their teaching careers in terms of practical suggestions and resources. Theory-based courses provide a foundation for novice teachers but often lack practical suggestions for how to effectively implement such knowledge; this text now fills that void.

Navigating the English Language Classroom is ideal reading for a practicum course and for newly minted instructors, but even seasoned teachers will find practical and useful suggestions in this text; all language programs should have this text in their library as a teacher resource. The strength of this text is that it focuses on real-life teaching concerns that many courses and programs do not address in such an effective and honest manner. Additionally, although the title states the English language classroom, this text will prove useful for any and all language instructors across a variety of levels from beginning to advanced levels.

Approaches and Organization

The authors' many years of teaching experiences in the United States and abroad competently inform *Navigating the English Language Classroom*. The text contains sixteen chapters that are divided into five sections. Each chapter template creates a layout that suits the information in a very accessible manner. The format of each chapter includes: *context, case studies, common concerns, effective practices, the big picture and the bottom line, food for thought, and references.* The authors are well aware of the concerns and worries of novice teachers, and as a result this text provides concrete advice and practical solutions for a host of issues such as lesson planning, assessment, technology, and professionalization. The chapters provide real-life scenarios that novice instructors can relate to and the "Effective Practices" sections contain very practical information that links theory to practice in a concrete manner. The tables and charts provide a wide variety of information from classroom activities and assessment tools to up-to-date websites; these practical classroom resources will prove to be very useful for both new and experienced classroom teachers. The "Food for Thought" sections are appliable to both individual reflection and pair or group work in a pedagogical course.

Features

This text does an excellent job of considering a variety of viewpoints, histories, and perspectives of underrepresented groups from teachers and students, and provides excellent references for further reading in these areas. The practical suggestions carefully consider the various perspectives of classroom instructors and students alike. The authors are well aware of the multicultural backgrounds and variety of learning styles in our classrooms and include very concrete suggestions for paying attention to and honoring this diversity. For example, the authors include suggestions for considering gender and sexuality awareness when creating classroom activities. "Section V: The Professionalization Process" is especially refreshing and honest. The authors' suggestions reflect how far our field has come in terms of applying best practices for championing student diversity.

This text is based on sound scholarship and research. The authors, as university faculty, have strong backgrounds in both current research and best classroom practices. Each chapter contains appropriate citations without feeling overly dense. Cited articles are from an array of scholars from various language backgrounds and institutions; citations include "old chestnuts" as well as very recent publications.

I know of no other teacher education text such as *Navigating the English Language Classroom: Effective Practices for Novice Teachers* that is so comprehensive and digestible; it's both scholarly and practical, and it's up-to-date and inclusive. This text is ideal as a capstone in a teacher education program, as well as a practical guide for those beginning to teach in language programs and for those who have years of teaching experience, since all language teachers, who commit to being lifelong learners, can continue to learn from their fellow instructors.

Linda Jensen Darling
Retired lecturer
University of California, Los Angeles (1988–2015)
University of California, Berkeley (2015–2020)

Authors

Lía D. Kamhi-Stein is a professor and coordinator of the MA in TESOL program at California State University, Los Angeles, where she teaches courses in methods of second language teaching; the integration of technology in the language classroom; educational sociolinguistics; and the teaching practicum. Lía has published chapters in edited volumes, edited and coedited several books, and authored many articles published in peer-reviewed journals. In recognition of her teaching, Lía has received several awards, including the TESOL Association Excellence in Teaching Award and the California State University, Los Angeles Outstanding Professor Award. Her areas of research interest are non-native English-speaking professionals, novice teacher identity and preparation, and the role of English in the Americas. Lía was born and raised in Argentina, where she learned and taught English as a foreign language.

Bahiyyih Hardacre is an associate professor of TESOL at California State University, Los Angeles. She has over 25 years of experience teaching EFL and ESL. She also has extensive language teacher training experience, has supervised student-teachers in teacher credential programs in California, and has served on the Board of CATESOL since 2016. Bahiyyih was born and raised in Brazil, where she taught English as a foreign language.

Jeremy Kelley serves as the associate director of UCLA's writing programs, UCLA's academic home for both English composition and English as a second language courses. In addition to being a seasoned English language educator, he teaches the language teacher training seminar for graduate student ESL instructors and mentors new graduate instructors through their initial teaching appointment. He also teaches the core language pedagogy seminar for the writing programs' graduate certificate in writing pedagogy.

Acknowledgments

The three of us are teacher educators who are English language teachers at heart. We love the classroom and the many students we have had the privilege of teaching, from our English language learners in both English as a second language and English as a foreign language settings, to the diverse group of graduate students and novice instructors who have helped to inspire the overall shape of this volume. Our identity as educators is without doubt the realization of our interactions with these amazing students and colleagues. Their willingness to share insightful questions and valuable experiences have made this work all the richer. As it should be, our most sincere thanks go to those from whom we have learned and from whom we continue to learn over our many years in the profession.

We also want to thank the University of Michigan Press (UMP) for their patience and support. We have immensely benefited from Katie LaPlant's feedback and constant encouragement. She has been our rock through the book writing and editing process. Our appreciation also goes to Kelly Sippell, former UMP ELT Director, who immediately recognized the value of our proposal when we approached her about this book project. We are also grateful for the support we received from Katie's team at UMP. It has been a pleasure to work with Annie Carter, on the production team, and Danielle Coty-Fattal, on marketing and publicity.

Our heartfelt appreciation also goes to our friend and colleague Linda Jensen Darling for writing the foreword for this book. We are also indebted to our manuscript reviewers, whose valuable feedback and words of support meant so very much to us. Finally, special thanks to Natasha Guerrero,

Nathaniel Fifield, and Suky Kaur for sharing example materials that were used in the chapter about pedagogical technology.

Last but certainly not least, we want to acknowledge our families who have supported us throughout our project. Without their patience, love, and support, this passion project would not have been possible.

Lía, Bahiyyih, and Jeremy

Introduction

"I find myself spending more time developing my lesson plans than teaching from them. I always feel I am not prepared enough."

—Teacher 1

"Although I am teaching an intermediate-level class, my students' level of proficiency is very mixed, so some students complete the assigned tasks very quickly and others need much more time. I feel some students are wasting their time."

—Teacher 2

"I am required to use the textbook, but I also want to integrate authentic activities. However, I am worried about not completing the book."

—Teacher 3

These three statements are not unique to the novice teachers with whom we have worked over our many years in the field of teaching English to speakers of other languages (TESOL). They are common among novice English language teachers around the world. Although language teacher preparation programs expose future teachers to a variety of approaches, methods, and techniques; prepare them to analyze and conduct research; involve them in reflective tasks aimed at initiating their professional identity formation; and provide them with teaching opportunities through their field experience, the transition from training environments to real classrooms is not a straightforward one.

When teachers-in-preparation graduate from their programs, they have an idealized view of the language classroom, which often clashes with the realities of the actual classroom (Farrell, 2006, 2012; Kanno & Stuart, 2011; Zonoubi et al., 2017). This volume is designed to bridge the gap between a highly theorized view of the language classroom presented in language teacher preparation programs and the first years of teaching. Much development occurs during these times, when novice teachers have to adjust to their new role as classroom teachers. To achieve this goal, the volume is written in accessible language and filled with principled pedagogical practices that are designed to inform teachers as they enter the TESOL profession.

This volume is designed to meet the needs of several populations. First, it is written for novice English language teachers working in English as a second language (ESL) and English as a foreign language (EFL) settings. Novice teachers in these two settings face similar challenges, ranging from practical issues including, but not limited to, answering students' questions, managing the classroom context, and teaching from a set curriculum, to issues of teacher burnout and language teacher identity development. In addition, the volume is designed for teachers-in-preparation, including students enrolled in graduate certificate programs and teacher credentialing programs, and students enrolled in master's and doctoral programs. In fact, given the wide range of topics addressed in the volume, we see it as an exceptional resource that can be used across the curriculum of teacher preparation programs. Finally, because of its easy-to-access language, the volume can be used with undergraduate students enrolled in TESOL minors or certificate programs.

Organization of the Volume

The volume has sixteen chapters organized into five sections that focus on independent yet interrelated themes. Section I, "The Classroom as a Whole," has three chapters: "Building a Social Context," "Navigating Classroom and Institutional Policy," and "Working with and without Set Curricula and Textbooks." "Building a Social Context" focuses on developing the classroom as a social setting with real and evolving relationships. "Navigating Classroom and Institutional Policy" explores the overarching policies that shape and structure the language learning environment. "Working with and without Set Curricula and Textbooks" seeks to understand the instructor's role in constructing day-to-day learning objectives.

Section II, "The Teaching Situation," has three chapters: "Planning Lessons," "Delivering Lessons," and "Fostering Motivation and Participation." The first chapter in this section, "Planning Lessons," delves into the process of lesson planning. The second chapter, "Delivering Lessons," is designed to help novice teachers transition from lesson planning to lesson application in the language classroom. The last chapter in this section, "Fostering Motivation and Participation," discusses how to promote motivation within the language learning classroom.

Section III, titled "The Role of Assessment in the Language Classroom," has three chapters: "Understanding Classroom Assessment," "Implementing Assessment Expectations and Outcomes," and "Managing Feedback." The first chapter, "Understanding Assessment," situates the concept of assessment as a core classroom component that is often underestimated. The second chapter, "Implementing Assessment Expectations and Outcomes," discusses the role of classroom expectations in developing assignments and writing task instructions. The third chapter, "Managing Feedback," seeks to address the concerns that novice teachers have to assess student performance.

Section IV, containing four chapters, is titled "The Integration of Technology in the Language Classroom." The first chapter in this section, titled "Using Corpora as a Resource," focuses on the application of corpora as a useful tool for independent learning. The second chapter, "Using Digital Tools in the Language Classroom," explores the use of digital tools for the purpose of improving language learning outcomes. The third chapter, "Integrating Learning Management Systems," is designed to help novice teachers understand the various learning management systems that can be used to enhance the classroom experience of ESL/EFL learners. The final chapter in the section, "Teaching beyond the Face-to-Face Classroom," explores how a variety of online learning environments can be exploited to promote equitable student participation and interactivity.

The last section in the volume, Section V, titled "The Professionalization Process," has three chapters. The first, "Building a Professional Identity," addresses the importance of developing a positive self-image to be an effective teacher and discusses the need for new instructors to establish a living yet evolving sense of professional presence. The second chapter in this section, titled "Balancing Responsibilities with Life," focuses on the importance of having teachers develop realistic self-expectations to avoid teacher burnout. The last chapter in the volume, "Additional Resources for Professionalization and Teaching," describes the various sources that teachers can tap into to identify instructional resources and engage in professional development activities.

The volume ends with an epilogue titled "End as Beginning."

We hope the chapters in this volume contribute to the knowledge base of teachers-in-preparation, novice and experienced teachers, and teacher educators. We welcome feedback and comments on the volume since, as teacher educators, we are lifelong learners.

Lía D. Kamhi-Stein, California State University, Los Angeles
Bahiyyih Hardacre, California State University, Los Angeles
Jeremy Kelley, University of California, Los Angeles

References

Farrell, T. S. C. (2006). The first year of language teaching: Imposing order. *System, 34*(2), 211–221. https://doi.org/10.1016/j.system.2005.12.001

Farrell, T. S. C. (2012). Novice-service language teacher development: Bridging the gap between preservice and in-service education and development. *TESOL Quarterly, 46*(3), 435–449. http://www.jstor.org/stable/41576062

Kanno, Y., & Stuart, C. (2011). Learning to become a second language teacher: Identities-in-practice. *The Modern Language Journal, 95*(2), 236–252. https://doi.org/10.1111/j.1540-4781.2011.01178.x

Zonoubi, R., Rasekh, A. E., & Tavakoli, M. (2017). EFL teacher self-efficacy development in professional learning communities. *System, 66*, 1–12. https://doi.org/10.1016/j.system.2017.03.003

SECTION I

The Classroom as a Whole

CHAPTER I

Building a Social Context

Contextualization

Novice teachers are often concerned about their lesson planning and delivery skills. However, they also need to consider the important role that the classroom climate plays in promoting a positive learning environment. In addition, to be effective teachers, novice instructors need to build a sense of teacher–student trust so that English learners (ELs) feel emotionally safe as they engage in classroom activities. In this chapter, we describe a variety of practices that novice teachers can implement to promote a positive classroom social climate, build teacher–student trust, and inform them about their students' learning preferences and wants.

Case Study

A few months ago, a recent MA in teaching English to speakers of other languages (TESOL) graduate—whom we will call Pedro—met with his former advisor to share the good news that he had been hired to teach English as a second language (ESL) at a local community college. Although Pedro still had a lot to learn about the teaching profession, he felt well prepared to teach the grammar and reading for academic purposes classes he had been assigned to teach. To be hired, he had to give a demonstration lesson, which the community college administration evaluated to be well planned and delivered. Despite all of these positive facts, our teacher felt very nervous about his teaching assignment. He was no longer a student-teacher enrolled in a practicum course in which his mentor teacher and ESL students were rooting for him. Now, Pedro, our novice teacher, had the responsibility of leading his class. He knew that to be an effective instructor, his lesson planning and delivery skills would not suffice; to succeed, he would need to create a positive classroom social climate that would be conducive to his students' goal of English language learning. Given the importance that the classroom climate plays in the language classroom, this chapter describes the often taken-for-granted strategies that experienced teachers implement to promote a safe and inclusive classroom climate

Common Concerns

The questions below are designed to uncover many of the unwritten practices that experienced teachers implement to ensure that they create a classroom atmosphere of camaraderie and trust that are indispensable to the positive functioning of a class.

- *Q1. What strategies should teachers implement to build a positive social classroom climate?*
- *Q2. What strategies should teachers use to build students' trust?*
- *Q3. What strategies should teachers use to learn about their students?*

We understand that these questions do not cover all of the concerns ESL and English as a foreign language (EFL) teachers may express as they prepare for their first years of teaching. However, the questions are meant to address the most basic, taken-for-granted practices that effective teachers implement to create a classroom climate conducive to learning. In the next section, we address the three questions and identify a variety of practices that novice teachers can implement to promote a positive classroom atmosphere and create an atmosphere of trust.

Effective Practices in Building a Social Context

• *Q1. What strategies should teachers implement to build a positive social classroom climate?*

While the social classroom climate is built over time, the first day of class is an important one since it sets the tone for the rest of the term. The first day of class is when novice teachers and their students start working towards the construction of the student–teacher relationship. This construction is

Building a Social Context 9

dependent on a variety of factors, which range from practical issues, such as the classroom's physical layout, to more philosophical factors, like the novice teacher's beliefs about their role in the classroom.

The first factor that contributes to a positive classroom climate involves using the classroom's physical space effectively. In preparation for the first day of class, teachers should visit their classroom and determine how they will use the classroom space to engage their students actively in learning, because interaction, proximity, and contact act as "gelling agents" (Dörnyei, 2014, p. 528). Novice teachers should become familiar with their classroom floor plan and ask themselves questions like: Are there individual desks, and are these desks bolted to the floor or can they be moved? Are there rows of desks or long tables in the classroom? Will instruction be delivered in a lecture hall with ascending seating? Questions like these will help novice teachers strategize how the floor plan will be used to maximize student involvement in classroom activities. For example, if desks are bolted to the floor and novice teachers are planning to have their students work in dyads, they will need to be prepared to have their students work with their partners to their left (or in front or behind them) and then interact with those to their right (or behind them or in front). If the classroom has movable desks, strategizing how to get students to interact may not be as difficult, since desks could be moved to form dyads or small groups and then returned to their original location. In summary, understanding the layout of the classroom before the first day of class will allow teachers to think strategically about the different grouping arrangements.

Novice teachers will also need to take note of the position of the teacher's desk and the instructor's computer station—if there is one in the classroom. If present, these elements may affect the teacher's view of the students and ultimately hinder the teacher's ability to communicate effectively. Traditionally, the teacher's desk is placed in the front of the classroom as this allows teachers to have a good view of the students. The situation with the computer station is somewhat more complex because, regardless of where it is located, it often blocks the students' view of the teacher; thereby creating a separation between the teacher and students. As novice teachers consider these factors, they will need to decide how they will use their action zone—that is, the area in which teachers successfully engage with students (Richards & Lockhart, 1994). To make this decision, novice teachers will need to ask themselves questions like: Can I stand in front of—rather than behind—the teacher's desk to reduce the physical and emotional distance between my students and myself? Will I be in close proximity with my students? And will my students be able to be near one another? Will I be able to make eye contact with all my students, or will some students be blocked from my view? How will

I avoid being positioned behind the computer station—if there is one? If I use slides, should I use a PowerPoint remote control to be able to move freely? Before the term starts, novice teachers need to keep these questions in mind. Keeping these questions in mind before the beginning of the term will aid in planning the teacher's strategic engagement with all students.

The last factor to consider concerning the classroom's physical layout is the location of the (white/black)boards. Are they placed in the front of the classroom? Are they partially (or completely) blocked by the instructor's computer station? Is there a screen blocking the (white/black)board? Given that ESL/EFL teachers need to do extensive writing on the boards, novice teachers will need to avoid making random decisions about their use of these very important instructional tools. In summary, canvassing the classrooms where novice teachers will teach will allow them to think strategically about the classroom space and how the space will be used to contribute to a positive learning climate.

The physical layout of the classroom plays an important role because it affects the extent to which students can engage in student–student and student–teacher interaction without any physical barriers. Although the physical layout is significant to the functioning of the class, a cohesive classroom climate is even more vital for student engagement. Students should feel they are members of a learning community focused on a common goal: learning English (Dörnyei, 2014). To this end, in preparation for Day 1, novice teachers should obtain a copy of the class roster and learn how to pronounce their students' given names, since they are associated with the students' identities and histories. Mispronouncing students' names usually has negative consequences for them because it produces a loss of identity or negation of the students' backgrounds or cultures (McLaughlin, 2016). In addition, to start the process of building a classroom community in which students start learning about one another straightaway, students could be asked to create name tents (with their preferred names and the pronunciation of their names, as well as their preferred pronouns—if this is a culturally acceptable practice in the novice teacher's environments) and display them on their desks for the first few weeks of class. This easy-to-implement strategy will facilitate both the teacher's and students' abilities to learn everyone's names in the class. In turn, this will contribute to building students' relationships (Davidson, 2014). Another simple, easy-to-implement Day 1 strategy designed to establish a teacher–student relationship involves welcoming students with a smile and a "Welcome to class." ELs may feel intimidated on the first day of class, and a simple welcome will contribute to a positive tone and a sense of connection with the teacher and the classroom (Cook et al., 2018).

Group cohesiveness can be further promoted by engaging students in activities designed to help them get to know one another (Dörnyei, 2014). This can be achieved by having students participate in motivating activities that are meant to foster student rapport and create safe learning spaces (Yeganehpour, 2017). One such activity is "Two Truths and One Lie," in which students share two facts and one lie about themselves and the class has to guess which is the lie. Another activity is "What's in a Name?" In this activity, students work in dyads or small groups and share their given names. Then, everyone in the dyad or group answers questions like: Why were the names given to you? Do the names have a special meaning? Do you have a preferred name? And are there other names you use? What do the various names mean to you? What would you like the class to call you? After students have shared their answers in their dyads or small groups, they share highlights of their conversations with the rest of the class.

Two other activities designed to promote a positive classroom climate and group cohesiveness are "What or Who's Your Favorite . . .?" and "Speed Interviews." These are low-risk affective activities that are meant to elicit students' positive feelings (Moskowitz, 1978; Richard-Amato, 2010). "What or Who's Your Favorite . . .?" can be adapted to different grouping arrangements (pairs, small groups, mixers, line-ups) and with different proficiency-level groups. For example, beginning-level students could be given complete questions (What's your favorite food? What's your favorite flower? What's your favorite place in the world? What's your favorite animal? What's your favorite name? What's your favorite TV program? Who's your favorite relative? Who's your favorite childhood friend?) and a word bank designed to help students answer the questions. Working in pairs or small groups, students ask and answer the questions. After the time is up, students work with different partners or groups. To bring closure to the activity, working as a whole class, students share some of the ideas they learned from their peers. By changing the verb tense from the present to the past tense (for example: What was your favorite food when you were a child?), the activity could be implemented with intermediate-level students.

The second affective activity designed to start building a sense of cohesiveness, "Speed Interviews," is an alternative to "What or Who is Your Favorite . . .?" In "Speed Interviews" students are asked to close their eyes (or pass if they do not feel comfortable closing their eyes) and think of a favorite memory (or food, place in the world, and so on). After this step, intermediate-level students would work in a line-up and interview their peers by asking and answering rapid questions about their favorite memories. In contrast to higher-proficiency language students, beginning-level learners would be given some time to formulate their questions in writing before conducting peer interviews. After the interviews, working as a whole class, students would introduce their peers and share a highlight about them.

The above activities, much like other affective activities, rely on the rationale that they can add a valuable dimension to the language-learning process. As noted by Moskowitz (1978) and Richard-Amato (2010), affective activities provide meaningful language-learning opportunities and, at the same time, serve as a means of student bonding. Although these activities have become very popular in the language classroom, as explained by Richard-Amato (2010), teachers who do not feel comfortable sharing their personal feelings should avoid engaging students in these kinds of activities. In addition, teachers should implement activities that are appropriate for their students' ages, proficiency levels, and cultural beliefs. Students should be given the right to pass, and the activities should be low-risk so that students do not feel threatened (Moskowitz, 1978). Finally, teachers should remember that the activities are meant to develop a positive and meaningful classroom environment and help students bond.

Establishing a common set of classroom rules also contributes to promoting classroom cohesiveness. On the first day of class, teachers usually share a list of classroom rules (also known as learning agreements or contracts), which describe the teacher's expectations regarding classroom participation, use of the phone, classroom attendance, and so on. Although this activity provides students with necessary information on how the teacher will lead and manage the class, having teachers *and* students engage in a collaborative activity designed to develop a set of joint expectations (Pentón Herrera & Martínez-Alba, 2021) will contribute to creating a climate of "this is our classroom and we build it together" (N. Issagholian, personal communication, February 15, 2018). In addition to promoting a sense of "this is our classroom," the joint development of the learning agreements contributes to increased student investment in the classroom since it promotes student awareness of the expectations for achieving success in the course (Dörnyei, 2014).

The development of the joint learning agreements could start with the teacher listing a couple of expectations and getting the class to share their ideas and come to a consensus about the final list. This activity requires students to have at least a high beginning level of proficiency in English, as defined by the A2 level of the Common European Framework of Reference for Languages (CEFR) (Council of Europe, 2001). Nevertheless, students who lack English language proficiency should still be able to participate in the activity by employing translanguaging strategies, which involve the use of multiple languages to create meaning (Vogel & García, 2017). In fact, translanguaging is a strategy that will contribute to a positive social climate because it will send the message that the students' home language (L1) brings value to the classroom setting. Table 1.1 shows a classroom contract that was developed in a low intermediate EFL classroom.

Although the joint development of the learning agreement promotes a sense of student investment, one issue that novice teachers should consider is their expectations for classroom participation and the extent to which these will promote or hinder increased language learner anxiety which, in turn, may result in a more positive or negative classroom climate. In this respect, novice teachers should consider their wait-time strategies, an issue of great interest in the teaching of English and other second or foreign languages (Nunan & Lamb, 1996). Wait time is the period of silence that a teacher allows after posing a question and before either providing an answer or moving on. English language teaching research has shown that teacher wait time is very short (about two seconds) (Nunan & Lamb, 1996; Smith & King, 2017). It has also shown that increased wait time does not necessarily result in more complex language use (Nunan & Lamb, 1996). However, from a practical standpoint, traditional, short wait time usually results in responses by the more vocal or confident students, while those who may need more time to frame their answers run out of time to do so. To address this issue, we propose that novice teachers implement a longer wait-time period and have the class wait to volunteer their responses until the novice teacher invites their answers. In doing this, the objective is not to have students produce more complex language; instead, what is promoted is a climate of what we

Table 1.1. Our Classroom Contract

Do's	Don'ts
Listen to your peers	Don't be afraid to make mistakes
Ask for help and give help	Don't laugh at your peers when
Respect your peers and your teacher	they make mistakes
Have fun	Don't' roll your eyes
Meet deadlines. If you know you can't, talk to me!	Don't interrupt
Participate	Don't use offensive language
Be open-minded	
Agree and disagree politely (let's discuss how)	
Working in small groups, add your ideas! We will add them to the list.	

call "more equal classroom participation." In doing this, the goal is to create opportunities for more balanced student participation, ensuring that every student in the classroom gets an equal opportunity to contribute.

The practical ideas in the previous paragraphs will help novice teachers as they strategize how to create a positive classroom environment. In addition, novice teachers will need to reflect on their beliefs about teaching and learning, since these will influence their instructional practices (Richards & Lockhart, 1994). This reflection, meant to help novice teachers begin to conceptualize their role in the classroom, will evolve as they gain teaching experience. Developing an initial theory of how their classrooms will function will help novice teachers bridge the gap between the theoretical knowledge gained in their teacher preparation programs and the real world in which they now function.

• Q2. *What strategies should teachers use to build students' trust?*

"Your writing resembles 'Chinatown English'."

This statement, made by an ESL teacher to Quy, a seventh-grade immigrant student from Vietnam, immediately destroyed the student's trust in the teacher and negatively affected the student's self-image.

This dramatic, though real, story points to the power that teachers hold over their students (Peirce, 1995). They can build them up or destroy their self-esteem. The question that teachers should ask themselves is: How can I be the exact opposite of our student's teacher? The simple answer is: Teachers who develop positive student–teacher relationships create classrooms where students feel they can trust their teachers and the learning situation (Rimm-Kaufman & Sandilos, 2015). But how can teachers do this?

At the beginning of the term, students will be watching their teachers. A single statement or a body signal by the teacher may affect their students' sense of security in the classroom (Brake, 2020). Therefore, novice teachers should make sure they treat all students in the same way, without any signs of favoritism or prejudice (unfortunately, that was not the case for Quy's teacher). At the beginning of the term, when students are still in the process of learning how their teachers operate in the classroom, they will be looking for clues that will help them understand how their teachers will treat them (Shindler, 2010). During the first weeks of class, students ask themselves questions like: Is my teacher judging me? Is my teacher judging my peers? Is my teacher fair or is my teacher showing favoritism towards some students? Is my teacher even-tempered or does my teacher get easily upset? Teachers need to keep in mind that their actions are constantly being watched by their students since they want to ensure their self-image is not questioned or negatively affected. At the same time, during the first weeks of the term, teachers should ask themselves: Am I making eye contact with all my students? Am I favoring the students to the right or the front of the classroom? Am I listening to all my students with the same intent? Am I paying more attention to males or females? Are there cultural differences in the way my students participate? And how do I ensure that everyone participates? Teachers should constantly be reflecting and acting on these questions (and others) to ensure that they are creating a classroom of inclusion and acceptance, which will ultimately result in a sense of teacher–student trust.

Teachers who are perceived as trustworthy have several qualities. First, they are consistent in their actions and decisions (Shindler, 2010). When students see that their teacher's decisions or actions are not random or subjective, they develop a sense of trust in their teachers, and this trust usually translates into the students' sense of "emotional safety and security" (Shindler, 2010, p. 53). For example, when a teacher is not well organized or makes unilateral decisions about assignment deadlines, students perceive their teacher to be unreliable or untrustworthy. Avoiding making unilateral decisions like these contributes to the students' feeling that their teacher cares about their opinions and wants to create a democratic classroom climate. This does not mean that the teacher does not have clear expectations for students. This means that the teacher is willing to share power and aims to create a participatory classroom environment by involving students in the decision-making process (Harris, 2005).

Second, throughout the term, teachers establish and maintain their students' trust when the instructional materials are culturally and linguistically inclusive. Specifically, in designing and implementing instruction, teachers need to consider the extent to which their learning environment reflects their students' cultural, linguistic, ethnic backgrounds (Brake, 2020; Gay, 2010) and accessibility needs (Tobin & Behling, 2018). The materials selected, the textbooks used, and the teacher's language and actions should promote inclusivity and connectedness. For example, when selecting textbooks or activities, teachers should consider questions like: Are there more males than females represented in the materials? And who is in a position of authority? Are there minoritized people in lower positions than the people in the majority groups? And what are the backgrounds of the people in the materials? Concerning the language teachers use in the classroom, questions like these should be considered: What language do I use to refer to different cultural and linguistic groups? What language do I use to refer to students with special needs? What language do I use to refer to minoritized groups (LGBTQ+ students, immigrant groups, among others)? When teachers disregard these questions, students ask themselves: "Does my teacher *see* me? Can I trust a teacher who does not acknowledge my culture (or language, ethnic background, and barriers to learning)? Is there a place for me in the classroom? If these considerations are overlooked, the answer to these questions would be "No!"

Third, teachers who show a caring attitude are perceived as being trustworthy. Teachers with a caring attitude are invested in their classes and their students. They have high expectations for student performance and provide students with the necessary support to reach such expectations (Gay, 2010). Teacher support can be given by providing students with consistent expectations for student performance. This can be achieved through the use of well-designed rubrics that students should be able to access in advance of assignments (a topic we address in Chapter 8). Rubrics, then, become checklists that students can use to determine whether they have met their teacher's learning targets as they prepare to complete course assignments or projects. Trust is also gained or lost when teachers contradict themselves and go back on their words. Not only does this create a feeling of student uncertainty, but it also leads students to feel that their teachers are unreliable.

Fourth, students trust their teachers when they are given a choice: that is, when their teachers are willing to listen to and act on their students' feedback (Brake, 2020). When multiple students question a recurring activity with comments like "Teacher, are we doing this again?," teachers should consider modifying their lessons to change the classroom mood or pace. In these cases, teachers could ask students to express their feelings regarding the activity (Let's talk about this. How do you feel about this activity? Should we continue with it? Modify it? Make suggestions!). Sometimes, rather than being vocal, students will signal their lack of motivation or interest in completing a classroom activity with nonverbal communication. Students may drag their feet to complete the task, take too long to join their groups, or simply show boredom. If this happens, teachers should feel comfortable stopping the activity and leading a discussion on the activity. Again, teachers could prompt a conversation by saying: Let's have a frank discussion. What's going on? What should we do? What do you suggest we do? If students' concerns are valid, teachers should change their course of action. While this is a decision teachers will need to make on a case-by-case basis, the fact that teachers are willing to listen to their students sends the message that they have a say in their learning.

Fifth, teachers could also build students' trust by creating an atmosphere that shows that students should listen to their peers and agree or disagree with them, though in doing so they need to be constructive rather than judgmental or critical (Brake, 2020). Teachers working with CEFR B2 (high intermediate) or higher proficiency levels could ask students to work in groups and brainstorm ideas on how they will show agreement or disagreement. The groups could be asked questions like: How do you show agreement with your peers? How do you show disagreement? How do you show respect for your peers when they are talking? When this discussion is over, the different groups share their ideas with the teacher, who consolidates the class suggestions into a handout or a classroom poster. Lower-level English language proficiency students (CEFR B1 and below) may lack the vocabulary to disagree using nonjudgmental language. In this case, teachers may have different alternatives depending on their teaching situation. Specifically, teachers working in a monolingual classroom (which is often the case in EFL settings), could have students complete the same group activity—as the one just described—in the students' L1. The teacher would then translate the students' ideas into English and create a poster with the students' ideas written in English. In ESL settings, where classes are often multilingual, students could participate in a whole class activity in which they practice how to show respectful agreement or disagreement through the use of frames; for example, students could be given a handout with frames like: "I agree with you because _____." "Good point! But I disagree because _____ ." Working with the teacher, the class would brainstorm the language they would use to complete the sentences. As the class engages in this brainstorming activity, the teacher will create a poster containing the frames, which will be made reference to throughout the class meeting

Sixth, though teachers are not trained counselors, it is common for ESL/EFL students to confide in them. When students trust their teachers, they may be willing to share sensitive information. In these instances, novice teachers should show empathy by listening to their students and referring them to professionals who can provide them with qualified assistance.

In sum, trustworthy teachers commit to implementing a pedagogy where students have a voice, and power is shared by teachers and students. Given the important role that teacher–student trust plays in the classroom, teachers should observe, reflect on, and pay close attention to their classroom actions, practices, and interactions. Doing this should be an ongoing process since a commitment to building student–teacher trust requires consistency and intentionality.

• Q3. What strategies should teachers use to learn about their students?

In addition to working towards the creation of a classroom climate in which teachers and students feel they have a common goal and will work towards that goal, teachers should get to know who their students are so that they can treat them as individuals. A starting point towards this objective involves administering a student profile form: a document designed to have students answer questions such as their preferred names, preferred personal gender pronouns, goals for learning English, and activities they do in their L1 and English. Teachers should try to obtain other relevant information, such as their students' academic standing in their programs (number of classes they have taken, length of English study), technology tools they use, and so forth. Ideally, the student profile form should be administered in a language in which students can freely express their ideas. Teachers working in EFL settings, where they often share the students' L1, could administer the form in the students' home language or English—as long the students' level of proficiency will not prevent them from sharing their ideas. Teachers working with multilingual students, which is often the case in ESL settings, may not know all of their students' L1s. This lack of knowledge can make it difficult to administer the form in the students' home languages. In this case, the form could be revised to include images representing the questions on the survey. An even more practical solution would be to have students complete the form in the students' L1 and translate it using Google Translate. Figure 1.1 displays a sample student profile form that can be adapted to meet the instructor's needs.

The administration of the student profile form could be followed by the scheduling of short individual teacher–student meetings to obtain more detailed information about the students and, at the same time, build teacher–student rapport. In these meetings, students usually open up regarding a variety of issues that may range from concerns about classroom participation and time management to concerns regarding the school culture and future career goals. Due to time limitations, sometimes it may be difficult to get students to meet with their teachers. To address this issue, teachers could treat the meeting as a classroom assignment in which students get credit or extra credit toward the final course grade.

The student profile form and the follow-up teacher–student interview would give teachers information on their students' goals and, more importantly, would inform teachers of the potential barriers to learning their students may face. Knowing this would help teachers understand the types of adjustments (deadlines, homework assignments, technology access) they will need to make for their students to be successful in their classes.

Building a Social Context 19

Student Profile Form
Term

Course in which students are enrolled (to be filled out by the teacher)

What's your full name?_____

What do you want to be called in class?_____

What pronouns do you want me to use with you? (he/she/they/other) _____

What language(s) do you use at home? _____

What language(s) do you use with your friends? _____

Why are you taking this class? _____

What class did you take before this one? Who was your teacher? _____

What do you expect from this class? _____

What's your phone number? _____ I will only call you in an emergency.

Do you regularly use email? If you do, what's your email address? _____

What is your preferred medium of communication? Check all that apply.

Email WhatsApp WeChat Text messages Cell phone Social media (FB, Instagram, TikTok)

In what language do you communicate in your preferred medium? _____

How do you do your homework? By hand On a cell phone On a tablet On a computer On a laptop

Where do you do your homework? At home At work At the library In the classroom Other? Where?

If you do, how many hours per week do you work? Give an approximate number of hours_____

What language(s) do you use at work? (If you do not work, leave blank)_____

How many hours per week do you spend in classes? _____

What else should I know about you? _____

Figure 1.1. Sample student profile form.

Another strategy designed to help teachers learn about their students and, at the same time, promote better language learning, involves working on the notion of multiple intelligences (MI) (Christison & Kennedy, 1999). The theory of MI, proposed by Gardner (1993), supports the idea that humans learn and acquire information in different ways. Therefore, to learn about their students' MIs, novice teachers could administer MI surveys that would allow students to report on their preferred learning modalities.

Locating MI surveys should not be a difficult task since the web is filled with surveys that can be used by ELs at different proficiency levels. When working with very low English language proficiency classes, teachers could have students complete the surveys in different languages. These surveys could be administered in class and submitted to the teacher for analysis of individual students' preferences. As an alternative, a more meaningful and informative follow-up activity would be to have students participate in a small group activity designed to share their top preferences, as well as their commonalities and differences. This type of activity would make students aware (or enhance their awareness) of their preferred learning styles.

Another way of getting students to share information on their MIs involves engaging students in group activities designed to have them share their likes and dislikes concerning the various intelligences. To this end, students could participate in a modified version of the "Find Someone Who . . ." activity (Moskowitz, 1978). Figure 1.2 is a sample activity designed for low-level proficiency students.

After completing the activity, students would be asked to work in small groups and tally positive answers. For instance, students would say, "Two students, Chen and Teresa, like to draw. Five students like to meditate." Then, working with the teacher, the class would create a tally of the whole class preferences that the teacher could use as a resource for materials development throughout the term. As an alternative, the teacher could ask students to submit their "Find Someone Who . . ." handout so that the teacher can get a better understanding of the students' likes and dislikes. While this activity enables students to interact with peers and learn about one another, it also offers insights into their diverse interests and learning styles.

The notion of MI should not be limited to learning about the students' preferred learning styles. In designing their lessons, teachers should integrate a variety of intelligences because students will learn better when they are processing incoming information from different perspectives. However, it would be unrealistic to expect one lesson to integrate all nine intelligences in Gardner's (1993) theory (that is, linguistic; logical/mathematical; visual/spatial; bodily/kinesthetic; musical; naturalistic; interpersonal; intrapersonal; existential). Instead, as teachers plan their lessons, they should keep in mind the idea that their teaching does not solely rely on one or two intelligences, and instead, have students apply a combination of intelligences, since this will promote better learning.

Figure 1.3 provides a checklist that educators can employ to evaluate the degree to which various intelligences are addressed in their weekly classes. As teachers use this checklist, the goal is to make sure that they implement a balanced approach to MI integration.

Find Someone Who

Instructions: Walk around the classroom and ask the questions below:
Student A; Do you like to….?
Student B: Yes, I do. Or No, I don't.
      If your peer answers no, ask a different question until you get a positive
      answer.
      Then, move on to a different peer.

Do you enjoy music? Do you read poetry? Do you do puzzles? Do you read books? Do you like to draw? Do you enjoy learning new words? Do you do crossword puzzles? Do you like to sing? Do you play a musical instrument? Do you like to organize your books? Do you play chess? Do you like to learn languages? Do you play any sports? Do you like to watch sports games? Do you like to fix cars? Do you like to do arts and crafts? Do you calculate sums in your head? Do you like to go to parks? Do you like plants and flowers? Do you dance? Do you like to work independently? Do you like to meditate? Do you play memory games? Do you take pictures on your phone? Do you play charades? Do you like to draw?

Figure 1.2. Find Someone Who . . .

| Area | Warm-up | Presentation | Practice | | Evaluation | Comments |
			Guided	Independent		
Verbal-Linguistic (e.g., partici-pating in group and whole class activities; listening to the teacher's input; asking and answering questions, etc.)						
Musical (reading & writing poetry; listening to & talking about music; participating in and writing Jazz Chants, etc.)						
Logical-Mathematical (analyzing grammatical patterns; studying grammar rules; writing Haiku poems or rhymes; writing and participating in Jazz Chants, etc.)						
Spatial-Visual (creating mind maps and drawings; participating in multi-media projects, etc.)						
Bodily-Kinesthetic (playing TPR games; participat-ing in mixers; playing charades; engaging in yoga and mindfulness activities, etc.)						

Figure 1.3. Teacher self-assessment on weekly multiple intelligences use in the language classroom.

Area	Warm-up	Presentation	Practice		Evaluation	Comments
			Guided	Independent		
Interpersonal (participating in group activities; doing team-work; engaging in peer teaching activities; participating in role-plays, etc.)						
Intrapersonal (keeping a journal, strategizing for learning; reflecting on one's values, etc.						
Naturalistic (participating in field trips; participating in activities focusing on nature, including plants, animals, and the environment, etc.)						
Existential (participating in activities that help students make connections between the classroom and the real world, show different points of view, etc.)						

Figure 1.3. (Cont.)

To end this section, let us ask the following question: Why are we placing such strong emphasis on the importance of knowing your students and the various ways in which they learn? Teachers' pedagogical practices matter. To be a good teacher, teachers need to have pedagogical knowledge and their instruction needs to reflect this knowledge (Shulman, 1987). However, this knowledge alone does not make a good teacher. It's also crucial for teachers to understand their students so that their instruction capitalizes on their students' strengths, fosters new skills, and is meaningful and applicable to their lives.

Big Picture and Bottom Line

This chapter was designed to describe various strategies, often taken for granted, that experienced teachers implement to ensure their classrooms promote conditions conducive to learning. While good lesson delivery is central to the learning process, equally important are the social factors that affect the classroom climate, since these can ultimately contribute to the success or failure of the class. By consciously and intentionally preparing to establish a positive classroom climate starting on Day 1, novice teachers will be on their way to meeting their students' needs by creating a community of learners.

Food for Thought

1. After reviewing the information in this chapter, interview two experienced teachers to learn about:
   a. Day 1 classroom activities designed to create a positive classroom climate.
   b. Strategies they implement to build their students' trust.
   c. Strategies they implement to resolve conflict in the classroom.
2. Drawing on the information in this chapter, reflect on your experience as a language learner or as a student in your teacher preparation program. Recall a situation in which you felt you lost trust in an instructor. What were the instructor's actions that led you to lose confidence in them? How do you think your instructor could have acted to keep your trust?

References

Brake, A. (2020). Right from the start: Critical classroom practices for building teacher–student trust in the first 10 weeks of ninth grade. *The Urban Review, 52*(2), 277–298. https://doi.org/10.1007/s11256-019-00528-z

Christison, M. A., & Kennedy, K. D. (1999). *Multiple intelligences: Theory and practice in adult ESL.* Center for Applied Linguistics. Retrieved May 2, 2023, from https://essentialsoflanguageteachingnet.files.wordpress.com/2018/08/christison-kennedy-multiple-intelligences.pdf

Cook, C. R., Fiat, A., Larson, M., Daikos, C., Slemrod, T., Holland, E. A., Thayer, A. J., & Renshaw, T. (2018). Positive greetings at the door: Evaluation of a low-cost, high-yield proactive classroom management strategy. *Journal of Positive Behavior Interventions, 20*(3), 149–159. https://doi.org/10.1177/1098300717753831

Council of Europe. (2001). *Common European Framework of Reference Languages: Learning, teaching, assessment.* Cambridge University Press.

Davidson, J. (2014, January 24). *Activities for helping students learn one another's name.* Faculty Focus. Retrieved May 2, 2023, from https://www.facultyfocus.com/articles/teaching-and-learning/activities-helping-students-learn-one-anothers-name/

Dörnyei, Z. (2014). Motivation in second language learning. In M. Celce-Murcia, D. M. Brinton, & M. A. Snow (Eds.), *Teaching English as a second or foreign language* (4th ed., pp. 518–531). Heinle Cengage Learning.

Gardner, H. (1993). *Multiple intelligences: The theory in practice.* Basic Books.

Gay, G. (2010). *Culturally responsive teaching: Theory, research, and practice* (2nd ed.). Teachers College Press.

Harris, S. (2005). *Bravo, teacher! Building relationships with actions that value others.* Routledge.

McLaughlin, C. (2016, September 1). *The lasting impact of mispronouncing students' names.* NEA Today. Retrieved May 2, 2023, from https://www.nea.org/advocating-for-change/new-from-nea/lasting-impact-mispronouncing-students-names

Moskowitz, G. (1978). *Caring and sharing in the foreign language class: A sourcebook on humanistic techniques.* Newbury House.

Nunan, D., & Lamb, C. (1996). *The self-directed teacher: Managing the learning process.* Cambridge University Press.

Peirce, B. N. (1995). Social identity, investment, and language learning. *TESOL Quarterly, 29*(1), 9–31. https://doi.org/10.2307/3587803

Pentón Herrera, L. J., & Martínez-Alba, G. (2021). *Social-emotional learning in the English language classroom: Fostering growth, self-care, and independence.* TESOL Press.

Richard-Amato, P. A. (2010). *Making it happen: From interactive to participatory language teaching: Evolving theory and practice* (4th ed.). Pearson.

Richards, J. C., & Lockhart, C. (1994). *Reflective teaching in second language classrooms.* Cambridge University Press.

Rimm-Kaufman, S., & Sandilos, L. (2015) *Improving students' relationship with teachers to provide essential supports for learning.* American Psychological Association. Retrieved May 2, 2023, from https://www.apa.org/education-career/k12/relationships

Shindler, J. (2010). *Transformative classroom management: Positive strategies to engage all students and promote a psychology of success.* Jossey-Bass.

Shulman, L. S. (1987). Knowledge and teaching: Foundations of the new reform. *Harvard Educational Review, 57*(1), 1–23. https://doi.org/10.17763/haer.57.1.j463w 79r56455411

Smith, L., & King, J. (2017). A dynamic systems approach to wait time in the second language classroom. *System, 68,* 1–14. https://doi.org/10.1016/j.system.2017.05.005

Tobin, T. J., & Behling, K. T. (2018). *Reach everyone, teach everyone: Universal Design for Learning in higher education.* West Virginia University Press.

Vogel, S., & García, O. (2017). Translanguaging. In G. Noblit & L. Moll (Eds.), *Oxford research encyclopedia of education.* Oxford University Press. Retrieved May 2, 2023, from https://ofeliagarciadotorg.files.wordpress.com/2018/01/vogelgarciatr lng.pdf

Yeganehpour, P. (2017). Ice-breaking as a useful teaching policy for both genders. *Journal of Education and Practice, 8*(22), 137–142. Retrieved May 2, 2023, from https://files.eric.ed.gov/fulltext/ED577116.pdf

CHAPTER 2

Navigating Classroom and Institutional Policy

Contextualization

This chapter delves into the intricate yet often delicate relationship between teacher planning and larger notions of policy within classrooms, departments, and institutions. Educators commonly aim to put their personal touches on their lessons as they administer them. But depending on the program, as well as the institution, new teachers may find this a difficult task to accomplish, especially in cases where levels must be observed, examinations are standardized, and learning outcomes inevitably dictate what there will and will not be time for. In this way, policy represents a shaping force in education and can be envisioned in its realization as both freeing and restrictive at the same time depending on its degrees of flexibility and rigidity, respectively speaking.

To fully understand how policy unfolds in the language classroom, this chapter explores policy implementation through the many official documents that teachers create as well as the lasting impact those documents have on classroom dynamics. The chapter also explores hidden policy-related concerns that provide the foundation for these documents but which may not be overtly apparent or articulated for whatever reason. Policy is thereby positioned as the central guiding principle behind instructional actions, where it acts as both a formative instrument in a course's design and a culminating set of benchmarks for an instructor's educational moves.

Case Study: When Personal Policy Is in Conflict with Institutional Policy

In a recent ESL course within a summer study-abroad program at a Los Angeles university, a first-time graduate student instructor encountered a case of plagiarism, or rather, what she had deemed to be plagiarism. The instructor had included basic information on plagiarism in her syllabus which echoed the policies shared by the university, only in a reduced and more accessible manner than one would likely find on a Dean of Students' official website. Her wording essentially positioned plagiarism as the use of another's words without credit given. She then offered examples of plagiarism, followed by a note expressing that any plagiarized assignments would be assessed according to the degree of severity. In this case, the student had written their paper in their native language and translated it in full through an online Korean–English translator. When she attempted to give the student a failing grade, given that the entirety of the paper was inconsistent with what the student was able to produce in all other assignments, she was told by the Office of the Dean of Students that she should not take action until a full hearing had taken place to determine malintent.

In the official plagiarism hearing, the student was essentially let off the hook because the syllabus in question did not explicitly state that a student could not write their paper in their first language and then convert the document into English using an online translator. For the instructor and their supervisor, such an act indeed meant that the work was not in the student's voice, as evidenced by the fact that there was a significant discrepancy in performance between what the student was known to produce in class and the near perfect phrasing in her translated writing. For the student, such an act meant that they were indeed using their own ideas, not those of another, and so the language was in fact theirs to use as they wished. Needless to say, this led to the supervisor implementing a programmatic change in which all instructors were given standard language to use moving forward so that a clear policy could be established that met the university's expectations and avoided a repeat scenario. This was not necessarily a negative experience, since it led to productive advancements in terms of the program's take on plagiarism, but given that students were verbally warned in class against the use of translators beyond simple words and short phrases, it was at least partially disappointing that a student was essentially able to manipulate the system, unethically bypassing failure due to a technicality.

Common Concerns

The questions below cover some of the more frequent questions that emerge when navigating policy at the classroom, programmatic, and institutional levels. As an area of inquiry that spans territories of knowledge that are at times less overt, and in many ways assumed, policy can be tricky to master. In many cases, it can be downright opaque given the fact that different entities can indeed read policies in different ways. The common questions that will shape this chapter's exploration include the following:

- *Q1. As a new teacher, what is essential to know about classroom, programmatic, and institutional policy?*
- *Q2. How can a new teacher work to implement institutional and programmatic policies effectively within their classes without sacrificing their individuality as a language educator?*
- *Q3. How much information should go into a syllabus? How much is enough?*
- *Q4. How can new teachers meaningfully showcase their personal teaching philosophy? What role do "personal" policies play?*

Effective Practices for Understanding and Implementing Policy

• *Q1. As a new teacher, what is essential to know about classroom, programmatic, and institutional policy?*

The most important thing to know about policy and its impact on curriculum is that in most cases it is governed by three distinct policy levels: the institutional (education with respect to society); the programmatic (where institutional policy is operationalized); and the classroom (implementations of curriculum collaboratively conceived through teacher and student interactions) (Doyle, 1992), though some have characterized institutional and programmatic as more closely intertwined due to their closer connections to society (Westbury, 2000). When we examine more closely the interactions between these three policy levels, we frequently see that programmatic policy supersedes classroom policy, just as institutional policy supersedes programmatic policy. Knowing this is vital to any new teacher's success, as conflict between the various levels can lead to miscommunications between students and instructors that can wield significant influence over grading practices, disciplinary actions, and general interactional dynamics, among others.

With regard to the institutional level, general policies focus on issues that apply across programs. Such institution-spanning issues, which are often connected to accreditation standards (Wergin, 2005) and national/governmental policy (Gornitzka, 1999) can often include enrollment restrictions, attendance policies, plagiarism policies, workload policies, and disciplinary action policies. For instance, if a teacher tells students that they must leave class if they are caught using a cell phone, they might in fact want to check the institution's position on this policy before attempting to enact it, especially given that students are using technology more and more in the classroom given contemporary shifts toward digital learning. Though research has shown that students use cell phone technology for a number of reasons, many of which result in counterproductive distractions from classroom initiatives (Tindell & Bohlander, 2011), students today commonly use them as real-time dictionaries. Implementing a simple technology ban in this way could, therefore, lead to a legitimate grievance on the students' part. In other words, the institution may see this classroom policy as a violation of a student's right to use widely accepted and pedagogically effective technological tools in ways that further their immediate educational goals. Notice also that this is an issue that could be applied across programs (making it institutional), though it could in many cases be delegated to the program or classroom setting depending on the institution in question's role and approach. Table 2.1 demonstrates the overarching principles that govern institutional levels, as well as a nonexhaustive list of example shaping forces and institutional policies.

In terms of the programmatic level, policy issues typically revolve around notions of standards, subject-specific curricula, and learning outcomes. Similar to the institutional level's preference for covering all academic units within an institution, programmatic policy aims to cover the ground across individual courses and sections that comprise a family or body of ideas with similar disciplinary objectives and outcomes. In other words, they are focused on program-spanning policies that are intrinsic to their internal courses and not to the courses of other academic units within the institution. To exemplify programmatic policy, teachers might mention policies that address standards for a given course that feed into another course within the unit. For instance, if courses constitute a series of levels, then programmatic policy might dictate that certain benchmarks be mastered before a student can be designated as passing a given course. Likewise, academic programs might designate prerequisites or corequisites that a given course requires in order to be seen as valid in terms of its completion. Such discipline-specific policies are often too granular or idiosyncratic to warrant concerted scrutiny by

Table 2.1. Overview of Institutional Policy Level Characteristics

Policy level: Institutional
Governing principle: The institutional level of curriculum encompasses what "schooling should be with respect to society," characterized by discourse on curriculum policy at the intersection of schooling, culture, and society." (Deng, 2010, p.384).

Examples of shaping forces	Examples of institutional policies
Institutional policy is shaped by • National educational standards and laws (e.g., the United States passed the No Child Left Behind (NCLB) Act in 2002; this was replaced by the 2015 Every Student Succeeds Act (ESSA)) • State/local educational standards (e.g., in 2022, the state of Florida in the United States approved the Don't Say Gay bill, limiting LGBTQ+ educational initiatives) • Accreditation standards and practices associated with the institution (e.g., the University of California follows institutional guidance outlined by the Western Association of Schools and Colleges (WASC))	**Institutions typically** • Affirm that academic disciplines meet nationally and regionally accepted standards (e.g., ensuring that language programs align with regional standards of achievement) • Establish term enrollment restriction policies (e.g., course enrollment cut off dates within a semester) • Approve instructional format change requests (e.g., turning face-to-face courses into hybrid/online courses) • Formulate plagiarism policies that affect all units (e.g., requiring formalized hearings) • Control disciplinary action procedures (e.g., enacting safety protocols in cases of confrontation) • Provide guidance on students with disabilities (e.g., issuing protocols for accommodations based on need)

the institution, all the while being too broad for the goals and outcomes of an individual course. To put it more bluntly, programmatic policy occupies the liminal ground between the macro (institutional) and micro (classroom) environments on either end of its boundaries. And though it is intrinsically connected to each, it is typically separate in terms of its scope given its tendency to prioritize the academic discipline as a whole before all other concerns. With regard to the aforementioned issue of cell phones in class, a program might dictate that there are some acceptable uses of technology that do not apply to other units. For instance, a cell phone can for all intents and purposes replace heavy dictionaries and glosses that were typical of the very same students a generation before. In this way, the program might generate internal protocols that better align with their discipline's norms and behaviors but diverge from policies on similar topics in other programs.

Table 2.2 provides a snapshot of programmatic characteristics, as well as a nonexhaustive list of example shaping forces and policies at this level.

Finally, the classroom level of policy is primarily concerned with the specific learning outcomes of an individual classroom that is populated by like-minded students pursuing a specific set of goals that all students must demonstrate sufficient mastery over. At the classroom level, policy tends to address the most granular aspects of education. Here, the course's design is established by instructors who find themselves working with a given program, which is itself within a given institution. In this way, to merely say that the classroom level stands alone as it relates to planning would be erroneous given that the higher levels often provide shape for how classroom curricula can in fact be realized. Nevertheless, there is agency at the classroom level that cannot be overlooked. As Ball et al. (2012) posit, "Policy is done by and done to teachers; they are actors and subjects, subject to and objects

Table 2.2. Overview of Programmatic Policy Level Characteristics

Policy level: Programmatic
Governing principle: The programmatic level of curriculum occupies "the intermediate level between institutional and classroom curriculum," and "translates the expectations and ideals embedded within an institutional curriculum into operational frameworks for schools," connecting "the abstract institutional" with the "enacted classroom." (Deng, 2010, p.384).

Examples of shaping forces	Examples of programmatic policies
Programmatic policy is shaped by • Institutional policies (e.g., at California State University, Los Angeles, departments must follow institutional guidance when establishing online or hybrid instructional formats within individual programs) • Accreditation standards and practices associated with areas of specialization or disciplines (e.g., the Writing Programs at the University of California, Los Angeles follow composition and rhetoric specific guidance outlined by the Western Association of Schools and Colleges (WASC))	**Programs typically** • Establish standards for learning outcomes for a given course (e.g., multiple sections of the same course taught by different teachers would follow the same outcomes) • Decide curricular standards (e.g., aligning ESL levels with the American Council on the Teaching of Foreign Languages (ACTFL—see Chapter 3 for more details) • Determine proficiency benchmarks (e.g., acceptable TOEFL scores for international graduate students) • Outfit educational spaces associated with a given discipline (e.g., setting aside budgets for language labs)

of policy. [. . .] Policy is complexly encoded in texts and artifacts and it is decoded (and recoded) in equally complex ways" (p. 3). To exemplify, let us return to the examples of cell phones. Indeed, a program might aim to allow cell phones in class for the very reasons outlined in the previous segment on programmatic policy; however, an individual instructor might take the policy further by actually outlining what can and cannot be done on a cell phone. In taking such action, teachers might provide language that positions non-course-related actions as distractions that are subject to reduced participation scores or to disciplinary actions by programmatic or institutional leaders. The classroom policy level is, therefore, the locus in which the language of the policies of all levels, in unison, takes shape and becomes a window of interpretation for all stakeholders. Table 2.3 summarizes the general characteristics of the classroom policy level, including a nonexhaustive list of examples that showcase shaping forces and actual classroom policies.

Table 2.3. Overview of Classroom Policy Level Characteristics

Policy level: Classroom	
Governing principle: The classroom level of curriculum represents "the enacted curriculum" that is "jointly developed by a teacher and a group of students within a classroom." It is an "evolving construction resulting from the interaction of the teacher and students" and "involves transforming institutional and programmatic curriculum embodied in curriculum documents and materials into educational experiences for students." (Deng, 2010, p.385).	
Examples of shaping forces	**Examples of classroom policies**
Classroom policy is shaped by • Programmatic policies (e.g., in community college French language courses, content is subject to level-based benchmarks such as teaching the past/present perfect, present, and future tenses in level one so that students are prepared for level two, where these tenses become assumed knowledge) • Instructor policies (e.g., based on their experiences, an instructor might determine that late assignments in their classroom receive a grade reduction of 10% per day after a predetermined amount of time has passed since the original due date)	**Classrooms (i.e., teachers) typically** • Specify participation practices (e.g., each student is expected to orally contribute during class meetings) • Determine deadlines (e.g., instructors set the day/time for all homework and major assignment benchmarks) • Convey assignment submission protocols (e.g., all essay drafts must be submitted to the learning management system where they are subject to plagiarism scans) • Establish grading percentages (e.g., the instructor determines how much each course element will be worth—note: this could also be a programmatic policy)

With regard to official classroom documents, the syllabus and course calendar are where policy levels take meaningful shape. These documents often act as a type of contract between instructors and their students, where some instructors even mandate that students sign off on the terms (Wasley, 2008). Despite such legalistic approaches, the idea of these documents as contracts is in some ways fitting for several reasons. First, the contract lays out the general trajectory for the course so that all parties feel informed, reducing the notion of contractual surprises in favor of contractual predictability. Second, the contract provides all parties with general guides for approaching potential conflicts between students and teachers that might stem from individual interpretations of course policies. Third, the contract establishes methods of actionable recourse that instructors can pursue when a given student is negligent of the policies that have been put in place. And fourth, the contract paves the way for actions that students may take when the terms of the contract are breached by the instructor. In short, the syllabus and calendar work to establish practical realizations of policy at the classroom level that are in fact informed by the programmatic and institutional levels within which the classroom operates. Table 2.4 lists typical syllabus categories and how they may align with policy levels.

Beyond these two essential documents and the role that they play in realizing policy within the classroom, it is equally important to understand each individual policy level in terms of its scope and educational mandate, given how their scope and interactions with one another inevitably give shape to educational outcomes (Johnson, 2012). In this way, the interplay between policy levels informs official classroom documents that instructors put into motion.

- *Q2. How can a new teacher work to implement institutional and programmatic policies effectively within their classes without sacrificing their individuality as a language educator?*

Creativity in the classroom is always welcome, especially given that resources are often scarce, and thoughtful innovation keeps activities current and engaging. Yet creativity frequently contends with supraordinate programmatic and institutional policies, which tend to win out in moments of conflict. Despite this pecking order, creativity can at times prevail when applied in ways that accept established protocols as essential while also simultaneously seeing such protocols as opportunities for subtle adaptation. This is not to say that all policy is negotiable, nor is it to say that the classroom is immune from certain policy-based standards; rather, it is to say that policy,

Table 2.4. Possible Syllabus/Calendar Components with Typical Corresponding Policy Levels

Components and Typical Corresponding Policy Levels
Class name/number: Programs typically determine these under institutional guidance that lays out frameworks for consistency (e.g., English 101: Expository Writing)
Day/time/location: Programs typically decide these (unless scheduled centrally, which may require the institution's input) (e.g., Fridays, 1–2pm, Building X)
Instructor information: Programs typically require these; classrooms typically require these (e.g., name/title; office number; office hours; email address; phone number)
Course description: Programs typically determine these; classrooms might provide input, especially in variable topics/themes courses (e.g., "This course is designed to. . .")
Learning objectives: Programs typically determine these (e.g., "Students will learn to. . .")
State or national standards alignment: Institutions may require these; programs may require these (e.g., learning objective 3 corresponds to state standard X)
Materials: Programs or classrooms typically determine these (e.g., course textbooks)
Grading criteria/percentages: Programs or classrooms typically determine these (e.g., "This course uses holistic assessment"; "Participation is worth 20% of the course grade")
Task descriptions: Classrooms typically articulate these under program guidance (e.g., "Essay 1 is an evaluative summary, and will be submitted as a draft and final revision")
Classroom policies: Classrooms typically articulate these (e.g., Cell phones can only be used for X, Y, and Z; student–teacher conferences are mandatory for each drafted paper)
Broad student body policies: Institutions typically set such protocols; programs or classrooms sometimes construct these under institutional guidance (e.g., Plagiarism includes X, Y, and Z; absences will be excused only when preapproved or medically documented)
Campus resources: Classrooms typically decide on what to include; programs may mandate (e.g., The learning center is located at X, and its hours of operation are from Y to Z)
Schedule of daily themes/content: Classrooms typically determine these; programs may mandate (e.g., Week 1, Day 1: English greetings; Module 6: Revising for comprehensibility)
Due dates: Classrooms typically determine these (e.g., Portfolio draft due date: May 1st)

for all its rigidity, often leaves space for applied interpretations that can allow individual creativity to take hold in meaningful ways.

One activity that certainly allows for individuality in the establishment of protocol is the concept of student–teacher collaborative understanding, which can establish a form of collective sense-making. Such co-constructions have been explored in terms of collaborative syllabus development (Shugurova, 2020) as well as collaborative readings and annotations in distance learning (Kalir, 2020), but the same principles can be applied, to varying degrees, to most classroom documents. Collaborative understanding means that important documents can be impacted through strategic sessions designed to generate collective interpretation. For instance, rubrics for graded assignments are most likely not a concern at the institutional level. They are, however, often a concern for the programmatic level given that courses across an academic unit often have internal standards that must be respected by all instructors. At the classroom level, a teacher may not have the ability to physically change a rubric, as this might endanger consistency across sections; however, the teacher may be able to impact interpretation by conducting a whole-class collaborative interpretation session, whereby the classroom community enters into deep discussion to agree on the general merits of the rubric and its inevitable application. Collaborative interpretation sessions reveal the instructor's understanding of the document and allow students to come to a similar understanding of how the rubric will be used. Such collaborative sessions help instructors respect the standards laid out before them, while also respecting the fact that it is ultimately an individual educator who will be responsible for implementation. By positioning the language of the rubric as an object of collective interpretation, subtle shifts can be made at the classroom level that respect the unique intellectual composition of a given classroom population, while also recognizing that classroom microcosms are still a part of a larger population of like-minded individuals. The bottom line is that the classroom level will always be beholden to supraordinate policies, but this does not render subtle adjustments impossible to achieve.

Some classroom policy-related matters may be more instructor-driven than others, however. Take, for example, the notion of materials selection. When courses are a part of a system of proficiency levels, there is often much-needed collaboration among colleagues in deciding on instructional materials, an act which constitutes a form of policy in terms of programmatic materials selection. Conversely, in courses that are stand-alone in nature, such as a single course designed to enhance pronunciation features across proficiency levels, individual instructors might retain greater agency in not only choosing materials but also establishing internal policy. Likewise, when training on specific content-focused or level-based aspects of a course is not adequately established within programmatic or institutional policies, identified gaps can provide instances for the invocation of teacher agency (Ollerhead, 2010). In such scenarios, individual teachers may have greater agency in the educational materials that they will offer to students, the prompts that they will use to solicit student performance, the rubrics that they will use to establish standards of assessment on individual performance, and the micro-level policies of general conduct they will apply in order to ensure that the course's learning objectives have been successfully and equitably met.

One additional tactic that new instructors can make use of to generate windows for individuality in policy management is to review all policies in great depth and have a clear and easy-to-wield explanation at the ready for each. This implies that any policy that a teacher includes in a syllabus should be easily explainable and, thus, easily enforceable. For instance, if an instructor says that up to two absences are granted without excuse before participation will be reduced, then there needs to be a clear understanding of exactly what a potential third absence would mean. How many points will be taken away? What will the student have to do to make up the time? Can they make up the time and also regain all points, or are they only able to regain a fraction of the total points lost? If educators cannot explain their own policies, then how can they hold students accountable? To paraphrase, all policies should be clear from beginning to end in the mind of the teacher, and if there is even the tiniest room for doubt or contradictory interpretation, then more work needs to be done on each policy's general articulation.

In truth, the notion of individuality in policy making can be hard to achieve, and this is not surprising given that the classroom level is at the bottom of the policy pecking order. This does not mean that individually derived policy is some sort of unattainable goal (Huang & Yip, 2021); rather, it means that individuality in policy is quite simply a delicate topic that must be handled with care. Too much focus on individuality can create conflict at supraordinate policy echelons, while too little focus on individuality can leave students feeling as if they are but cogs in a rigid machine that does not care about the immediate composition of their environment. The bottom line is that educating oneself on policy-level interactions will inevitably help to ensure success.

• Q3. How much information should go into a syllabus? how much is enough?

When it comes to policy, knowing how much to add or remove is always a concern. New teachers may think that they have laid out a policy in clear terms, only to find that when it is put to the test, it doesn't actually have the impact they would have hoped for. In such cases, students are often given the benefit of the doubt, and teachers are left to revise their syllabi once more after the conflict, adding more specificity as needed to ensure that incongruent interpretations are rendered clear, lessened, or in the most ideal of scenarios eradicated in full.

For all intents and purposes, precision is the ultimate key when it comes to knowing how much or how little detail to express. Nevertheless, when achieving precision presents as problematic, teachers can't simply beat themselves up, as no one can possibly know how every situation will play out. When policy challenges emerge, teachers must remember that every interaction, be it bad or good, negative or positive, carries with it the potential for growth. If, to illustrate, an instructor states X as policy and then does Y in reality, students will indeed have legitimate grievances in terms of classroom policy. In such instances, instructors, by their own hand, set themselves up for conflict or challenge. If a grievance is legitimate, the teacher is often better served by giving students the benefit of the doubt and circling back to the articulation of policy in subsequent iterations so that continued incongruencies can be efficiently negated.

The ultimate goal when contemplating the degree of detail in conveying various policies is, thus, to ensure that what is offered is enough for the students to clearly understand, but not so much that it leads to shut-down due to convolution or heavy-handedness. For newer teachers, lack of experience in terms of how much language is needed for clarity can be counterbalanced through in-class review. In other words, spending extra time on major policies, especially at the onset of a course, can provide interactional space in which to clarify important points before they come into question. Below are a few review practices new instructors might find useful:

- When introducing students to the course, and by extension the policies that support the course, instructors can model a "share the air" approach that invites students to interact and actively process policy language through open question-and-answer formats designed to tease out nuance. Here, establishing a "no

Navigating Classroom and Institutional Policy   39

dumb questions" stance frees students to ask questions that they might otherwise avoid asking.

- o Extension: Carry the discussion forward by addressing respectful communication as a core value of a classroom community. By doing this, the "no dumb questions" rule becomes a benchmark for all subsequent classroom interactions.
- Discuss what condensed participation language means and solicit micro-level realizations from students that can be listed on the whiteboard/chalkboard. Document their ideas so that they become active in the establishment of participation policies.
  - o Extension: Refine their contributions in real time so that misunderstandings can be rectified before they fossilize into misconceptions with negative consequences. Add any additional points that students do not raise by framing them as, "Oh, one other thing . . ." type supplements that complement the students' suggestions.
- Walk students through the syllabus, calendar, and learning management systems in a manner that ensures that they know where everything is located. This sets up a policy in which not knowing is not an acceptable excuse. If other policy-driven measures will be used, take the time to review them so that no one can claim ignorance at a later date.
  - o Extension: A follow-up activity to location walkthroughs is to set up a scavenger hunt where students work together to locate and explain specific classroom policies that are articulated in official classroom discourse and documents. The scavenger hunt is a great way to fold all locations of knowledge into one through collaborative discussion and research. It is also just a more engaging and fun activity, as dry rules transform into interactive windows of exploration.

The point of these practices and extended actions is to demonstrate that policy can be much more than words that are consulted after the fact. If teachers can get their students to understand them as guides before, during, and after tasks and assignments, then educators can lessen the overall negotiability of the policy language and its accompanying implications.

It is worth noting that once a policy is firmly established, be it through written language or through interactional discourse in conjunction with written language, it is difficult if not impossible to make policy changes after the fact. This is why it is crucial for instructors to ask the right questions at all times and to seek supervisory and collegial guidance when even the smallest of doubts emerges. Take, for example, the scenario of due dates for assignments. Due dates are not typically seen as fluid and negotiable. Indeed, time constraints within language courses are frequently examination-driven, which implies that learning outcomes have to be addressed at specific times in order to allow the student population to collectively move on to the next set of learning outcomes that must be mastered, especially at lower proficiency levels. If an instructor shifts a date, it can impact the overall flow of objectives throughout the remainder of the course, and this might in fact endanger the larger set of learning outcomes; this in turn could affect the next course in a larger series. In addition, if the dates are applied in different ways depending on individual students and individual needs, then the notion of policy standards in the course can be thrown into jeopardy, as policies, in such scenarios, are applied in varied ways that do not respect fairness across the population. All of this is to say that policy consistency is of the utmost importance in all that language teachers do in their classrooms.

• Q4. How can new teachers meaningfully showcase their personal teaching philosophy? What role do "personal" policies play?

For every official policy that is codified in the written language of the syllabus, calendar, learning management system, and supplemental course documents, there are twice as many unofficial policies lurking beneath the surface, waiting to be encountered and addressed as scenarios warrant them. In many cases, these more idiosyncratic policies might reside entirely within the instructor's mind, rendering them inaccessible to students. Because of their invisibility, unofficial policies often present as obscurely embedded within a teacher's psyche.

One less commonly articulated policy area in terms of classroom interaction is the notion of cold calling. Research has shown that cold calling can in fact improve a student's question-asking ability as well as their overall responsiveness (Dallimore et al., 2012). While some see cold calls as a dynamic interactional method for ensuring that all student voices are heard, many teachers frown upon them, as they see them as intrusive, placing students into defensive positions from the onset of the interchange. Regardless of the position an instructor takes, it is vital that students be given insight into how their instructor plans to interact with them. If cold calls are to be used in a course, the teacher can let the students know this early; the instructor can then let the students know what shape the cold calls will take.

Teachers might also have their own internal policies on extended communication practices. For instance, if students email without putting their name on their message or without a clear subject line (especially when their email address is not transparent), it might make a formal response from the instructor somewhat more difficult. Likewise, if a student asks an overly broad question in an email that cannot be reasonably answered with short, direct writing, then an internal, hidden policy that sees such requests as unfair might present as sheer negligence to a student who is expecting an official response. In a similar vein, students may email their instructor for help three hours before an assignment is due, leaving an instructor with little to no time to assist. The teacher's failure to provide assistance may be interpreted as an unwillingness to help. Finally, texting and chat forum culture has in many ways created expectations that teachers are on call and will provide immediate assistance when requested. This is untenable for countless reasons, but unless it is explained to students, they may never fully understand the rules of engagement. In all of these communication scenarios, teachers might be best served by simply sharing their philosophy towards communication practices in a proactive manner so that students understand what is considered acceptable and unacceptable behavior.

Some newer teachers might also have strong personal ideas about what is considered acceptable or not acceptable in terms of instructor flexibility. To illustrate, new teachers may see all deadlines as firm, with no room for negotiation. Others might see absences as unacceptable, except in extreme, medically supported circumstances. Still other teachers might see the classroom as a space in which only classroom-related matters can be addressed. In each, the common thread is that a new teacher may not be as flexible as others who have been around the block and understand that life happens, daily. New teachers should remember this notion: life happens, and it often happens at the most unexpected moments. For instance, death is a natural part of life, and deaths frequently occur, not only in the lives of teachers but also students. If a given teacher takes a one-size-fits-all approach to handling cases of family death, then that teacher runs the risk of erasing important situational nuances that might impact students in different ways and with different consequences (for example, a student who is a primary caregiver for someone who dies might experience severe trauma that is not easily understood by an outsider). In a similar example, sometimes a student awaits a very important phone call that could be life-changing (an interview for admittance into a program, for instance), so to simply say that no calls are allowed may be tantamount to destroying an opportunity of great importance. This is not to say that the classroom should be managed as if it were a lawless nation; rather, it is to reiterate the phrase that *life happens*, not only to students but to educators as well. If a given teacher can step out for an important call from time to time (and this is not uncommon or far-fetched), then it stands to reason that their students might need to do the same occasionally. In other words, rigid policies that neglect contextual gravity essentially equate to rules for the sake of having rules, which can ultimately run the risk of damaging the greater classroom ethos.

Teachers are all human, and life, as well as its many twists and turns, continues to happen, every moment of the day, whether it is wanted or not. An instructor's teaching philosophy is important, just as are the many unarticulated policies that help to formulate that philosophy. New instructors can avoid the ethical traps of articulated versus nonarticulated policies by simply making personal philosophy transparent at all possible turns.

Big Picture and Bottom Line

The role of policy in language classrooms cannot be underestimated. Though dry by comparison to other topics, its scope influences virtually all actions and reactions within the classroom community. To navigate policy, it is essential that new instructors familiarize themselves, to the fullest extent possible, with all institutional-level policy matters that must be accounted for in classroom actions. The same is true for all programmatic policies, as they too wield influence over a teacher's courses of action. Ultimately, the most granular level, the classroom—where enacted policies reside and personal philosophy is realized—is the locus in which all policies converge into a single voice, setting up the educational space as a proverbial battlefield where policy always realizes its existence in conjunction with authentic interactions.

Food for Thought

1. Imagine that a student turned in a final assignment after its due date. On your syllabus, it says that "no late work will be accepted." However, the institution's official policy is that "work submitted late must be accepted, and a reduced score may be applied by the instructor." Your official policy has no clear mechanism for

determining what the reduction in score would be or how it might be applied, leaving you open to conflict with the student in question. How would you go about addressing this situation, and what specifically would you convey to the student so as to abide by the university's wishes without sacrificing the integrity of your course?

2. Decide on a classroom level and context. Students then generate private slips of paper with policy issues labeled on each. Each student will draw from the pool and share the policy, while also providing their take on how they would address or implement the policy. Compare everyone's perspective and then collaboratively research the policy at two to three comparable institutions. Reassess perspectives based on what is found. Contemplate how this would impact each person's official syllabus language.

References

Ball, S. J., Maguire, M., & Braun, A. (2012). *How schools do policy: Policy enactments in secondary schools*. Routledge.

Dallimore, E. J., Hertenstein, J. H., & Platt, M. B. (2012). Impact of cold-calling on student voluntary participation. *Journal of Management Education, 37*(3), 305–341. https://doi.org/10.1177/1052562912446067

Deng, Z. (2010). Curriculum planning and systems change. In P. Peterson, E. Baker, & B. McGaw (Eds.), *International encyclopedia of education* (3rd ed., pp. 384–389). Elsevier Science. https://doi.org/10.1016/B978-0-08-044894-7.00062-2

Doyle, W. (1992). Curriculum and pedagogy. In P. W. Jackson (Ed.), *Handbook of research on curriculum* (pp. 486–516). Macmillan.

Gornitzka, Å. (1999). Governmental policies and organisational change in higher education. *Higher Education, 38*(1), 5–31. https://doi.org/10.1023/A:100370 3214848

Huang, J. & Yip, J. W. C. (2021). Understanding ESL teachers' agency in their early years of professional development: A three-layered triadic reciprocity framework. *Frontiers in Psychology, 12*, Article 739271. https://doi.org/10.3389/fpsyg.2021.739271

Johnson, E. J. (2012). Arbitrating repression: Language policy and education in Arizona. *Language and Education, 26*(1), 53–76. https://doi.org/10.1080/09500 782.2011.615936

Kalir, J. H. (2020). Social annotation enabling collaboration for open learning. *Distance Education, 41*(2), 245–260, https://doi.org/10.1080/01587 919.2020.1757413

Ollerhead, S. (2010). Teacher agency and policy response in the adult ESL literacy classroom. *TESOL Quarterly, 44*(3), 606–618. https://www.jstor.org/stable/27896749

Shugurova, O. (2020). Co-constructing a learner-centered, democratic syllabus with teacher candidates: A poetic rendering of students' meaning making experiences. *Inquiry in Education, 12*(2), Article 3. https://eric.ed.gov/?id=EJ1279504

Tindell, D. R., & Bohlander, R. W. (2011). The use and abuse of cell phones and text messaging in the classroom: A survey of college students. *College Teaching, 60*(1), 1–9. https://doi.org/10.1080/87567555.2011.604802

Wasley, P. (2008, March 14). The syllabus becomes a repository of legalese: As dos and don'ts get added, some professors cry "enough." *The Chronicle of Higher Education, 54*(27), p. A1. https://www.chronicle.com/article/the-syllabus-beco mes-a-repository-of-legalese/

Wergin, J. F. (2005). Higher education: Waking up to the importance of accreditation. *Change, 37*(3), 35–41.

Westbury, I. (2000). Teaching as a reflective practice: What might Didaktik teach curriculum. In I. Westbury, S. Hopmann, & K. Riquarts (Eds.), *Teaching as a reflective practice: The German Didaktik tradition* (pp. 15–39). Erlbaum

CHAPTER 3

Working with and without Set Curricula and Textbooks

Contextualization

This chapter seeks to describe the different possible scenarios that can constrain the degree of freedom an instructor may have in constructing day-to-day learning objectives. These scenarios range from educational contexts where both the curriculum and the textbook(s) are set by a program coordinator, school principal, or school director (administrators), to where both are set by the instructor. This chapter first aims to describe what a curriculum entails and what the teacher's ultimate limits would be within said curriculum. Adopting a curriculum set by school administrators requires that teachers adhere to classroom materials that have been provided by publishers, institutions, or peers, and include predetermined day-to-day lesson plans, programmatically adopted textbooks, collaboratively established forms of assessment, and so forth.

This chapter also addresses the concept of textbook adoption, especially in terms of scenarios in which instructors are expected to choose between selecting a published textbook or creating their own teaching and assessment materials. When it comes to the latter, this chapter weighs the advantages of incorporating authentic materials into lessons and within the larger curriculum, offering novice teachers advice on how best to manage innovative materials development without feeling overwhelmed or overburdened.

Case Study: When a Textbook Is a Novice Teacher's Best Friend, and When It's Not

A textbook can be a novice teacher's best friend at a new job. When not very familiar with a new educational setting and its students, it is usually best to rely on the textbook assigned for the class, or on one whose intended level corresponds to the learners' proficiency level. A textbook that comes with a teacher's manual that provides good teaching suggestions can help a novice teacher get their bearings and learn the ropes of classroom interaction. This is the scenario in which a novice teacher found herself when she started teaching English as a foreign language at a binational center in Brazil. This teacher in particular had just been hired to teach a beginner's class and was given a copy of the textbook *Interchange 1* by Jack Richards, published by Cambridge University Press—very popular at the time. She was also given the teacher's manual, the student's workbook, and all the accompanying tapes (yes, cassette tapes!). Being new at the job and not yet very proficient at creating her own materials, she opened the teacher's manual in search of suggestions of how to set up the activities contained in the textbook. She realized that the teacher's manual was very comprehensive, and it offered suggestions for fun warm-ups, activity lead-ins, transitions, how to get students to participate, fun game-like activities, how to offer feedback, types of assessments, and even how to explain grammatical topics by providing short scripts and diagrams. This teacher recollects that the teacher's manual was a lifesaver during her first semester teaching because it covered all the basics of best teaching practices. After following those guidelines to teach the content and involve students in the learning process during that semester, she eventually felt confident enough to create variations of the textbook's activities and materials that she felt would be more suited for her students.

In this particular case, this novice teacher was working with a thorough and well-designed beginners' textbook that came with an equally well-designed teacher's manual. But what if she had chosen a less adequate textbook for the level and purpose of the class? Would it provide sufficient teaching and learning support for her students? Probably not. And this second scenario is exactly what happened with an English composition instructor at a higher education institution in Southern California. By design, the course she taught did not adopt a textbook in order to encourage instructors to evaluate their students' needs and cater to them each semester. Instead of taking advantage of this flexibility, she chose to pull activities from a textbook she had used before. This decision was not based on clear planning or careful curriculum development, and therefore had no sense of purpose paired with thoughtful consideration of her students' needs and how they would benefit from those materials. The course she taught was an upper intermediate writing class designed to prepare students to take English courses in the following semester. In order to be prepared to take an English course at that university, students must be able to write at an advanced level. Therefore, the main objective of this preceding course is to help students be ready to succeed in their English courses when they take it. Nevertheless, the instructor in this example chose to adopt a textbook that contained basic academic writing practice more geared for lower intermediate courses. So adopting such a textbook for an upper intermediate university writing course that had the purpose of preparing its students for advanced writing required by English courses in that institution was a serious mistake and a disservice to her students. This is why it is important to keep in mind what the entire curriculum is, and how each course connects to others.

Common Concerns

First, let us briefly introduce what a curriculum is. A curriculum is a collection of academic content, lessons, assessments, and other pedagogical guidelines that conveys what instructors at a given educational setting need to cover. The concept of a curriculum is usually broadly defined as the totality of programmatic student experiences that occur in an educational setting (Rao et al., 2021; Wiles, 2009). The term often refers specifically to a planned sequence of instruction, or to a view of the student's experiences in terms of the educator's or school's instructional goals; but a curriculum may also incorporate the planned interaction of students with instructional content, materials, resources, and processes for evaluating the attainment of educational objectives.

A curriculum can be set by a national or state educational board or organization, by the school administration, and sometimes by the coordinators of a specific academic program, but it is not usually a decision made by a single teacher. Although it is meant to provide instructional guidance and a uniform and equitable experience for all students, it can be perceived as a constraining mechanism that limits a teacher's freedom to select content that might be better suited for their students. Being able to decide on a course curriculum and on required textbooks and materials to be adopted in such a course can have its benefits, but it also poses challenges. The questions

48   Navigating the English Language Classroom

below showcase some of the most common concerns expressed by a number of teachers-in-training and novice teachers.

- *Q1. The home department requires that teachers follow a very specific curriculum and use a textbook that was selected by others. How can a teacher be successful within a context that leaves little room for creativity?*
- *Q2. A teacher was asked to teach a class that already has pre-established course objectives and student learning outcomes, a syllabus that has been created by a program coordinator in conjunction with previous instructors, a suggested calendar that maps out themes and assignments, but there is no textbook assigned for the course. How should this teacher decide whether to go with a textbook or not in such a case?*
- *Q3. A class has an adopted textbook, but there are no curricular standards that have been laid out for the courses in the program. How can a teacher make their course effective in relation to the other courses the program offers while using an already adopted textbook in their course?*
- *Q4. A course seems to be a complete free-for-all. Teachers are free to do whatever they want. Where should they start?*

Effective Practices for Working with and without Set Curricula and Textbooks

- **Q1. *The home department requires that teachers follow a very specific curriculum and use a textbook that was selected by others. How can a teacher be successful within a context that leaves little room for creativity?***

When a class has a preset curriculum with a preset textbook at a school, it is typically so that several sections of the same course are uniformized, which means that all teachers are to cover the same content and use the same guidelines and pace, a necessary condition when a school has multiple sections of the same class. In addition, when a school has several subsequent levels, there is a need for students to meet student learning outcomes for each level before moving on to the next one. This would be the case of a school that offers courses that range from A1 to C2 (see the Common European Framework of Reference for Languages [CEFR]; Council of Europe, 2001) throughout the span of two to three years.

The class overhead may be decided for the instructor of record without their input or without surveying students about their ability to afford them. The first downside of a preset curriculum that adopts published textbooks is the potentially high cost factor. When some of the students are not able to afford the textbook, the teacher may have to pair them with those who do so that they can do the practice activities during class. Alternatively, teachers may choose to provide those students with photocopies of the pages they will use in a lesson, but access to a photocopier might be restricted or onerous. In addition, an important consideration when photocopying pages from a textbook pertains to breaking the publisher's copyright, so teachers need to make sure to observe fair use rules. A solution would be to suggest that students buy used textbooks or older editions, both of which are typically cheaper than new ones.

Another downside that is associated with a textbook being selected by a school administrator is that they may adopt a text that the class instructor may not be comfortable with. There are a number of factors that may lead to one not being comfortable with a textbook, such as that it may require the use of a methodology that the teacher is not familiar with, or it contains topics that the teacher is less familiar with, or it presents content in a manner that the teacher disagrees with (for example, when the content is culturally inaccurate or culturally insensitive, or when it is linguistically inaccurate or misleading).

Moreover, a textbook selected by someone other than the class instructor may not necessarily be the best option in the market for the students' specific needs. When a textbook is not the best match to the students' needs and characteristics, the teacher should try to supplement the textbook with materials that replace inaccurate or insensitive information, and with the adequate support that students need to thrive and achieve their goals.

When the teacher is not offered the opportunity to select a textbook for the class they will teach, not all is lost. This lack of choice is not without some advantages. It makes teaching the class more straightforward because textbooks come with preset lessons and course designs. Besides, the teacher still has the ability to make it their own. Activities from the textbook can be adapted and replaced on an as- needed basis in order to improve student engagement; teachers can select more current topics, add games and fun interactive activities, or create expansion activities that reinforce content taught. These little freedoms allow for some creativity in a seemingly constrained system.

It is common for textbooks to have a lot of controlled and guided activities, so it might be a good idea to supplement it with more free production activities, especially when teaching lower levels. For example, if the textbook contains a simple activity in which learners add relative pronouns that are missing (controlled), followed by another activity in which students write missing relative clauses (guided), the teacher can add an activity after that asking students to write entire true/false sentences with relative clauses to trigger free communicative practice. This could be followed by having students work in pairs to guess if those sentences are true or false, ending this practice series with a meaningful free production activity.

- *Q2. A teacher was asked to teach a class that already has pre-established course objectives and student learning outcomes, a syllabus that has been created by a program coordinator in conjunction with previous instructors, a suggested calendar that maps out themes and assignments, but there is no textbook assigned for the course. How should this teacher decide whether to go with a textbook or not in such a case?*

This scenario describes a course with a set curriculum without a set textbook, and this course is going to be constrained by program learning outcomes (PLOs) or student learning outcomes (SLOs). When there is no set textbook, the teacher will have to decide between choosing one or creating materials to use instead of a textbook.

When deciding whether to adopt a textbook in this scenario, teachers should take into account the following considerations—each of which will be further discussed in the paragraphs that follow:

1. What is the program's philosophy on textbook adoption? In other words, does the program encourage teachers to choose a textbook for their own courses as long as they fit the curriculum, PLOs, and SLOs, or are teachers required to create their own teaching and assessment materials?
2. Is it possible to find a textbook that aligns well with the school's teaching philosophy and that does not deviate from the program's curriculum design?
3. Will students be allowed to use older or different editions of the textbook if one is selected?
4. Are there electronic textbooks that are cheaper or free of charge, and if so, are they preferable and will students have access to them?
5. If free educational resources are opted in lieu of a textbook, or as a supplement to a textbook, how would they be accessed in the classroom or at a school site?

6. How much of the textbook will be useful when taking into account important variables such as students' needs, their ability level, and time constraints? (When the purchase of a textbook is required in a course but only a fraction of it is actually used, students might resent having to pay for it, especially when it is expensive.)
7. Are there textbooks available that are culturally responsive to the educational context?

First, it is important to find out about the school or language program's stand on textbook adoption. The fact that there is a set curriculum for the course but not a textbook could be an indicator that their philosophy is to not use a textbook and go with alternatives instead. This could be part of their teaching philosophy or be based on student opinion surveys, for example. Therefore, before even considering starting a search for a suitable textbook, it is important to talk to the program coordinator and senior faculty (who might have institutional memory and can explain the underlying reasons for the school's teaching philosophy on textbook adoption). The program or previous course instructors might have decided to forgo the use of a textbook if the adoption of a textbook is discouraged by the program by virtue of being too costly or not compatible with the PLOs or SLOs. If that is the case, the options are then to create materials from scratch, or to adapt materials from existing sources. If a teacher decides to create teaching and assessment materials from scratch, they should keep in mind that this option can be time-consuming; the upside, however, is that these materials can be completely tailored to students' needs. On the other hand, searching for existing premade teaching handouts, worksheets, quizzes, and other materials on the internet will also be quite time-consuming. In addition, even though existing electronic resources such as text corpora can be used to develop lessons that match the PLOs or SLOs, teachers may have to deal with copyright issues. Another point to note is that even though there are a lot of educational electronic resources on the internet, most of them need to be revised, corrected, or adapted to suit specific students' needs. It is very important that teachers verify that the materials they found elsewhere match their students' proficiency level, learning objectives, academic needs, cultural background, and so on, before they distribute them to their students. Finally, all sources should be referenced, because intellectual property is a big concern in some countries like the United States. The name of the original author can be written at the top or at the bottom of the handout or worksheet (for example, it can say "Retrieved from X" or "Adapted from X").

Next, not deviating from the program's curriculum design is a major factor in this decision. The textbook selected should contain all the content areas and skills and subskills to be covered in the course, and it should support teaching and cater to students' needs and goals. According to Byrd and Schuemann (2014), selecting a textbook is "a complex process carried out in different ways in different settings" (p. 382). This is because students' needs and goals will depend on the setting, age group, and career goals, among many other potential variables. More experienced teachers might enjoy the freedom of not adopting a textbook and creating their own materials, and novice teachers might prefer to lean on the expert-designed structure of a solid textbook.

Another equally important—yet more fundamental—consideration is the school's teaching philosophy and mission. An educator's teaching philosophy describes their core beliefs about teaching and learning (see Chapter 2). It is typically a statement that describes their views on the practice of pedagogy and the process of learning in general, which may range from teaching methods and pedagogical theories to classroom communication and interactions. In the same way, a school can have a teaching philosophy, which sometimes can be gathered by reading their "mission statement." While a statement of philosophy defines the values and beliefs of a school or program, a mission statement defines its pedagogical purpose and educational activities. The latter should provide a unifying force, a sense of direction, and a guide to decision making for all levels of management. Ideally, a school's vision and mission would emerge from the foundation created by its philosophy, and these are elicited and developed through deep conversation and reflection with all stakeholders, from the school founders to its directors, level coordinators, teachers, and students. Therefore, it is important to make sure that the textbook selected for a course aligns with the school's philosophy and mission first and foremost. For example, there are some schools that strongly subscribe to the audio-lingual method, or even to the grammar–translation approach; when that's the case, teachers would not be able to use a textbook designed to be used in a task-based classroom that aligns with the communicative approach.

The third question addressed the existence of older editions of a textbook and whether to allow students to buy them instead. When a textbook with older editions is adopted, it is common for students to ask if they can buy one of those older editions instead of purchasing the latest and often more expensive edition. Older editions are often still available for purchase on online stores and textbook thrift stores. Teachers contemplating the adoption of a textbook that has previous editions should consider allowing

Working with and without Set Curricula and Textbooks 53

students to buy an older edition and save some money if the content hasn't been updated or if the exercises that will be assigned for classroom work or homework have not been revised.

The fourth question was related to the use of electronic textbooks. Sometimes they can be cheaper than a printed textbook, or even free of charge. Being cheaper or free of charge would most definitely be very important variables to consider in the selection of teaching materials for a course. But teachers need to consider whether this choice would create inequities in their classroom. Being cheaper or even free would be seemingly beneficial for most students, unless it is an option that would not only require that students have their own smart devices (smart tablets, laptops, computers) to bring to class or with which to work from home, but that the devices have access to the internet for the entire duration of the course. Therefore, what initially seemed to have been a cheaper alternative can pose a financial burden or an additional challenge (such as having to find public computers in order to do the work assigned for out of the classroom) to some students. Taking the financial imposition and issues of access and equity aside, electronic textbooks are also easier to transport around than printed textbooks. Oftentimes students don't bring their textbooks to class simply because they didn't want to carry them that day. But if they have their own tablets or laptops, they typically don't leave home without them!

When considering supplementing or forgoing a textbook and using free educational resources to create teaching and assessment materials, teachers must consider the technological resources available they have at home (in order to plan and create materials), in the classroom, and at the school site (in order to implement their lesson plans). Some examples of technological resources they might need in the classroom are computers and projectors in the classroom, a whiteboard, screen, or a white wall on which to project images and electronic worksheets. Having a computer and projector in the classroom will also allow the use of interactive media such as PowerPoint, Keynote, Prezi, Google Slides, among others (the latter two options are free). If there is a photocopier available at the school, handouts can be printed and distributed to students in class. If students have access to a computer lab at the school or to a personal computer at home, files created can be uploaded to a learning management system (such as Google for Education, Canvas, Moodle, Blackboard, and so on), as long as copyright and fair use rules are respected. Whenever internet activities are used even as inspiration to develop other materials, teachers must give credit where credit is due by adding the original hyperlink and/or by mentioning the original author's name. Creating teaching materials from existing materials requires learning what the copyright laws are for the materials found. Photocopying and copyright restrictions can vary in different countries. For example, in the United States a teacher can only photocopy materials up to 10% of a book when intending to distribute the copies to their students and not charge for it under fair use. The US Copyright Office website defines it as:

> Fair use is a legal doctrine that promotes freedom of expression by permitting the unlicensed use of copyright-protected works in certain circumstances. Section 107 of the Copyright Act provides the statutory framework for determining whether something is a fair use and identifies certain types of uses—such as criticism, comment, news reporting, teaching, scholarship, and research—as examples of activities that may qualify as fair use.
>
> (US Copyright Office, n.d.)

Other important considerations when deciding to go with a textbook are whether one can be found that is a good fit for students' needs, learning goals, and ability level, and that at least most of it can be used within the course term. A textbook is only a tool to mediate learning, so it needs to be one that aligns with students' learning goals and needs, and one that matches their proficiency level. If it so happens that a teacher can't find a textbook that satisfies these conditions, then creating their own materials for the course might be the best course of action. Finally, when teachers require that students purchase a textbook but only a fraction of it is actually used, students will resent having to pay for it, especially when it is expensive.

An ideal textbook should also be culturally appropriate and responsive. In normative multilingual educational contexts in which English is taught as a second language, nondominant cultural and ethnic representations are either absent or are superficially or incorrectly represented (Boruah, 2022). Because of this trend, Thornbury (2013) argues that commercial language textbooks are "fundamentally flawed" and "detrimental" to language teaching, "hindering rather than helping the business of language learning" (p. 205). Aligned with this perspective, Gray (2016) argued that commercially produced textbooks are "cultural artefacts which serve to make languages mean in a particular way" (p. 2). Grant and Wong (2018) added that "ELT curriculum, textbooks, and supporting materials represent those cultural authorities, norms, and values that the United States and other countries where English is spoken as a first language, accept and acknowledge" (p. 1). It is clear that there are those who believe textbooks should be more culturally sustaining in order to represent underrepresented minorities and thereby to include the populations who might be utilizing the book. For instance, Boruah (2022) proposes that English teaching materials be used to develop inclusiveness, cultural acceptance, and responsiveness (p. 14). Bowen and Hopper (2022) add that because textbooks can be powerful socialization agents, allowing for adequate inclusivity in educational materials is a matter of ethics and fairness, as well as a means to maximize learning processes (p. 1).

In sum, the adoption of a textbook comes with advantages and disadvantages, and so does not choosing one. Table 3.1 provides a quick summary of some of the considerations to take into account if an instructor has the choice.

Table 3.1. Pros and Cons of Adopting a Textbook

When it's better to adopt a textbook	When not to adopt a textbook
Price: Cost will not pose a problem for you or for your students.	Your students cannot afford the high cost of textbooks.
Ready-made: You don't have time to create your own materials from scratch.	You prefer creating your own teaching and assessment materials from scratch, and you have the time to do it.
Content: You are not sure what you should teach students at a certain level, and a textbook would help remove the guesswork.	Any particular textbook you may have access to does not exactly match your students' learning needs and goals.
Resources: No access to a printer, photocopier, or computers and projectors, prohibiting the reproduction of various focused exercises and text that could be used on a lesson.	Your educational setting offers a printer, photocopier, overhead projector, and/or computer and projector, so pulling materials from different online resources or different textbooks is possible.
Copyright: Compiling the materials you need to use would involve asking for permission from their publishers and paying copyright fees, making it too complicated and less desirable.	The materials you would like to use are copyright-free, or you would be able to apply the fair use rule.
Curriculum: The textbook selected is a great match to the curriculum you were given.	You do not need to follow a set curriculum, or no textbooks available on the current market include all the content areas you need to cover in class.

- ***Q3. A class has an adopted textbook, but there are no curricular standards that have been laid out for the courses in the program. How can a teacher make their course effective in relation to the other courses the program offers while using an already adopted textbook in their course?***

This scenario is different from the previous two because it has a set textbook but no set curriculum. This situation is common in nonaccredited programs—that is, programs that were not vetted and approved by a third-party organization that oversees the quality of education in schools of different kinds. This scenario may also be the case of private tutoring contexts, as teachers often go along with the immediate requests and needs of the one student who has hired them and don't necessarily develop a whole curriculum for it. Not having a set curriculum can be a little problematic in the case of language schools where students are supposed to move up to higher levels. For example, if a school has six levels, and textbooks were selected by school administrators who are not in the classroom, there may be issues in maintaining the quality and integrity of each level while teachers work in individual vacuums unconnected to one another. When there is no guidance in terms of an overarching curriculum, an isolated class design will be shaped by the design of the textbook adopted. With no sense of curricular needs for an evolving set of proficiency levels within a school program, the selected textbook becomes the default in approaching the structure of a course, and the textbook's lesson and chapter objectives become the course's curriculum.

To navigate having a text with little direction on how it would fit into a larger curriculum or with other courses in the same school, a novice teacher can seek out thoughtful conversations with other teachers who work there. Knowing what other teachers are doing in their classes below and above their course level can help delineate the boundaries of those levels and create a sense of flow. By comparing notes with their peers, they can decide how to better approach the textbook as their framework. This collaborative community of teachers can also work together to develop and coordinate curriculum standards and create supplementary materials. They may decide to develop lessons together, compare activities, discuss students' performance in activities and in said lessons, and so on. Some peers might have been working at that place a little longer and therefore might have a little more experience than them (choosing to be humble, asking for help, and using this opportunity to ask questions usually works well as embracing the fact that they're new leads to being allowed—and expected—to ask questions.). This joint effort can even have other advantages, such as having more weight

Working with and without Set Curricula and Textbooks 57

to approach administration about a curriculum review, or helping one another to create opportunities for professional development.

Another problem that a lack of a set curriculum might create is that a course without a curriculum is also not well or fully aligned with an international standard for language proficiency like CEFR (Noijons et al, 2011), or the American Council on the Teaching of Foreign Languages' (ACTFL) World-Readiness Standards for Learning Languages. When that is the case, a course title might not represent very well the actual level of the students in that course; for example, a course called "Advanced Conversation" that is not aligned with CEFR, can have students ranging from lower to higher intermediate (Levels B1 and B2) instead of having C1 and C2 students.

Finally, another problem caused by a lack of predetermined curriculum at a language school with different courses supposed to cater for students at different levels is that it might be harder to place students correctly. When school administrators don't go by a set curriculum, it becomes easier to misplace students. When an instructor teaches under these conditions, they should consider conducting diagnostic tests of their students' speaking, listening, reading, and writing skill level at the beginning of the term, and then compare the results they obtain to the learning objectives of the textbook they will use in that class. If they have students who excel or who do extremely poorly on the diagnostic tests, they should consider moving them up or down accordingly, if permissible.

• Q4. A course seems to be a complete free-for-all. Teachers are free to do whatever they want. Where should they start?

This is the last of four different scenarios involving curricula and textbooks, and in this case, it is the one with no set curriculum and no set textbook. This is typically the case for one-off classes, like a non-leveled conversation class without a textbook. Teachers in institutions of higher education also have a very high degree of freedom when designing curricula. They make decisions on learning objectives, content, content organization, teaching arrangement, and assessment. A "no set curriculum with no set textbook" provides the teacher with the highest degree of freedom. But this greater freedom poses greater responsibility. The teacher holds in their hands all the decisions related to their students' ultimate achievement and success. For this reason, an initial diagnostic of students' levels will be even more critical as they will help inform the teacher's teaching approach and how to execute that approach, allowing students' needs that emerge from diagnostic tests to inform the course curriculum and textbook adoption decisions.

When a teacher has the freedom to choose a textbook and to design a course curriculum from scratch, they should consider relevant factors that will help them narrow down a list of possible learning objectives:

1. What is the educational setting?
2. What is the class format?
3. Is this a private lesson, as in one-on-one tutoring?
4. What is the course objective?
5. What are the students' needs?
6. Is there a need to match the class to a proficiency standard framework like the CEFR?

It is possible that this apparent lack of a larger structure and overarching curriculum would leave novice teachers not knowing what to include or exclude from their syllabus. When they feel there is no obvious structure to guide them, there are a few things that they can do. First, they can ask peers if they would be open to having them as a visitor in their classrooms so that they can observe how they make decisions in terms of course objectives and day-to-day objectives, what materials and resources they are using, what seems to be working well with their students, and so forth. Next, they can hunt for available syllabi that might give them inspiration and ideas for things they can do. For example, they might be able to adapt existing syllabi, covering "family terms" and "colors" in beginning levels, "relative clauses" in intermediate, and "writing tone and style" for advanced levels.

When working for a language school, teachers should check in with a school director, a program coordinator, or course supervisor to ensure that their curricular plans are aligned with the program's philosophy and mission (see Chapter 2 for information about institutional, programmatic, and classroom policies). Another way to gather formative feedback on curricular decisions is to ask students for their opinions in student satisfaction surveys; making use of different types of feedback tools, such as mid-course evaluations, anonymous satisfaction surveys, anonymous polls, among others; and ask students frequently what are the things that they think should be calibrated to better suit their needs. For example, they can be asked if they want the teacher to spend more or less time on certain topics, or practice more certain skills and subskills, or add certain content not originally included in the syllabus.

The "no set curriculum and no set textbook" scenario will require that teachers create their own materials, and fortunately sources abound. As a rule of thumb, authentic materials should be favored over made-up content, and topics related to what is particularly meaningful and interesting to students should be prioritized. Teachers can create a course reader with the materials selected and retrieved for use by the students in the course (respecting copyright laws). But when putting a course reader together, teachers must keep in mind that it may involve having to pay copyright fees, leading to transferring the cost to students—that is, selling the readers to the students in order to cover copyright fees, which can lead to readers becoming a costly alternative. To avoid having to pay copyright fees, teachers can search for materials that are open access and use images that are in the public domain (images usually come with information about copyright restrictions, such as "available to use only," "available to use and post," "available to use, post, and sell," and so on). Another option is to use free interactive and educational software (such as Google Docs and Google Slides, Prezi, Canva, Pinterest, ClassDojo, Schoology, Kahoot, Padlet, among others) to create teaching and assessment activities; and they can share (via email, a learning management platform such as Canvas, or through a cloud-sharing platform such as WeTransfer, Google Drive, or Dropbox) the links of such educational resources to their students so they can access them before and during class.

Developing their own teaching materials provides teachers with opportunities to grow professionally (Gao & Cui, 2023). It may raise their awareness about their students' needs (Bouckaert, 2019); improve their linguistic, subject, content, and pedagogical knowledge (Zeegers, 2012); improve their understanding of teaching methods and theories (Masuhara, 2006), and it produces an outlet to externalize their beliefs, identities, and emotions (Gao et al., 2022). Therefore, although it can be a daunting task, teachers should take on the task knowing that it cannot only help them tailor their teaching materials to their students' needs, but also help them become better teachers.

On the other hand, the "no set curriculum and no set textbook" scenario may also allow the selection of a textbook, but where should this decision-making process start? The following suggestions may require some advance planning and time, but they are worth considering in the long run. First, teachers can plan to attend publishers' textbook workshops in their area or attend professional conferences that invite publishers to showcase their textbooks in the exhibit hall, where they would be free to browse through multiple textbook options in one place. Teachers can also reach out to publishers and ask for desk copies to be sent to them in the mail. Another option is to explore (ESL/EFL) language sections in physical or online libraries where there might be additional resources that teachers could use that would otherwise be under their radar. But the cost of a textbook can be expensive, so if a teacher is going to use one, they should make sure that it is a worthwhile investment for the students and that they will get promising returns for their investments.

Big Picture and Bottom Line

Teachers' beliefs and attitudes regarding curriculum design affect decision-making and planning processes, teaching approaches, and their relationships with students (Shieh & Reynolds, 2021). According to Borg (2003), "teachers are active, thinking decision-makers who make instructional choices by drawing on complex, practically-oriented, personalized, and context-sensitive networks of knowledge, thoughts, and beliefs" (p. 81), but this freedom can be limited when the curriculum is preset by the institution(s) where they work. In addition, ESL curriculum design may be considered even more challenging because students often are learning through a second language, and because it can have a wide-ranging set of learning objectives, ranging from—for example—English for academic purposes (EAP) to proficiency test preparation courses (Nation, 2013).

For this reason, it is important to understand how to make the best of every teaching context and then have a positive attitude about tackling the challenges that come with that context. This chapter discussed four different teaching scenarios ranging from extreme rigidity to extreme freedom. The most rigid context is the one in which the school sets the curriculum and the textbook on behalf of teachers. The freest context is the one in which teachers have the freedom to create their own curriculum and choose the textbook or materials they would like to work with. The other two scenarios involve a set curriculum without a set textbook, and a set textbook without a set curriculum. Each of these four scenarios will bear both advantages and disadvantages or challenges that novice teachers must learn to navigate. The teaching context (that is, the degree of curriculum and textbook flexibility) should not prevent anyone from applying for a teaching position. Every teacher must learn to make the best of every teaching scenario, always keeping in mind what is best for their students.

Food for Thought

1. Imagine that you were just hired to teach an advanced reading class (CEFR C2 level). You were given the freedom to choose your own materials or pick a textbook. In small groups, discuss the pros and cons of each alternative, making reference not only to some of the issues raised in this chapter, but also specific issues related to the demands of teaching a higher-level reading class, what your

students' needs might be, and what your course design and student learning outcomes might be.

2. You were just told that the following semester you will be offered an upper intermediate level (CEFR B2) academic writing class to international students who are also freshmen at a community college. You have a few months to design your syllabus, but you were told you will have to use the textbook that the program wants you to use, which is the *Academic Writing for Graduate Students*, 3rd edition, by Christine Feak and John Swales, published by the University of Michigan Press. You know this is a very popular textbook among university-level graduate writing courses, but you fear that it will be too advanced for your students. Knowing you can't change the textbook, that your students will buy it, and that you will have no choice but to use at least some of it, what are some solutions you can think of that will help your students be successful and make progress in your class despite the fact that the textbook is a little too advanced for them?

3. Regardless of where, what level, and under which conditions we teach, there will always be some need to supplement our courses with more current or more adequate materials here and there. Discuss the advantages and disadvantages of creating your own materials from scratch versus creating them from existing materials and language corpora.

References

Borg, S. (2003). Teacher cognition in language teaching: A review of research on what language teachers think, know, believe, and do. *Language Teaching, 36*(2), 81–109. http://doi.org/10.1017/S0261444803001903

Boruah, P. B. (2022). Visibility as validation: A case study of culturally responsive materials development for TESOL. *The CATESOL Journal, 33*(1), 1–16.

Bouckaert, M. (2019). Current perspectives on teachers as materials developers: Why, what, and how? *RELC Journal, 50*(3), 439–456. https://doi.org/10.1177/0033688218810549

Bowen, N. E. J. A., & Hopper, D. (2022), The representation of race in English language learning textbooks: Inclusivity and equality in images. *TESOL Quarterly, 57*(4), 1013–1040 https://doi.org/10.1002/tesq.3169

Byrd, P., & Schuemann, C. (2014). English as a second/foreign language textbooks: How to choose them—how to use them. In M. Celce-Murcia, D. M. Brinton, &

M. A. Snow (Eds.), *Teaching English as a second or foreign language* (4th ed., pp. 380–393). Heinle Cengage Learning.

Council of Europe. (2001). *Common European Framework of Reference for Languages: Learning, teaching, assessment.* Cambridge University Press.

Gao, Y. & Cui, Y. (2023). Emotional tensions as rewards: An emerging teacher leader's identity construction in EFL textbook development. *TESOL Journal, 14,* Article e689. https://doi.org/10.1002/tesj.689

Gao, Y., Cui, Y., & De Costa. P. I. (2022). "Agree to disagree": Reconciling an English teacher's identity tensions in negotiating an educational reform through a community of practice perspective. *Language Teaching Research.* https://doi.org/10.1177/13621688221130125

Grant, R., & Wong, S. D. (2018). Addressing cultural bias in ELT materials. In J. I. Liontas (Ed.), *TESOL encyclopedia of English language teaching.* Wiley. https://doi.org/10.1002/9781118784235.eelt0315

Gray, J. (2016). ELT materials: Claims, critiques and controversies. In G. Hall (Ed.), *The Routledge handbook of English language teaching* (pp. 93–107) Routledge.

Masuhara, H. (2006). Materials as a teacher development tool. In J. Mukundan (Ed.), *Readings on ELT materials II* (pp. 34–46). Pearson Malaysia.

Nation, P. (2013). *What should every ESL teacher know?* Compass Publishing.

Noijons, J., Bérešová, J., Breton, G., & Szabó, G. (2011). *Relating language examinations to the Common European Framework of Reference for Languages: Learning, teaching, assessment (CEFR). Highlights from the manual.* Council of Europe Publishing. https://www.ecml.at/Portals/1/documents/ECML-resources/2011_10_10_relex._E_web.pdf

Rao, K. S., Rao, H. K. L., & Chaluvarayaswamy, R. (2021). Management of critical thinking abilities of teachers and learners in a dynamic futuristic environment. In B. Khan, M. Kuofie, & S. Suman (Eds.), *Handbook of research on future opportunities for technology management education* (pp. 1–17). IGI Global. https://doi.org/10.4018/978-1-7998-8327-2.ch001

Shieh, J., & Reynolds, B. L. (2021). The origin and impact of an ESL teacher's beliefs on curriculum design. *Asia Pacific Journal of Education, 41*(3), 574–593. https://doi.org/10.1080/02188791.2020.1832043

Thornbury, S. (2013). Resisting coursebooks. In J. Gray (Ed.), *Critical perspectives on language teaching materials* (pp. 204–223). Palgrave Macmillan. https://doi.org/10.1057/9781137384263_10

US Copyright Office. (n.d.). *About fair use.* U.S. Copyright Office Fair Use Index. https://www.copyright.gov/fair-use/

Wiles, J. (2009). *Leading curriculum development.* Corwin Press.

Zeegers, Y. (2012). Curriculum development for teacher education in the southern Philippines: A simultaneous process of professional learning and syllabus enhancement. *International Journal of Educational Development, 32*(2), 207– 213. https://doi.org/10.1016/j.ijedudev.2011.01.015

SECTION II

The Teaching Situation

CHAPTER 4

Planning Lessons

Contextualization

This chapter explores the preliminary concerns that must be considered and accounted for throughout the lesson planning phase. The aim of this chapter is to provide novice instructors with effective strategies for pinpointing planning areas that cause issues and to address the intricacies of these issues as instructors consider their impact on actual lesson builds. The distinction between building and planning is an important one, in that building relies on careful planning for success, so without a carefully crafted planning phase, our builds run a greater risk of being less impactful. The chapter also explores the idea of lesson planning as it relates to curricular agreement and flow, where micro-level lesson identity is realized through macro-level curricular execution. In this way, this chapter promotes investigation and foresight as primary tools in achieving successful lesson builds that are grounded in solid planning practices.

Case Study: I'm Having a Hard Time Sacrificing Because Everything Is Essential!

In a recent mentoring experience within a university summer intensive ESL program, a new lecturer spoke with her mentor about the flow of her lessons within and beyond individual days. It was her first time teaching in the program, as well as her first time teaching an academic reading and writing course, so naturally she was worried about how she would balance the program's learning objectives with the real-time dynamics of an intensive program. She felt strongly that all components were important for most assignments, while showing uneasiness in choosing where to place items she planned to address. In truth, she was apprehensive about assessing students on items that had not been covered, and as a result, her course calendar was heavily fronted, with little substance in the latter weeks. Her mentor was able to calm her nerves by reminding her that it was more realistic to hold students accountable for certain aspects as they were covered, incrementally adding more areas for assessment as more material is taught. Knowing she did not have to teach and assess everything all at once freed her to play around with her pace and test out her ability to conceptualize both individual and full-term lesson sequences that were realistic and implementable.

The reason that this lecturer's story resonates with many teachers is because all teachers go through this type of developmental preparation phase. Learning to plan and build out lessons is a skill that emerges through trial and error, and this takes time—and periodic aggravation—to accomplish. In the end, this lecturer had to rely on her previous experiences as well as the advice of her mentor to construct a pathway that sounded reasonable in terms of her workload while also remaining fair for her students and the struggles that they face.

Common Concerns

The questions below offer a glimpse into many of the recurring issues that arise when planning and building lessons. In reality, there are seemingly endless issues that could potentially arise when addressing lesson development, especially since lessons can interact with students in unpredictable ways; however, there are also general maneuvers within lesson planning and building that, when properly attended to, can make even the most difficult aspects less nebulous and easier to handle in terms of eventual implementation. The questions below shed light on some of the core issues that are frequently shared among many new teachers.

- *Q1: Where do novice teachers start in terms of planning lessons over a term of instruction?*
- *Q2: How do novice teachers manage lesson planning so that it is effective and not time-consuming?*
- *Q3: How do novice teachers make their lessons flow in a way that is logically progressive from day to day, while also taking into account the course's learning objectives?*

- *Q4: When lessons are not going to plan, how do novice teachers readjust the plan?*
- *Q5: Each class is different, so how do novice teachers plan lessons to keep all students engaged?*

Effective Practices for Planning Lessons

• *Q1: Where do novice teachers start in terms of planning lessons over a term of instruction?*

A crucial aspect that new teachers need to consider as they begin planning lessons is the setting in which they will teach. In the United States, for example, the educational landscape includes public and private institutions, spanning an extensive range that begins with preschools, primary schools, and secondary schools. The system then culminates with community colleges, four-year colleges and universities, and graduate and professional schools. This landscape also includes stand-alone public and private programs like community learning settings, adult education programs, and private language schools. The reason that settings are important for planning is because each brings with it different contextual considerations. For instance, preschools through secondary schools might have regimented lessons that are predetermined by state or local school boards. As Purgason (2014) notes, "institutions often specify the objectives, aims, goals, or outcomes that they expect teachers to implement" (p. 367), and this is most strongly seen in institutions that follow a more heavily prescribed educational trajectory, such as is found at foundational levels. Conversely, institutions of higher education—community colleges, four-year colleges, and universities—tend to have more freedom in how lessons are conceptualized, often relying more heavily on the instructor's pedagogical approach than standards that all instructors must follow. Of course, even when higher education instructors have more freedom, the program can still be regimented, as is often the case with language programs that adhere to distinct levels that function as a system.

Once the level of freedom in terms of institutional planning is understood, it is then helpful to consider lessons through two different programmatic planning pathways: outcome-defined (OD) and schedule-defined (SD). In OD, the ultimate goal is to satisfy an established set of learning outcomes using personal pedagogy to achieve programmatic requirements. This pathway potentially provides more planning freedom for instructors, but it can also require a great deal more creativity and effort. In SD, the course and its lessons are marked as if they were distance marker points along the roadside in a marathon, where the outcomes are premapped onto a well-defined schedule that acts as a roadmap for progression. In this pathway, teachers might find the burden of creativity and effort somewhat lessened, as the planning work is more under the scope of the program than the classroom itself. This does not preclude personal pedagogy, but it does mean that personal pedagogy must fit within a more regimented set of progressive benchmarks.

The purpose of considering both the institutional setting and the programmatic pathway is to understand the weight of obligations as a teacher addresses planning. Settings and pathways help to shape pedagogical decisions, and if teachers want to be good team players within their respective programs, it is crucial that their decisions align with any preset planning expectations. Discrepancies within the system could in fact result in a counterproductive flow of progression for students. For instance, higher educational settings could be regimented (language programs at a university, for instance), just as primary school settings can be freer at times, as might be the case in private primary school settings (such as charter schools). Whatever the situation, each planning scenario will require investigation and open discussion with superiors and colleagues to ensure that the team approach is observed and that the individual's lesson planning fits nicely within the program's established scope and structure.

Lastly, teachers should consider whether planning within a program requires, prefers, or allows for deductive or inductive approaches, or whether there is freedom to shuttle between the two. Deductive lessons are those that first explicitly teach target rules or structures (Gollin, 1998; Takimoto, 2008); this teaching phase is then followed by an activation phase where the rule or structure is put into practice through relevant activities. Table 4.1 offers two examples of deductive lessons.

To the contrary, inductive lessons first ask students to grapple with contextually salient material, to dive in and see what patterns or structures can be gleaned, so to speak (Hammerly, 1975; Shaffer, 1989). After the student formulates their thoughts on the materials, the teacher then enters a more traditional recap of the rules and structures to ensure that students accurately understood the target language items embedded within. Table 4.2 offers two examples of inductive lesson plan actions.

Both deductive and inductive lessons are valid approaches to lesson planning, but both affect the progress of a lesson in different ways. To

Table 4.1. Sample Deductive Lesson Plan Activities

Actives and Passives	
1st - Instruction: An instructor explains the grammar of active sentences, which places the true subject within the first sentence slot and the object in the third (the object/complement slot). They then explain the grammar of passive sentences, which places the object in the first sentence slot (typically the subject slot) and the subject in an optional "by ____" structure that typically occurs in the object/complement slot (the third slot).	**2nd - Practice**: The instructor asks the students to examine a series of ten sentences. The series is made up of an equal number of active and passive sentences (five actives and five passives). The instructor then asks the students to implement the previous rules by identifying which sentences are active and which are passive. Students then share their responses with classmates afterward.
Indirect Object Preposition Inclusion	
1st - Instruction: An instructor explains the placement rules for direct and indirect objects. The lesson focuses specifically on how indirect objects that precede direct objects lose their initial preposition (I gave her the letter) but keep it when they come after the direct object (I gave the letter to her.).	**2nd - Practice**: The instructor asks students to work in groups on a passage that includes several verbs with both direct and indirect objects. She then asks the students to rewrite each sentence with this pattern into its oppositional form, paying close attention to the rule of prepositional inclusion.

better understand the logic behind this statement, it is useful to consider the two approaches in terms of teacher energy. Inductive lessons require more effort and insight on the instructor's part, as they must carefully weigh the students' ability to detect encoded items without a foregrounding of rules and structures. Deductive lessons, on the other hand, require less up-front creativity, as the rules and structures take center stage. In the practice phase that follows, however, creativity is essential, as it is often necessary to encourage students to remain invested now that they are familiar with how a given item functions. When choice is an option, teachers might want to vary their approach depending on what they are teaching and what is at stake. If something is less consequential in terms of assessment, it might provide an opportunity to go fully inductive, allowing students to play with the material and learn through their experiences. Conversely, in a standards-driven setting, a more deductive approach might be what is needed to ensure that the students are adequately prepared for any subsequent assessments.

70 Navigating the English Language Classroom

Table 4.2. Sample Inductive Lesson Plan Activities

Understanding Transitions and Logical Connectors	
1st - Practice: An instructor in an advanced ESL composition course provides students with two excerpts on the same topic. One effectively uses transitions and logical connectors within and between sentences. The other contains a general lack of these resources. After students read each silently, she asks them to work in groups and compare each based on the following questions: Which of the two flowed well? Which helped you follow the author's thinking with ease? Which allowed you to best understand the overall meaning conveyed?	**2nd - Instruction**: The instructor allows the students to share their thoughts in an open class forum, writing their responses on the board. After the discussion, she tells them she wants to focus on a few of their talking points in greater depth. She focuses on instances in which the students pinpointed language devices that connect ideas and link the message across sentences in productive ways. She then reviews a range of categories that span this body of knowledge (e.g., items that create opposition: but, however, and so on).
Examining the Grammar Used in Business Slogans	
1st - Practice: An instructor provides students with a list of fifty corporate slogans of companies within the United States. Some ask questions, while others use statements, commands, and fragments. Some are gendered, and others pit formal English against colloquial English. He then instructs students to work with a partner to fill out a worksheet that requests three different patterns that they collaboratively identify among the slogans, focusing precisely on structural similarities they see across them.	**2nd - Instruction**: The instructor asks students to share their results with the class. While they speak, the instructor creates categories on a shared classroom document. After each of the pairs offers an item or reasserts what another group offered, the instructor moves into a business English lesson on the different grammatical and lexical shapes used within slogans in the United States. Connections are made to the examples the students identified, and the instructor supplements missing patterns.

- *Q2: How do novice teachers manage lesson planning so that it is effective and not time-consuming?*

Once teachers understand their obligations in terms of institutional or programmatic planning (see Q1), teachers must begin to consider the many moving parts of a lesson and how these parts can be satisfied in the most efficient manner possible. For most teachers, lesson planning efficiency ultimately boils down to the concept of time management practices, and lucky for new teachers, there are a few concrete practices that are easy to adopt.

To begin lesson planning in efficient ways, teachers should first and foremost remember that planning happens at multiple levels, from reflections while walking the halls to focused instances of intense planning (Purgason, 2014). They should also begin by exploring the resources at their disposal and the potential role they might play in their lesson planning outcomes. For instance, does the teacher have all of the tools they need, such as boards, handouts, presentation software (PowerPoint, Keynote, for example), textbooks, videos, and so on? By understanding the tools and resources available to educators, teachers ensure that their plans are grounded in the reality of their teaching scenario. Having a solid understanding of the complete environment makes planning less of a guessing game and more of an exercise in applying what the teacher knows and is equipped for, which in turn makes the process more productive.

Another core area that teachers can focus on when lesson planning is the notion of good record-keeping, which in turn aids in time efficiency and materials reusability in lesson implementations. New educators often underestimate the need to develop and maintain repositories of material resources and online informational sites, where helpful handouts often fall into the bin after use and useful sites typically fade into the ether. However, by training ourselves to keep thoughtful records, these resources can be recycled and repurposed across large swathes of time and vast stacks of lessons. One common record keeping method involves creating a physical filing system that allows educators to organize materials into readily accessible go-to resources that can be reviewed at a moment's notice. This is useful when teachers consider the time constraints that they are often under when planning lessons. The more they know where things are, the more they can make use of them when needed. This also extends to digital resources, where keeping running lists of sites, either through lists or through browser bookmarks, renders materials easily accessible for quick and instantaneous retrieval. Some digital resources are also stored on personal hard drives, and in these instances, a digital filing system that is logical and easy to remember is key (such as organizing by course number, by term, or by skill). Whether physical or digital, investing in a personal set of resources yields immeasurable returns, so the time spent creating these repositories, while also adding to the overall time burden for teachers, ultimately has a way of improving teacher efficiency over time.

To build such repositories, it is important to consider where trusted resources reside. This is where interpersonal relationships with coworkers become crucial. Indeed, to make lesson planning more efficient, it is necessary to seek out the advice of more experienced teachers, program administrators, or librarians. Chances are they know the students very well and can point new teachers in the direction of valuable materials. In some cases, this might mean sharing physical resources, but in others it might mean sharing online sites. Regardless, interacting with colleagues is a great way to expand a new instructor's resource pool, so educators should not underestimate the need to make connections and to engage colleagues for assistance as soon as possible. In other words, novice teachers shouldn't be afraid to ask for help. And though some colleagues will inevitably be less amenable to sharing, others will likely jump at the chance.

Building on the notion of sharing, teachers new to the field should not underestimate the trusted resources that they themselves have already started amassing in their studies, internships, or previous positions. For instance, in teacher training programs, mentors commonly provide teachers trainees with a range of useful techniques and strategies for addressing the needs of students within lesson builds. Sample textbooks that have been encountered typically offer myriad examples of how to teach certain items or skills, while sometimes also providing useful handouts that are ready-made and easily adoptable. There are also endless materials-sharing websites that most teachers have encountered and that can easily be found through simple internet searches (while writing this, a quick search for "free ESL lessons" instantly turned up a wealth of online resources). These sites, which are sometimes free, paid, or trade-oriented in their sharing design, allow teachers to proactively and continuously attain additional resources that might in turn add ingenuity and enrichment to their existing resource pool. These resources then become valuable commodities in a collegial environment that often depends on good-natured sharing among peers, giving new teachers more to offer in the exchange.

When planning lessons, teachers should also ask themselves, realistically, how much time it would take their learners to complete a given task. In the early attempts at teaching a course, this can take time to gauge. In fact, this may take a little trial and error, especially if an instructor is brand new to the classroom. Once a teacher does this a few times, however, they start to see what their students can and cannot do in a given timeframe. This is something that even seasoned teachers need to contemplate from time to time, as student groups always bring with them their own classroom identities. What is important is that lesson planning can be rendered more thoughtful and comprehensive by maintaining a realistic outlook on our students' abilities and on the amount of time that will be needed for any actionable item.

One tactic that can foster a strong ability to gauge lesson component timing is through reverse engineering activities (Lambert, 2004). Reverse engineering, which shines light on the many task-oriented twists and turns that will essentially shape the task in question, helps teachers understand how much time may inevitably be needed to properly execute a given task. It accomplishes this by prompting the instructor to consider each component lodged within a given activity. For instance, the teacher has to consider all components that must be taught in order for the student to effectively execute the assignment. They may need to explain, teach, workshop, and conference as needed, but they may also need to expand once in the throes of the process. The general assumption, however, is that they should enter the larger task with an understanding of the core items needed to facilitate student success while leaving space for adaptation as unforeseen issues emerge. Figure 4.1 provides a closer look at the foundational components and instructional moves that might be found within a summarization activity. It begins with the end result and descends into a series of steps that may be needed to set up the assignment.

As Figure 4.1 shows, reverse engineering classroom actions has the potential to shed light on the many underlying steps that must be in place for a given task, simple though it may seem, to be successful. Importantly, these steps illustrate how much time and effort are warranted in bringing a given learning objective to fruition. They also provide additional insight into how larger spans of lessons should be paced in order to establish the foundational steps that will lead to student success. Though labor-intensive, reverse engineering should be considered essential for most major classroom activities,

Culminating stages of the assignment

- Students produce a final summary of their selected reading
- Students revise based on feedback received from peer and instructor
- Instructor reviews student work; one-on-one student conferences
- Students share feedback through in-class workshop and peer review
- Students enter core writing phase for the activity
- Students begin drafting their summary in an in-class activity
- Students formulate outlines in an in-class activity
- Students work with partners to identify items needed in their outline
- Instructor offers a lesson on outlining a summary
- Students select a reading to summarize for the assignment
- Instructor workshops sample summaries to locate effective strategies
- Instructor teaches strategies in summarization (e.g., paraphrase)
- Instructor introduces the summary writing assignment
- Instructor considers what students have learned up to this point and considers what will be needed in each of the subsequent steps

Initial stages of the assignment

Figure 4.1. Reverse engineering a task to understand timing and necessary steps.

especially when new teachers are learning to manage their time within lessons. Once this process has been conducted over several assignments, lessons, and courses, the overall planning commitment tends to become easier as one's experience grows and familiarity with the time needed for certain tasks or activities becomes accessible—the long-term payoff of the teacher's efforts then becomes much more evident.

Another action that new teachers can take to help make lesson planning more time-effective is to come to terms with personal boundaries and find a pathway for placing these boundaries in harmony with work expectations. For instance, depending on a person's life, they may not have all night or weekend to plan. This is where certain meta-planning tactics can come in handy. First, teachers should set a schedule that is realistic for them, one in which planning is prioritized, but not to the detriment of personal life. If a teacher only has a certain window each day to plan, they should ensure that the workspace is devoid of distractions and properly stocked with any materials that will be needed (including treats, as this is a common excuse to meander away from the workspace). The teacher can also turn off phone calls, text messages, and email alerts to keep the limited window of time focused and on task. Second, teachers can study the learning outcomes and schedule for their course well in advance of teaching so that a great deal of the overall course planning can be done ahead of time. This is, of course, with the understanding that daily planning curveballs will arise here and there. In many cases, the initial weeks of a course can be mapped out in advance of actual teaching, lessening the burden over the subsequent weeks and helping to balance the overall time commitment in the midst of teaching. Third, after each lesson that is taught, teachers can make notes for revision immediately after class. Retyping lesson plans may not take place until the end of the day, but by taking real-time notes, teachers ensure that effective teaching practices are always treated in the moment, before memory or out-of-class distractions can become a hindrance. Real-time note-taking makes the revision process more effective in terms of pedagogical accuracy while also rendering it easier to execute at the end of the day when there are only a few extra minutes to spare. The implication, thus, is that the teacher must set aside dedicated time after teaching to quickly address lesson changes. Finally, teachers can develop templates that are effective and reusable. By taking the initial time to develop accessible approaches to lessons, instructors can reduce overall preparation time by having a set approach that is easily recognizable and iterative through predictable repetition. In short, teachers have to be proactive and decisive when it comes to their time, as careful *life planning* often leads to better overall *lesson planning* (see Chapter 15 for more details on effective work–life balance).

- **Q3: How do novice teachers make their lessons flow in a way that is logically progressive from day to day, while also taking into account the course's learning objectives?**

One of the greatest struggles new teachers face is learning to envision lessons as interconnected cogs in the same machine. In the previous questions, our exploration has primarily focused on individual lessons, but now we look at how lessons fit within a larger course as a set of ideas that work in unison to achieve learning objectives.

One area that can serve new teachers well in terms of planning lessons beyond individual days is the idea of double-dipping. No, this isn't referring to chips and dip at a party; rather, it is referring to how teachers can maximize the use of a single pedagogical item by exploiting it in subsequent lessons. Not only does this save time, but it can allow for additional exposures with course content, providing in turn additional opportunities for growth and learning (Lynch & Maclean, 2000). For instance, if a reading is used to demonstrate the relationship between topic sentences and paragraph development in one lesson, the same reading can then be used in a follow-up lesson to pivot into transition devices between sentences within a paragraph. Similarly, the reading used in the previous lesson could become an object of comparison with the current day's reading. In this way, the reading is maximized in terms of its educational yield, lessening the need for additional new readings while reinforcing the students' preexisting schema. Such recycling is common given its benefit; in fact, reusing materials has been shown to positively impact vocabulary development through extended exposure (Zimmerman, 2014) and to improve both item and contextual memory through encounters over time (Chen & Yang, 2020). The bottom line is that double-dipping not only makes materials more accessible and learnable for students but also renders the lesson planning process more productive. In this way, double-dipping can positively impact the overall time dedication required for effective lesson development. Pedagogically speaking, this strategy becomes an easy tactic that saves planning time while reexposing students to material for additional learning opportunities.

When teachers are not restricted in terms of building lessons, they should consider the general shape of an effective lesson. The teacher will ultimately be responsible for initiating, developing, and concluding a lesson's contents in a manner that satisfies the learning goals while also remaining on track in terms of overall course planning (that is, other lessons in the same course). Logically, a lesson should have an opening segment that makes sense, such as a homework review to connect back to a previous lesson or a warm-up activity to connect forward by getting the students relaxed while also revealing a potential preview of the content to come. Virtually all aspects of a given lesson should be in service of moving the learning objectives forward, especially given that each lesson embodies a part of a larger whole of lessons. Both backward-facing and forward-facing segments ask educators to consider the lessons surrounding the one in question. Because of the interconnected nature of lessons, if a new instructor designs a lesson that does not consider its sisters, that lesson might result in a disjointed effect that is counterproductive to learning objective progression. That lesson might also end up causing the instructor to expend more effort than is needed over time, simply because the relationships between *all* lessons were not effectively considered. In other words, to build *an* effective lesson, the instructor needs to hold *all* lessons for the course in their line of sight.

When teachers have less control over how they apply materials—such as in highly preset systems with distinct levels—some of the lesson planning guessing game is actually removed. These regimented plans in turn place a greater deal of the planning burden on the program or collective as opposed to the individual. This type of system can seem restrictive when considering lesson planning, but it can also be helpful in providing good structure and a more readily accessible timeline, meaning that the lessons—and how they work together as a family—are more clearly defined for the teacher well in advance of teaching. The more fleshed-out nature of a preset curricular system inevitably means that the shape of the lessons as a whole will emerge more clearly, reducing individual effort in favor of established protocol.

Nevertheless, when working within more restrictive programs, teachers still need to rely on ingenuity, as each class will carry its own identity, complete with strengths and weaknesses. This statement implies that some degree of flexibility is required within rigidity, which means that even in the most rigid of programs, there will always be moments of teacher agency in terms of planning. Planning within rigidity may amount to only subtle shifts, such as how a teacher emphasizes aspects of a lesson, spends more or less time on a segment of a lesson depending on need, or rearranges segments to alter the flow to a more suitable progression that aligns well with the proficiency of the students. These are all things that the course instructor better understands given their working relationship with the students. To condense this into something actionable, the learning objectives and standards that the program requires should be a first consideration before deviating too far from a defined path, but there are likely subtle shifts that can occur in even the most rigid of settings.

• Q4: When lessons are not going to plan, how do novice teachers readjust the plan?

This question, unfortunately, is one that really has to be experienced to truly understand its answer. It isn't until educators are in the classroom that they start to feel the impact of a plan that is—for lack of better wording—derailing. However, educators can always rely on their experiences as students and their training as professional educators to lessen planning hurdles.

One way that teachers can rely on training to help them address planning micro-adjustments is by remembering that, by and large, novice teachers enter into their profession through extensive experiences. In terms of *experiences*, teachers not only consider their teacher training programs but their time as learners more generally. As general learners, new teachers will come to understand that they have all been in situations in which a mentor's lesson failed to realize its anticipated impact. It is to a given teacher's advantage to reflect deeply on these experiences and how they unfolded at the time. Was the activity done away with, or did the teacher push through, to everyone's chagrin? Was the activity not explained well, and the teacher merely had to rehash the instructions through paraphrase in order for the lesson to connect with the students? A new educator's preexisting time as a learner can provide them with endless insight into what works and what does not work from the learner's perspective. This is useful for educators new to the profession because they can draw on these experiences to inform their own moment-to-moment micro-adjustments, basing their decisions more on lived experience than on conjecture.

Similarly, as trained professionals, teachers can rely on best practices that they have encountered in lectures, discussions, textbook interactions, and assignments that they have tackled to get them to this point in their career. Likewise, new teachers should not underestimate the simple suggestions from peers that they encounter from time to time; for just as the suggestions change with time, so too does the identity of the classroom. What would have been unconscionable in one class may be just the thing in another, so educators should always remain open to trying different tactics at different times and in different groups or settings. Indeed, seemingly inconsequential advice or comments always stem from the experiences of others, so it is not unreasonable to think that, over time, the right situation will emerge for the advice given. And in this way, the notion of adaptation—or more overtly, an ability to grow and change—becomes crucial for any new teacher entering the field (Shishavan & Sadeghi, 2009; Al-Mahrooqi et al., 2015; Al-Seghayer, 2017).

Teachers new to the field can also rely on more concrete lesson planning adjustment tactics to navigate less-than-perfect classroom moments. To illustrate, a teacher could use the idea of reframing to take a given lesson's action and shift it into a new light. For example, if this teacher is teaching the English modal verb system, they might begin by talking about the system's role in producing politeness within interaction (as one of many modal uses). If this description is not enough for the students to internalize the material, they might then *reframe* this aspect of the modal lesson to notions of social obligation or logical possibility, the two dominant paradigms within which most modal verbs function (Master, 2017). This reframing action might also be thought of as a type of *pivoting* action, where the teacher makes subtle shifts into different subaspects of the feature under review. If the reframing or pivoting is insufficient, then aspects of the lesson may need to be, quite simply, *replaced* in real time. Such maneuvers imply that it is advantageous to come into any lesson with a fallback option just in case something doesn't work. As an example, if the aforementioned action on modals is still not getting through to the students, then the teacher might replace a simple list with a more refined chart depicting the continuum-like nature of the system. The teacher can also build on this replacement with *referencing*, in which they reference material that the students have already learned to help make connections that will render this new material more accessible.

Just as it is important to navigate issues within parts of a lesson, so too is it important to conceptualize the overall lesson as a unit before entering the classroom, as this can help to facilitate a larger contingency plan. With regard to contingency, certain lessons as a whole can sometimes run long or short. Before entering class, it is helpful to reflect deeply on *omission*, or what can be cut, if the lesson is in fact taking longer than expected. If nothing can be cut due to assessment benchmarks or programmatic mandates, then it is equally useful to consider how a given aspect can be transformed into a homework assignment that can then become a quick warm-up for the next class. Predicting what can be scrapped, in advance, allows the lesson to be shortened without accidently sacrificing any necessary content. Conversely, it is equally useful to consider what can be done if the lesson runs short. In such cases, the teacher relies on the concept of *extension* to help them determine ways in which they can add to the lesson without making the addition feel detached from the content. For instance, returning to the example of modal verbs, if the teacher reaches the end of the class and has ten minutes to spare, they might have a few stock sentences at the ready that would ask students to transform a single modal verb (*must*, for instance) into its phrasal equivalent (*to have to*), and vice versa. By attempting to predict what might be possible with too little or too much time, the teacher recognizes that each lesson requires tactical tools at the ready to remedy the range of situations that might occur.

Teachers must also remember that with each lesson planning experience, they will inevitably learn something. New teachers sometimes underestimate the benefit of actually writing up physical lesson plans for their courses, as a thorough write-up involves substantial time investment. Nevertheless, it is an exceptionally useful exercise to go through, especially the first time that a course is taught, as the returns over time are significant. By planning lessons out fully and with depth, new teachers learn to feel the lesson, to understand what presents as reasonable or unreasonable, and to develop resources in ways that are productively reusable. So even though it is a huge time commitment, it is one that yields great returns throughout the span of a career.

• Q5: Each class is different, so how do novice teachers plan lessons to keep all students engaged?

One of the most effective planning actions that new teachers can take is to be responsive to the vibe of the students (Johnson, 1992). If students are confused, then something might need more time. If they didn't read the assigned readings, the instructor might have to rethink how they will approach the activity and whom they will call on. Based on one's experiences in the classroom, and the developing relationships with students that result from those experiences, teachers might need to add additional scaffolding devices to assist weaker students who are struggling. If the first paper in a reading and writing course was done without a prewriting activity, then the next paper might need one factored into its lesson, either as an in-class workshop or as a take-home task. If teachers consider this well in advance, they will likely have time to fold it into the plan, as long as they have the creative license to do so. In more rigid systems, foresight is even more crucial, and it often takes the form of what has been articulated in disabilities studies as "proactive classroom management strategies" (Nagro et al., 2019, p.131–140). When language instructors are proactive in their planning, they might perform premeditated tasks such as reallocating the seating by mixing students up so that weaker students are given opportunities to work with more advanced others. Teachers might also rethink the sequence of a general lesson simply because they know the students and they know what they need to encounter in succession in order to be successful. Regardless of the tactic taken, being proactive is a great strategy for gaining freedom within an otherwise restrictive system.

Despite the usefulness of gauging instruments such as exams or assignments, student variation in terms of proficiency will remain a constant concern, as people learn at their own pace and in their own ways. If a teacher knows their students, they will also begin to see who is good at reading, or who is good at writing, or who is the best speaker in the class, or who always seems to get the grammar. Learn to play to their strengths and how to gently shepherd the students into more advanced areas of content as they become ready to advance. This can increase their sense of achievement in incremental ways that will eventually add up and promote a healthier outlook for students who might be struggling. From the teacher's perspective, this will also provide useful tools for navigating a lesson that may not be going to plan or that may require a shift in thinking. As an example, when no one answers a question that has been posed, it can lead to excessive wait-time segments. In these moments, a given teacher might pivot more quickly to one of their better speakers in the class, especially if they know they can handle the question. Such pivots can save time and help the lesson remain on track in terms of execution. Just keep in mind that pivoting excessively might rob students who need more processing time, so there should always be balance. If an instructor is pushing students forward in their learning, and they aren't exactly ready, then it may mean that more attention should be paid to the planning process overall. In essence, the teacher in question has to look at the lesson plan as a living, breathing figure in the classroom, and by treating it as such, they begin to see each class session as something that can be planned but also something that will inevitably require maintenance to attain full engagement and to ensure all are ready to progress.

Big Picture and Bottom Line

When it comes to planning lessons, what this chapter is really discussing is a game of trial and error. New teachers have to find their footing in the classroom through experiences, for better or worse, because no amount of training can possibly cover the immense spectrum of issues that could potentially arise within a given setting. Teachers can ask questions and adopt strategies that have been suggested by peers, but planning is by its very nature preliminary, which implies that its realization in the classroom will always be somewhat predictable and somewhat unpredictable depending on the identity of the class.

By considering lesson planning as a crucial first step in terms of classroom preparation, new teachers are better positioned to enter their teaching assignments with confidence, all the while recognizing that this confidence might be shaken from time to time by new experiences that require new thought processes and approaches. Such shakes to confidence should not be seen as a step backwards, though, as they are a crucial point of entry into teaching. In short, trial and error is something that all teachers go through, as are shakes to confidence, so the best thing they can do in terms of lesson planning is to embrace at least some degree of uncertainty as a part of the job, not as something not to overcome, but as something to navigate.

Food for Thought

1. Pull a lesson plan that you have created for class or taught from in your own classroom setting. Rewrite the lesson from one of the following perspectives to see how it might transform to meet the new demands.
   a. Change the lesson to a lower or higher proficiency level (for example, if the class was originally working with low intermediate learners, then consider making it a beginning level or advanced level class and see how this impacts the lesson).
   b. Change the lesson to a different educational setting (if the class was in a primary school setting, for instance, then consider making it a university setting).
   c. Change the lesson to a different set of time constraints (so, if the class originally met for two hours, then consider making it one and a half hours or three hours in length)
2. Review the contents of this chapter on lesson planning, and then envision yourself as an instructor teaching its message to new teachers. How would you design a stand-alone lesson that is two to three hours in length? Using your preferred lesson plan template, imagine this chapter, in abbreviated form, while attending to sequence and pace. Be sure to build in mini activities to help students activate the knowledge as you cover it.

References

Al-Mahrooqi, R., Denman, C., Al-Siyabi, J., & Al-Maamari, F. (2015). Characteristics of a good EFL teacher: Omani EFL teacher and student perspectives. *Sage Open, 5*(2). https://doi.org/10.1177/2158244015584782

Al-Seghayer, K. (2017). The central characteristics of successful ESL/EFL teachers. *Journal of Language Teaching and Research, 8*(5), 881–890. http://dx.doi.org/10.17507/jltr.0805.06

Chen, H., & Yang, J. (2020). Multiple exposures enhance both item memory and contextual memory over time. *Frontiers in Psychology, 11*, Article 565169. https://doi.org/10.3389/fpsyg.2020.565169

Gollin, J. (1998). Key concepts in ELT: Deductive vs. inductive language learning. *ELT Journal, 52*(1), 88–89. https://doi.org/10.1093/elt/52.1.88

Hammerly, H. (1975). The deduction/induction controversy. *The Modern Language Journal, 59*(1/2), 15–18. https://doi.org/10.2307/325441

Johnson, K. E. (1992). Learning to teach: Instructional actions and decisions of preservice ESL teachers. *TESOL Quarterly, 26*(3), 507–535. https://doi.org/10.2307/3587176

Lambert, C. (2004). Reverse-engineering communication tasks. *ELT Journal, 58*(1), 18–27. https://doi.org/10.1093/elt/58.1.18

Lynch, T., & Maclean, J. (2000). Exploring the benefits of task repetition and recycling for classroom language learning. *Language Teaching Research, 4*(3), 221–250. https://doi.org/10.1177/13621688000040303

Master, P. (2017). *Systems in English grammar: An introduction for language teachers* (2nd ed.). CreateSpace.

Nagro, S. A, Fraser, D. W., & Hooks, S. D. (2019). Lesson planning with engagement in mind: Proactive classroom management strategies for curriculum instruction. *Intervention in School and Clinic, 54*(3), 131–140. https://doi.org/10.1177/1053451218767905

Purgason, K. B. (2014). Lesson planning in second/foreign language teaching. In M. Celce-Murcia, D. M., Brinton, & M. A. Snow (Eds.). *Teaching English as a second or foreign language* (4th ed., pp. 362–379). Heinle Cengage Learning.

Shaffer, C. (1989). A comparison of inductive and deductive approaches to teaching foreign languages. *The Modern Language Journal, 73*(4), 395–403. https://doi.org/10.1111/j.1540-4781.1989.tb05319.x

Shishavan, H. B., & Sadeghi, K. (2009). Characteristics of an effective English language teacher as perceived by Iranian teachers and learners of English. *English Language Teaching, 2*(4), 130–143.

Takimoto, M. (2008). The effects of deductive and inductive instruction on the development of language learners' pragmatic competence. *The Modern Language Journal, 92*(3), 369–386. https://doi.org/10.1111/j.1540-4781.2008.00752.x

Zimmerman, C. B. (2014). Teaching and learning vocabulary for second language learners. In M. Celce-Murcia, D. M., Brinton, & M. A. Snow (Eds.), *Teaching English as a second or foreign language* (4th ed., pp. 289–302). Heinle Cengage Learning.

CHAPTER 5

Delivering Lessons

Contextualization

This chapter is complementary to Chapter 4 since it focuses on the language lesson; that is, the enactment of the lesson plan in the language classroom. The language lesson has three different dimensions: its opening, its sequencing, and its closure. These dimensions interact and contribute to the effectiveness or failure of the instructional process. This chapter focuses on the three dimensions of the lesson and also addresses pacing, a factor that contributes to establishing and maintaining the momentum of the language lesson. Furthermore, the chapter addresses the relationship between the lesson plan and its delivery in the language classroom. The chapter concludes with a discussion of the common challenges faced by novice teachers as they deliver their lessons.

Case Study: I Am Afraid My Lesson Will Flop!

A few months ago, a student-teacher enrolled in her English as a foreign language (EFL) teacher preparation program's practicum course met with her mentor teacher regarding the first one-hour solo lesson she was scheduled to teach. Our student teacher had planned a very good lesson and had received her mentor teacher's feedback regarding the lesson objectives and activities. Despite all of this, our student-teacher felt very nervous. She continuously strategized about the opening and the closing of her lesson. She was also nervous about how she would pace the lesson to maintain momentum. Although our student-teacher had taught several mini lessons, this was the first time she would be fully responsible for leading a whole-class

84   Navigating the English Language Classroom

one-hour lesson. Therefore, our student teacher felt tremendous pressure to deliver an effective lesson.

Concerns like those of our student-teacher are very common among novice teachers. They understand that well-designed lesson plans can flop if the lesson delivery is not effective. In fact, a feature that characterizes good teaching is the intentionality with which teachers deliver their lessons. This means that rather than improvising how they open and close their lessons, and how they pace and sequence the activities in their lessons, novice teachers need to take the time to review their lesson plans and prepare their lessons' delivery to maximize their effectiveness. Given these important issues, in this chapter, we offer a few suggestions on how to deal with the various dimensions of the language lesson and how to solve the problems that novice teachers may face when teaching their lessons.

Common Concerns

The questions below are designed to guide novice teachers as they prepare to deliver their lessons.

- *Q1. What is the relationship between the lesson plan and the language lesson?*
- *Q2. What are the various dimensions of a good language lesson?*
- *Q3. What strategies can novice teachers use to maintain momentum in their lessons?*
- *Q4. What are some common challenges faced by novice teachers as they deliver their lessons?*

Effective Practices for Delivering Lessons

• *Q1. What is the relationship between the lesson plan and the language lesson?*

Work in the ELT field has produced a variety of written lesson plan models. The first model is Harmer's (2001) three-stage lesson plan titled "Presentation, practice, and production" (commonly known as the PPP model), in which the teacher presents a language point that students practice in activities that go from guided to independent. The second model is the "engage, study, activate" (ESA) model, which is perceived as a more flexible alternative to the PPP model because it allows for multiple ESA cycles (Harmer, 2007, as cited in Purgason, 2014). Another lesson plan model, originating in the education field, is the Hunter model (2004). This model is flexible, sometimes integrating five steps, and depending on the focus of the lesson, it may integrate seven or even nine steps (Hunter, 2004, as cited in Purgason, 2014).

Despite the apparent differences among all of the lesson plan models described in the previous paragraph, they all share a common sequence. In fact, regardless of whether teachers use PPP, the five-step model, or the ESA model, for example, central to all of them is the fact that they flow from the presentation stage, where the teacher provides language input, to the practice stage, which flows from guided to independent practice. In turn, all of the lesson plan models can be adapted to include multiple cycles in which new language is presented and practiced. (For a sample lesson plan, see Appendix 5.1.)

Experienced teachers often have a preferred lesson plan model that they consistently use, though they will still adapt it to meet their teaching style and their students' needs. Adhering to one model may seem to be too boring; however, students benefit from the structure since it gives them a sense of security (Purgason, 2014; Richards & Lockhart, 1994).

While the lesson plan is typically a document produced—with more or less detail—on paper (see Chapter 4 for an extensive treatment of lesson planning), the enactment of the lesson plan in the actual classroom is known as the language lesson. As explained by Richards and Farrell (2011), the language lesson consists of various activities designed to meet established objectives. The language lesson is a professional genre (Swales, 1990), as it follows a structure easily recognizable by professionals in the English language teaching (ELT) field. The language lesson is characterized by three dimensions that will be the focus of Question 2.

• Q2. What are the various dimensions of a good language lesson?

Regardless of the lesson plan model implemented by novice teachers, "a language lesson consists of a sequence of activities that lead toward your lesson goals or objectives" (Richards & Farrell, 2011, p. 77). Although the starting point for a good language lesson is a well-developed lesson plan, the enactment of an effective lesson requires that novice teachers pay attention to how they structure their language lessons. What this means is that when teachers deliver their lessons, they have to attend to the three dimensions of the language lesson—the opening, the sequencing, and the closing—that can ultimately contribute to the effective delivery of the lesson

86 Navigating the English Language Classroom

(Richard-Amato, 2010; Richards & Farrell, 2011). In this section, we describe the three dimensions of the language lesson, as well as the factors that novice teachers need to pay attention to as they focus on each of these dimensions.

The Opening of the Lesson

Let's imagine a language lesson that opens with the teacher walking into the classroom and saying something like this: "Hello. Open your books to page ten. Let's start reading." What is the problem with this lesson opening? How would you react if you were a student in this teacher's class? Most likely, you would not be mentally prepared to start reading, as you would not have had an opportunity to tune into the lesson.

The opening, which involves how the teacher starts the lesson, usually takes place during the first few minutes of class and, as Crookes (2003) puts it, "is often said to be important in aiding learning" (p. 66) because it frames the lesson and prepares students for what is to come. The lesson opening can serve several purposes. One of these involves connecting the previous lesson with the current one by engaging students in a review activity, which serves as a warm-up to the current lesson. For example, in a lesson designed to teach students the items that need to be included in a first-aid kit, the teacher could lead students in a "Simon Says" Total Physical Response-like activity focusing on the parts of the body (see Appendix 5.1 for an example of how the activity fits into an actual lesson). Another engaging warm-up and review activity that can be used to connect the previous lesson with the current one involves students working as a whole class in a "hot seat" activity designed to review a grammar lesson on question formation. In this activity, the student in the hot seat becomes a famous character (usually a popular actor or historical figure) but does not disclose the name of the personality. The rest of the class has to guess who the person in the hot seat is by taking turns asking yes/no questions.

Besides connecting the previous lesson with the current one, the opening of a lesson can be used to establish lesson objectives by providing students with the day's agenda and explaining how the class will achieve those objectives. In this case, the teacher could introduce the day's objectives by enthusiastically saying something like this: "Last week, we learned the parts of the body. By the end of today's lesson, we will be able to give and receive advice using the items in our first-aid kit." (See Appendix 5.1.)

A third purpose of the opening of a lesson is to create a break between the outside world and the classroom environment. This can be achieved by engaging students in a motivating activity (for example, a memory game or

Kahoot game—a game-based learning platform). In addition, to create an imaginary wall between the outside world and the classroom, the teacher may choose to engage students in a meditation exercise, for example, as a means to promote a sense of well-being. In creating an imaginary wall or a break between the outside world and the classroom environment, the teacher's goal is to get students to immerse themselves in classroom activities rather than being preoccupied with their life concerns.

The opening of the lesson can also be used to help students develop or activate background knowledge on the topic of the lesson to be taught. For example, in a content-based lesson focusing on earthquakes and earthquake preparedness, students could be asked to brainstorm what an earthquake emergency kit should contain. In a lesson focusing on how to order food at a restaurant, students could participate in a bingo activity designed to review the names of different foods. Alternatively, in a lesson focusing on house chores, students could be asked to work in pairs, sit back-to-back, and take turns describing a room in their home. As one student in the pair describes a room, the other student draws the room on a blank sheet of paper. After both students have described and drawn a picture of their partners' rooms, they share and compare their drawings.

A further purpose of the opening of a lesson is to have students complete homework assignments. This is often the case in adult, community-based English as a second language (ESL) classes attended by immigrant students. These students oftentimes do not have time to do their homework due to their many competing life obligations. Therefore, to open their lessons, teachers may choose to allow students to collaborate with their peers as they complete (or review) homework assignments.

Lesson openings are expected to be brief: they are meant to set the stage for the main phase of the lesson, which is characterized by the sequencing of its activities (Richard-Amato, 2010; Richards & Farrell, 2011; Richards & Lockhart, 1994). However, deciding how "brief" lesson openings should be is a challenging issue since the length of the opening stage depends on a variety of factors, including, but not limited to, the length of the class, the students' level of engagement in the activities, the climate of the classroom, and so forth. Therefore, as novice teachers decide on the length of the opening stage of their lessons, they will need to attend to the above factors. At the same time, novice teachers will need to keep in mind that if lesson openings run for an extended period, they may slow down the flow of the lesson (Richard-Amato, 2010).

In summary, the opening of a lesson can serve different purposes. However, regardless of how novice teachers open the lesson, they should keep in mind that the opening sets the tone for what is to come. Therefore, in conceptualizing the lesson, the opening should not be an afterthought. Instead, novice teachers should pay attention to their opening strategies since they will contribute to the overall success or failure of the lesson at hand. In addition, as teachers implement the different strategies described in this section, they will need to reflect on the extent to which their openings contribute to the smooth functioning of the lesson. Finally, learning how to open a lesson is not an exact science. It requires that novice teachers engage in a process of trial and error: what works with one group of students may fail with another one. More importantly, learning how to open a lesson requires that teachers engage in a process of reflection designed to make them aware of the strengths and weaknesses of their lesson openings.

Now that we have covered the opening of the language lesson, we are ready to focus on the second dimension of the language lesson: its sequencing.

The Sequencing of the Lesson

The sequencing of the lesson involves the ordering of the activities that provide structure to the language lesson (Álvarez, 2008; Goldsmith, 2009; Richards & Farrell, 2011; Richards & Lockhart, 1994;). Usually, the lesson sequence is determined by the lesson plan. However, in sequencing lessons, there is a principle common to the various lesson plan models described in this chapter: Teachers should consider the level of complexity of the various activities in the lesson and sequence instruction from "easy" to "difficult" (Ellis, 2003, as cited in Baralt et al., 2014), with cognitively and linguistically simple (or guided tasks) presenting few memory and attention demands presented first, and followed by increasingly cognitively and linguistically complex (or less guided) activities (Robinson & Gilabert, 2007, as cited in Baralt et al., 2014). This rationale is based on the idea that language learners have limited attentional capacity; therefore, it is difficult for them to simultaneously attend to the various factors required to complete a task (Allaw & McDonough, 2019; Skehan, 1996, as cited in Baralt et al., 2014). (See Appendix 5.1 for an example of how the activities in the sample lesson go from guided to independent and, at the same time, go from less to more cognitively demanding.)

Besides sequencing lessons from simple to more complex tasks, there is another principle that guides ELT instruction. This principle supports the notion that in teaching reading (or listening) lessons, instruction should engage students in three stages: pre-reading (or listening), while-reading (or listening), and post-reading (or listening) (Field, 2002; Goh, 2014; Grabe & Stoller, 2014; Hedgcock & Ferris, 2018). The pre-reading (or listening) stage is meant to prepare students for the task that is to follow. In addition, this stage is meant to imitate what strategic readers (or listeners) do in real life: Rather than jumping into the reading (or listening) task cold, they reflect on what they know about the materials, brainstorm the purposes for which they will read (or listen to the materials), predict the focus of the reading (or listening) text, and so on. The second stage, while-reading (or listening), involves the exploitation of the materials by engaging students in several rounds of reading (or listening) activities. This stage is designed to promote increased comprehension, the development of strategic performance, vocabulary development, and more. The final stage, the post-reading (or listening) stage, which also involves several activities, is designed to get students to think critically about the reading text or listening passage.

As we have shown in this section, lessons are characterized by integrating a variety of activities that, regardless of the lesson plan model implemented, reflect a common sequence. To provide internal coherence to the various activities in a lesson, teachers implement transitions. Transitions play an important role in the lesson since they provide what Stoller and Grabe (2017) call "explicitly planned linkages" (p. 60). To transition between activities in a lesson, teachers working with lower-level proficiency students may choose to use signals that are meant to grab the students' attention. These signals include but are not limited to raising one's hand and keeping it raised until students make eye contact with the teacher; using a chime or bell to get the students' attention; turning off the classroom lights; remaining quiet until students are silent, and such like. With more advanced students, teachers may choose to make statements that signal the connection between an activity that students have just completed and an activity that will follow. For example, a teacher may choose to say something like: "We have just brainstormed what an earthquake preparedness kit needs to have. Now we will do a reading on earthquake preparedness and identify what supplies, other than the ones we identified, we need to have in our kit." Regardless of the language that teachers use to weave the various activities in a lesson, central to the notion of transitions is the idea that they should be overt, since this provides students with a cognitive map of the lesson's direction. At the same time, overt transitions contribute to relieving students of the mental pressure they have to experience to find the logical connections between the various activities in the lesson (Steinman, 2013).

Despite the important role that transitions play in delivering instruction, novice teachers often forget to use transitions in their teaching since they are often overwhelmed by the multiple demands of the classroom (Feldon, 2007). This oversight is problematic because transitions provide meaningfulness to the activities and, at the same time, bring coherence to the lesson (Stoller & Grabe, 2017). So how should novice teachers address this challenge? They should strategize how to alleviate themselves of the mental burden of doing transitions by planning how they will transition from one activity to the next. Besides planning, novice teachers could have bullet points on the daily agenda displayed on the board, reminding themselves to create transitions between the various activities in the lesson.

To conclude, as teachers prepare to deliver their lessons, they need to strategize how they will sequence their lessons for maximum effect purposes. They will also need to consider how the activities in their lessons will be connected to provide coherence to their lessons. Initially, planning for all of these classroom events will take time and effort. However, as novice teachers become more experienced and confident, the planning process will become more manageable and less time-consuming.

The Closing of the Lesson

Let's consider the following scenario: You are teaching a lesson and running out of time to bring closure to the day's activities. Consequently, you find yourself shouting out the homework assignment as your students are walking out of the classroom because they have to take the bus, they have another class to attend, or they simply are ready to move on to their next activity. While we have all made mistakes like these, we need to learn to avoid them, given that a well-executed closure prevents students from leaving the class "without a satisfying ending" (Ganske, 2017, p. 99) (a point also made by Purgason, 2014; Richards & Lockhart, 1994).

The closing of the lesson, much like its opening, serves multiple purposes. It can be used to facilitate a recap or a quick summary of what students have learned in the lesson. In turn, this recap or summary also serves as a brief formative assessment of student learning, carried out before students are assigned a real-world homework activity that may become the warm-up and review in the next lesson (Richard-Amato, 2010; Richards & Lockhart, 1994). Given these factors, it is important to end lessons on a high note that leaves students and teachers with a strong sense of accomplishment. However, this does not mean that the closure of the lesson needs to be lengthy or complicated. A simple "What is your takeaway from today's lesson?" or "Take thirty seconds and write down one idea (or vocabulary word, for instance) you learned today" followed by selected students' responses, would suffice. Another simple technique designed to close the lesson involves having students turn in an "exit ticket." This technique, usually seen in K-12 or adult ESL classrooms, involves having students quickly share an expression, or a vocabulary word, for example, they learned in class as they leave the classroom.

While the closing of the lesson seems to be straightforward, we have seen classrooms in which teachers, rather than the students, identify the vocabulary or grammatical structures taught in the lesson, for example. The closing of the lesson should work as a formative assessment of *student* learning; therefore, we recommend that students engage in a short activity that allows *them* to recap or consolidate their learning. This type of closure provides the teacher with opportunities to assess the extent to which their lesson has succeeded and, at the same time, promotes high student satisfaction.

In summary, a language lesson is similar to a theater play. It has a beginning (the opening of the lesson) that is designed to set the stage for the lesson. It follows an internal sequence consisting of several activities (the play's events) that have internal coherence. The lesson, much like a theater play, gets wrapped up by bringing closure to its activities. A good play leaves its audience with a sense of satisfaction. Much like a good play, a well-delivered lesson leaves students and their teacher with a sense of accomplishment. Thinking about a theater play and a language lesson as comparable events will help teachers understand the important role that the various dimensions of a good language lesson play in delivering instruction that promotes student satisfaction.

• Q3. What strategies can novice teachers use to maintain momentum in their lessons?

Momentum can be understood as "the lesson flowing without stops and starts, disruptions, or discontinuity" (Shindler, 2010, p. 205). To maintain momentum, teachers need to pace their lessons in such a way that they "communicate a sense of development" (Richards & Lockhart, 1994, p. 122). That is, instruction is orchestrated in a way that engages students in the lesson, ensuring the lesson is moving towards the objectives, and students are moving in concert with the teacher as they complete the lesson activities. Attending to these various factors can pose a challenge for novice teachers since they need to have what Shindler (2010) calls, "metaphorical eyes in the back of their head" (p. 205). Therefore, the question that novice teachers can ask themselves is: What strategies can they implement to keep their lessons moving and maintain the lesson momentum? Or to put it another

92   Navigating the English Language Classroom

way: What strategies contribute to the pacing of a lesson so that the teacher can keep the students' attention and the lesson flows? Following are several suggestions intended to contribute to achieving what Richards and Lockhart (1994) refer to as "suitable pacing" (p. 123). These suggestions are grounded in principled and widely accepted pedagogical practices in both the education and the ELT field (Alber, 2012; Farrell, 2006; Harmer, 2015; Richard-Amato, 2010; Richards & Farrell, 2011; Richards & Lockhart, 1994; Shindler, 2010).

1. Time activities and make students aware of the time allotted to them. At the same time, be flexible. If you observe students are highly engaged in the activities and need more time to complete them, allot extra time. Conversely, if you notice students are losing interest in the activities and are becoming distracted, shorten the activities. Central to the notion of timing activities is the idea that they should not drag on, causing students to lose interest and momentum. A rule of thumb provided by Gower and Walters (1983, as cited in Richards & Lockhart, 1994), is that as long as the objectives of an activity are reached, it is better to stop the activity when it is going well rather than when interest in the activity has waned. This approach will leave students with a sense of satisfaction and excitement, and, in all probability, will ensure that the next time a similar activity is implemented, students will be motivated to participate.

2. Engage students in a variety of activities within the same lesson. Doing so will provide the lesson with a sense of movement or flow that contributes towards achieving the lesson objectives. At the same time, engaging students in a variety of activities will contribute to avoiding a sense of boredom and prevent students from losing attention.

3. Vary the grouping arrangements within the same lesson. Having students work in different arrangements (pairs, small groups, one-centered, whole class, for example) will allow students to receive input from different peers and, at the same time, will contribute to building momentum in the lesson.

4. Provide clear instructions. Ensure that before embarking on an activity, students have a clear understanding of the activity's objectives and the steps necessary to meet them. Break down instructions into manageable steps. Avoid lengthy and winding oral instructions like "Now you will get into groups, I will give you a

handout, and, working in your groups, you will participate in a discussion that requires that you agree or disagree with the statements on the handout." A more effective approach to providing clear instructions is to break them down and have students follow them step by step: "Let's get into groups of four." (The teacher signals how the groups will be formed and quickly gets students to join their groups. The teacher moves on with instructions.) "We are going to do an exciting activity! Now, I will give each of you a handout." (The teacher quickly distributes the handout.) "Read the instructions on the handout silently. You have thirty seconds to do this." (The teacher waits until students look up from their seats.) (The teacher does a comprehension check.) "OK. What am I asking you to do?" (As a couple of students respond, the teacher writes what the students say on the board. Then, the teacher continues.) "Good. Let's model how you are going to complete the task." (The teacher models with a student). While it may seem that this step-by-step approach to giving instructions is time-consuming, in reality, it is very efficient as it prevents student confusion, which often results in the teacher having to repeat instructions to individual students during the activity.

5. Avoid lengthy presentations of new teaching points which are not supported by images or realia. As explained in this chapter, language learners, especially those with low proficiency levels, have a limited cognitive and language memory capacity; therefore, long explanations without visual support will likely confuse or lose them. This means that rather than, for example, defining what a book is ("A book is a written work which has pages . . ."), teachers should show students a book and say something like: "Look! This is a book!" (Teacher displays another book and says) "This is a book too! And look at your book! I love books!"

6. Be prepared for your lesson. This involves having all necessary handouts ready so that there is no "dead" time or time wasted between activities.

Central to the suggestions in this section is the idea that the language teacher needs to be tuned into the lesson to ensure that the pacing of the lesson contributes to maintaining its momentum. However, the responsibility for the lesson's pacing should not be limited to the teacher alone. In reality, students also have an important role to play since, for the lesson to be effective, they have to work in concert with the teacher. This means that

94   Navigating the English Language Classroom

the pacing of the language lesson is co-constructed by the teacher and the students in the classroom, who have to work together to meet the language lesson's objectives.

- **Q4. What are some common challenges faced by novice teachers as they deliver their lessons?**

As explained by Purgason (2014), no lesson goes exactly according to plan. As novice teachers deliver their lessons, they will have to make real-time or on-the-spot decisions to address unanticipated problems. While experienced teachers have developed strategies designed to help them deal with these problems, novice teachers often feel that the problems they face will derail their teaching. In this section, we identify five common problems that teachers often face as they teach their lessons.

The first problem that may often challenge the delivery of a novice teacher's lesson involves having developed a lesson that contains many activities and, as teachers deliver their lesson, they realize they will not be able to complete all of the activities as planned. To avoid this problem, as teachers prepare to deliver their lessons, they should decide which activities are a must-do and which ones can be skipped. At the same time, the activities that can be skipped should be saved for those times when a lesson runs short. If this is the case, then an activity that was left undone in a previous lesson can be used to provide language learners with language practice and, at the same time, fill the time in a meaningful way.

The second problem that novice teachers may face is that the lesson activities may be too complex—or conversely, too easy—to do, and students quickly lose motivation to complete them. When this happens, teachers should quickly stop the lesson and recalibrate it. This could be done by engaging students in a motivating game while the teacher is thinking of how to modify the lesson to get students to participate in an alternative activity. Doing this requires quick problem-solving and multitasking skills on the part of the novice teacher. Therefore, a more manageable solution for novice teachers may involve anticipating problematic activities at the time of lesson planning and strategizing how to adjust the level of difficulty of the activities (see Chapter 4 for ideas on this issue).

Novice teachers also feel challenged when a lesson may not be motivating, or there may be external factors that affect the lesson or the classroom climate. To address this issue, it helps to have a repertoire of backup activities that can be used to change the pace or the mood of the lesson. For example, for Common European Framework of Reference (CEFR) A1 students (beginning language learners), teachers could have students participate in a hangman activity designed to review the spelling of commonly used vocabulary. Another simple CEFR A1 activity involves having students work in small groups and participate in a category game competition. The teacher assigns students categories of nouns (vegetables, for example). Working in groups, students have to list six vegetables. The first group to complete the list shouts "Done!" CEFR B1 (low intermediate) students could participate in a calendar activity focusing on their previous week's activities. In this activity, students fill out their calendars for their previous week; then, working in pairs, students ask and answer questions about their past week. After the activity is over, the pairs share the activities that they had in common. CEFR C1 (low advanced) students could participate in a small-group problem-solving activity in which, for example, they have to think creatively to build a shelter on an island. In summary, novice teachers should always be ready for any contingency by having backup ideas if the lesson goes awry.

Fourth, lessons may go in an unexpected direction because a student raises a question in which the class shows great interest. These moments, known as "teachable moments," are extremely valuable because they have captured the attention of the class. Therefore, rather than continuing with the planned lesson and disregarding the students' concerns, teachers should take the opportunity to address the question.

Finally, a common challenge faced by teachers who integrate technology in their classrooms is a slow or intermittent internet connection or a technology tool malfunction. When this happens, teachers should avoid getting frustrated and instead, motivate students by getting them to think about a potential solution to the problem (Bennett, 2023). However, after spending a few minutes trying to find the solution, teachers should resort to a low-tech backup plan (a paper and pencil activity, for example) and continue with their lesson.

In summary, it is never too early to start developing a library of activities that can be plugged into a lesson that needs a change of pace or has lost momentum. On the other hand, having designed a lesson that contains too many activities is not a bad problem to have. Novice teachers can save those activities that have been unused and eventually implement them in a review or consolidation lesson.

Big Picture and Bottom Line

The effectiveness of a lesson depends on the factors that we have described in this chapter. Learning how to deal with them requires that novice teachers invest time and experiment with a variety of strategies. In addition, novice teachers will need to reflect on which strategies work for their students and their classes. Only when teachers do this will they become effective instructors.

Food for Thought

1. After reviewing the information in this chapter, select a lesson you recently taught. Then, identify the lesson's opening, sequencing, and closure and reflect on how these contributed to the lesson's effectiveness or ineffectiveness. Finally, identify any necessary adjustments you would make to the lesson.
2. Interview two experienced teachers and ask them about the challenges they have faced when delivering their lessons. Are their challenges different from those we identified in this chapter? Are there any challenges that can be added to the list described in this chapter?
3. Watch a video of a lesson you have delivered. If you do not have access to a lesson you have taught, then immediately after your next lesson, take notes on the strategies you have implemented to maintain momentum in your lesson. Reflect on the strategies you used and identify the ones that worked or didn't work. Decide what strategies you would modify to maximize the lesson's momentum.

References

Alber, R. (2012, December 17). *Instructional pacing: How do your lessons flow?* Edutopia. https://www.edutopia.org/blog/instructional-pacing-tips-rebecca-alber

Allaw, E., & McDonough, K. (2019). The effect of task sequencing on second language written lexical complexity, accuracy, and fluency. *System, 85*, Article 102104. https://doi.org/10.1016/j.system.2019.06.008

Álvarez, J. A. (2008). Instructional sequences of English language teachers: An attempt to describe them. *HOW, 15*(1), 29–48.

Baralt, M., Gilabert, R., & Robinson, P. (2014). An introduction to theory and research in task sequencing and instructed second language learning. In M. Baralt, R. Gilabert, & P. Robinson (Eds.), *Task sequencing and instructed second language learning* (pp. 1–34). Bloomsbury.

Bennett, C. (2023, April 5). *What to do when the technology fails in class.* ThoughtCo. https://www.thoughtco.com/when-the-technology-fails-in-class-4046343

Crookes, G. (2003). *A practicum in TESOL: Professional development through teaching practice.* Cambridge University Press.

Farrell, T. S. C. (2006). The first year of language teaching: Imposing order. *System, 34*(2), 211–221. https://doi.org/10.1016/j.system.2005.12.001

Feldon, D. F. (2007). Cognitive load and classroom teaching: The double-edged sword of automaticity. *Educational Psychologist, 42*(3), 123–137. https://doi.org/10.1080/00461520701416173

Field, J. (2002). The changing face of listening. In J. C. Richards & W. A. Renandya (Eds.), *Methodology in language teaching: An anthology of current practice* (pp. 242–247). Cambridge University Press.

Ganske, K. (2017). Lesson closure: An important piece of the student learning puzzle. *The Reading Teacher, 71*(1), 95–100. https://doi.org/10.1002/trtr.1587

Goh, C. C. M. (2014). Second language listening comprehension: Process and pedagogy. In M. Celce-Murcia, D. M. Brinton, & M. A. Snow (Eds.), *Teaching English as a second or foreign language* (4th ed., pp. 72–89). Heinle Cengage Learning.

Goldsmith, J. (2009). Pacing and time allocation at the micro- and meso-level within the class hour: Why pacing is important, how to study it, and what it implies for individual lesson planning. *Bellaterra Journal of Teaching & Learning Languages and Literature, 1*(1), 30–48. https://doi.org/10.5565/rev/jtl3.34

Grabe, W., & Stoller, F. L. (2014). Teaching reading for academic purposes. In M. Celce-Murcia, D. M. Brinton, & M. A. Snow (Eds.). *Teaching English as second or foreign language* (4th ed., pp. 189–205). Heinle Cengage Learning.

Harmer, J. (2001). *The practice of English language teaching* (3rd ed.). Pearson.

Harmer, J. (2015). *The practice of English language teaching* (5th ed.). Pearson.

Hedgcock, J. S., & Ferris, D. R. (2018). *Teaching readers of English: Students, texts, and contexts* (2nd ed). Routledge.

Hunter, R. (2004). *Madeline Hunter's mastery teaching: Increasing instructional effectiveness in elementary and secondary schools.* Corwin Press.

Purgason, K. B. (2014). Lesson planning in second/foreign language teaching. In M. Celce-Murcia, D. M. Brinton, & M. A. Snow (Eds.), *Teaching English as a second or foreign language* (4th ed., 362–379). Heinle Cengage Learning.

Richard-Amato, P. A. (2010). *Making it happen: From interactive to participatory language teaching: Evolving theory and practice* (4th ed.). Pearson.

Richards, J. C., & Farrell, T. S. C. (2011). *Practice teaching: A reflective approach.* Cambridge University Press. https://doi.org/10.1017/CBO9781139151535

Richards, J. C., & Lockhart, C. (1994). *Reflective teaching in second language classrooms.* Cambridge University Press.

Shindler, J. (2010). *Transformative classroom management: Positive strategies to engage all students and promote a psychology of success.* Jossey-Bass.

Steinman, L. (2013). The role of transitions in ESL instruction. *TESL Canada Journal, 30*(2), 46–54. https://doi.org/10.18806/tesl.v30i2.1141

Stoller, F. L., & Grabe, W. (2017). Building coherence into the content-based curriculum: Six Ts revisited. In M. A. Snow & D. M. Brinton (Eds.), *The content-based classroom: New perspectives on integrating language and content* (2nd ed., pp. 53–66). University of Michigan Press.

Swales, J. M. (1990). *Genre analysis: English in academic and research settings.* Cambridge University Press.

98 Navigating the English Language Classroom

Appendix 5.1

First-Aid Kit—Lesson Plan

Level of proficiency: CEFR A2, B1

Length of class: Two hours (lesson activities do not add up to two hours to allow flexibility).

Instructional setting: Community ESL class, students' level of English proficiency is somewhat mixed.

Objectives: By the end of this lesson, students will be able to: 1) identify the items in a first-aid kit (Band-Aids, thermometer, painkillers, gauze, ice pack, etc.); and 2) give and receive advice using the new vocabulary.

Prior knowledge/connections: Students are already familiar with some hospital- and pharmacy-related vocabulary. This lesson is specifically intended to build on the previous knowledge and introduce new vocabulary that can be used in everyday life.

Instructional techniques: Jazz chants, games, visuals, PowerPoint slides, memory game cards, handouts.

Appendix 5.1. First-Aid Kit—Lesson Plan

Steps (PPP)	Activity	Aim of activity	Patterns of interaction	Materials	Timing	Reminders
Warm-up and review	T has students play "Simon Says," focusing on body parts.	To review body parts.	Whole class	N/A	10 min	T models how to play the game.
	Ss lead small groups in a "Simon Says" game.		Small groups			
	Ss report back the names of the body parts.					
	T shows the day's agenda and goes over objectives.	To focus Ss' attention on the whole lesson activities.	Whole class	Agenda on the board	5 min	T points to the board.
	T shows a first-aid kit and introduces the new lesson with enthusiasm.	To introduce the topic.	Whole class	First-aid kit	5 min	We all need a first-aid kit (showing a kit), or Last week, we learned . . . Today, we will focus on . . .
Presentation	T presents the first-aid kit vocabulary terms in context.	T provides input	T-led	Slides + realia	20 min	T presents 7–9 terms.
	T shows slides and circulates realia as she presents the vocabulary.	T has students recognize the items.				
	T uses intonation and body language to emphasize new vocabulary.					
	T asks questions: • Yes/no • Either/or • Open-ended					

(*continued*)

Steps (PPP)	Activity	Aim of activity	Patterns of interaction	Materials	Timing	Reminders
Guided practice 1	T leads Ss in a jazz chant.	Ss produce new vocabulary.	Class as a whole	Slides	10 min	T has Ss read the jazz chant, then she removes the handout from Ss. Eventually, Ss recall the jazz chant. Jazz chant (initial lines): What should do if I cut my finger? Put on a Band-Aid. What should I do if I hurt my back? Use an ice pack. What should I do if I am wounded? Use gauze.
Guided practice 2	T has Ss play a memory game.	Ss practice the new vocabulary and body parts,	Pair work	Memory game cards	10 min	T models how to play the game. Ss model before playing the game.
Guided practice 3	T models how to ask for and give advice. A: I cut my finger. What should I do? B: Put on a Band-Aid.	To give and receive advice.	Whole class Pair work	Handout	10 min	T leads the whole class activity, then she has Ss work in pairs and ask each other for advice. Give frames: What should I do if . . .? and a word bank with the lesson vocabulary. T walks around and helps Ss as needed.

Appendix 5.1 (Cont.)

Steps (PPP)	Activity	Aim of activity	Patterns of interaction	Materials	Timing	Reminders
Independent practice	Ss participate in a scenario. Working in groups of 4, one student will be the pharmacist, the other 3 will be clients asking the pharmacist for advice.	To give and receive advice.	Group work	N/A	15 min	T works with students to avoid delays as Ss form groups.
Evaluation	T gives Ss a handout where they have to match questions and advice.	To assess the outcomes of the lesson.	Individual work	Handout	5 min	T has Ss report back their responses. To bring closure to the lesson, T enthusiastically repeats Ss' responses. She introduces the homework and dismisses the class.
Homework	Ss are asked to check their first-aid kits and make a list of the items in it.				5 min	The information Ss bring to class will be used in the warm-up/review.

Source: Suky Kaur

CHAPTER 6

Fostering Motivation and Participation

Contextualization

This chapter explores the role of motivation and participation in the language classroom to provide new teachers with effective ways of taking these seemingly nebulous concepts and turning them into something with visibly accessible shape. It begins by first revisiting key related concepts in an attempt to define them and understand their impact on classroom dynamics; it then explores issues of expectations, individual differences, personal preferences, biases, anxiety, classroom environment, and teacher–student/student–student interactions. The chapter concludes with a holistic reflection on why motivation and participation are essential classroom aspects that are highly connected to student agency and investment (Dörnyei & Ushioda, 2021).

Case Study: But I Was Listening the Whole Time!

In a graduate seminar from 2010, the course syllabus provided students with brief instructions on best practices for satisfying the participation requirement for the course. The practices were detailed in a simple manner, which the instructor thought would be accessible and simple to follow. For instance, students were told to volunteer questions in classroom discussions, to respond to peers when they offered commentary, to actively contribute to forum postings, to submit work completed with appropriate effort and dedication, to submit work on time and as instructed, and to perform any homework or general course preparation in advance of the class sessions in which it would play a prominent role.

From the teacher's perspective, the students had enough information to successfully navigate participation within the course; however, at the end of the quarter, it became evident that the policy on participation had not been fully interpreted as intended. Indeed, at the end of the quarter, one student of Eastern Asian descent who had performed very well on her other graded assignments in the course emailed the instructor to inquire about her final participation grade, mainly because she felt the lower score that she had received (in her case a B+) was unfair. She argued that she had been participating through "active listening" throughout the ten weeks of the course. Hearing this, the instructor felt compelled to take a closer look at the syllabus' language and to deeply reflect on what it means to participate in a North American college educational context, while also weighing this against the student's individual motivations for being in the course and how these motivations impacted her actions. This student was, for lack of better terminology, interacting with the class in a manner that reflected her upbringing, where her personal views of classroom interaction differed greatly from her instructor's due to the very different nature of her educational socialization. The cultural impact on her participation quickly became visible through these discussions, and it ultimately led the instructor to change the grade after he gained insight from the student's input.

The message in this case study is simple: teachers can't make assumptions about all students being a homogenous block, even when they may share the same history or background. Teachers should also be mindful that what might transpire as a lack of motivation to participate in classroom activities, or a lack of engagement with the course content, might actually simply be a misunderstanding on the part of the student about how to *perform* classroom participation. If participation is to be included as a factor in a language classroom, teachers' understanding of participation should be culturally informed through collective experience, all the while being realized moment-to-moment through complex individual experiences and actions.

Common Concerns

The questions below reflect some of the general concerns that are prominent in language teacher training scenarios involving motivation and participation. Despite the fact that there are additional subtopics that could be explored, the goal of these questions is to address some of the core aspects that are prolific in the training discussions the authors conduct. These questions aim to help new teachers, who are leaving the safety of simulated

104 Navigating the English Language Classroom

learning and becoming responsible for their own educational settings, to see how learner idiosyncrasies are often antithetical to monolithic, one-size-fits-all approaches to classroom interaction, and that this discrepancy can wield great influence on motivation and participation. Below are the core questions of this chapter.

- *Q1: What is the difference between the terms participation, engagement, motivation, and investment?*
- *Q2: What are some useful strategies to manage productive classroom participation? And how does participation management interact with student motivations?*
- *Q3: Why do some of the strategies for participation management work well for some students but not for others?*
- *Q4: How do new teachers effectively navigate their students' personal beliefs and motivations, markers of identity, or home culture so that individual investment can be enhanced?*
- *Q5: How do new teachers navigate the learning environment in ways that address participation challenges for the group, not just the individual?*

Effective Practices for Fostering Motivation and Participation

- ***Q1: What is the difference between the terms** participation, engagement, motivation, **and** investment?*

When it comes to discussing strategies to improve student learning outcomes, the second language acquisition (SLA) literature often refers to terms such as *participation, engagement, motivation*, and *investment*; these terms carry some conceptual overlap, and because of that they can sometimes be used interchangeably. However, each refers to a different aspect of students' characteristics that may or may not influence their classroom behavior; therefore, it is important for a teacher to have a good understanding of what these various terms mean.

Participation is defined as when students seize opportunities to engage with others during a class by asking and answering questions as well as making contributions during pair or group work with a specific task in focus. Student participation is one of the major components of teaching methods like the communicative language teaching approach, which actively promotes using the language through meaningful interactions. Some examples of activities that promote students' classroom participation are: role-plays, interviews, group work with assigned roles, information gap activities, opinion sharing, scavenger hunts, and project-based and task-based student collaborations with assigned roles.

In the education literature, the term *engagement* refers to the degree of attention, curiosity, interest, optimism, and passion that students show when they are learning or being taught. Student engagement has also been described as the tendency to be behaviorally, emotionally, and cognitively involved in academic activities. Consequently, compared to less engaged peers, engaged students demonstrate more effort, experience more positive emotions, and pay more attention in the classroom. In addition, student engagement has also been associated with positive student outcomes, including higher grades and decreased dropouts. Teachers can have a positive impact on student engagement through the demonstration of their enjoyment and confidence in their teaching, pedagogical efficacy, and affective orientations in the classroom.

Motivation has been described as the driving force that leads to engagement and investment, or as the fundamental determiner of people's behavior. According to Dörnyei (2014), research on motivation has treated it as both stable and transient, as related to both affect and cognition, and as a characteristic that could be either internal to the learner or externally determined by the immediate surrounding climate or environment. He argues that motivation determines the direction (orientation) and magnitude (intensity) of people's behavior, as in "*why* people decide to do something, *how long* they are willing to sustain the activity, and *how hard* they are going to pursue it" (p. 519). Some teaching strategies that promote motivational intensity (the effort learners are prepared to put in) suggest creating a pleasant and supportive atmosphere in the classroom, while strategies that promote motivational orientation (learners' long-term goals, which can be instrumental or integrative) suggest increasing the students' expectancy of success in particular tasks and in learning in general.

The last term to be defined is *investment*. This refers to the extent to which learners are engaged in their learning process and are able to describe where they are in their linguistic development, how they can grow towards their educational goals, and what they are willing to do in order to achieve them. This type of self-regulation is only possible when students clearly understand what they are trying to achieve, have a sense of what quality work looks like, and can adapt and revise their behavior in order to get closer to the learning goal. To promote student investment, teachers could share information with students about learning goals for lessons and pedagogical justifications

Table 6.1. Summary of Terms

Summary of the four key terms that govern student behavior	
Participation	Students ask and answer questions and make contributions during interactional coursework.
Engagement	Students pay attention and show curiosity, interest, optimism, and passion for learning.
Motivation	Students determine the degree of intensity, effort, and time they will apply to learning.
Investment	Students adapt and revise their behavior to get closer to the learning goal.

behind classroom tasks; they could also frequently report on assessment results and curricular adjustments based on observed student needs, while providing timely feedback on performance. Table 6.1 summarizes the four terms discussed in this question.

These four terms present challenges that all teachers experience throughout their professional career. If students are actively engaged in the various in-class activities, contributing to class discussions and tasks, helping each other during pair or group work, answering questions when prompted, then teachers will likely feel that their main goals have been accomplished. Nevertheless, a teacher might deliver a lesson in the same manner in two different sections of the same class with completely different outcomes. This is due to the fact that motivation and its in-class realization through student engagement and participation practices don't entirely depend on the design of a lesson plan; a lot of a lesson's success, which is typically reflected in displays of students' engagement and participation, depends on students' motivation and investment in the class as well as on the teacher's enjoyment and confidence.

- *Q2: What are some useful strategies to manage productive classroom participation? And how does participation management interact with student motivations?*

Effective classroom participation largely depends on transparent and strategic management. Some examples of managing student participation that require purposeful intervention are as follows: 1) having a clear syllabus or policy that explains what participation means; 2) making sure task instructions are very clear; 3) varying which students answer display and comprehension questions; 4) being mindful of teacher positioning and circulating in the room; and 5) considering the use of applications and online tools.

First and foremost, a teacher's expectation for classroom participation should be clearly laid out in the course syllabus. The description of what is expected in terms of classroom participation should be so obvious that students from any cultural background would know how the teacher defines participation. The syllabus should anticipate typical concerns, such as whether or not participation will be assessed and graded, what specific behaviors are acceptable, or what the rules of respectful classroom etiquette are (for example, use a respectful tone of voice, do not tease others, and so on). Novice teachers should keep in mind that the reason why some students are perceived as not contributing satisfactorily could be due to a discrepancy between the student's and the teacher's understanding of what participatory engagement entails (Cirocki et al., 2019). For instance, various countries have different practices for participation, and if those clash with a given educational setting, it can give the impression that a student is not participating, when in fact that student is simply following different socialization practices (as was the case in this chapter's opening case study). This is why it is imperative that instructors lead a discussion early in the quarter/semester/ term about the characteristics of effective participation, as this can reveal areas that students might need to attend to. Examples of interactional and metacognitive strategies that instructors can teach their students include the following: guidance on turn-taking practices to gain speakership, etiquette for expressing agreement and disagreement, and avenues for pursuing more information or gaining clarification.

Another way to increase classroom participation is to provide clear task instructions; otherwise, instructors run the risk of students not understanding what is asked of them. To counter such issues, they can check for students' understanding, break down complex aspects that are hard to digest, give examples, pause long enough to allow students to ask questions, and provide any additional information that is needed to scaffold the activity. If instructors ask students to start a task before they are ready, they will not be able to do what is expected of them until they get further clarification. One clue for the teacher would be when students are observed looking around with a confused facial expression or whispering to each other instead of gathering the required resources and materials to initiate the task.

Varying which students will answer display and comprehension questions is another way teachers can manage classroom participation. Students' ideas of active participation might differ dramatically depending on their socialization. For example, some students might believe that the expected behavior from them is to quietly listen to the teacher and their classmates while displaying agreement or disagreement by nodding or altering their facial expressions, while others may believe that one is expected to show their investment and engagement in the class by offering to answer all questions asked by the teacher. The result might be an unbalanced distribution of participation across the room. To avoid this issue, teachers should call on different students to answer questions provided that they are given sufficient time to prepare an answer.

A strategic way to manage classroom participation involves the teacher's positioning and circulation around the room. Observations of teacher trainees have shown that teacher movement within physical spaces has the potential, depending on teacher adeptness, to beneficially decenter teacher centrality when properly implemented (Cook et al., 2002). And moving around the room while students are working in groups might also help the teacher manage students' willingness to stay on task and use the target language if they know the teacher might walk by and monitor their participation. In addition, if a classroom is too large or has poor acoustics, which might make it difficult for a student making a verbal contribution to be heard across the room, the teacher can move away from that student so that they must speak up, rendering their volume more impactful for the class as a whole. If students can't hear one another, some might become frustrated or cease to pay attention, which is the opposite of what educators want to accomplish. In some cases, they may need to reiterate a student's contribution to ensure that everyone hears it, but the primary goal is to empower the students to participate willingly and effectively on their own.

Finally, classroom participation can also be promoted by tapping into student engagement with existing learning technologies and social media. Technology has a significant presence in the lives of students and therefore is potentially more engaging for them. For instance, teachers can use iClickers for voting electronically on multiple choice questions, use online surveys to conduct anonymous polls to collect students' responses and opinions, use documents shared in the cloud and online annotation tools to promote group work and task collaboration, and use online discussion prompts via social media feeds or a learning management system.

When we consider participation management, our approach should always be in relation to students' reasons and motivations for learning English as a second or foreign language, as well as the course objectives that govern the overarching learning outcomes. In this way, participation differs across educational settings and across the wider spectrum of students' reasons for being in the classroom, and these variations are at least in part linked to the diversity of motivations that underlie each student's educational journey.

To better understand the connection between participation management and student motivations, let us look to a college-level reading and writing classroom scenario. In such an environment, some of the students might take participation in prewriting tasks more seriously than participation in general warm-up oral discussion activities. That is not to say that some students wouldn't enjoy participating in a more casual conversational activity in a reading/writing course, but if it is not an essential element of the course, or if they are not personally invested in developing their general oral skills, other students might perceive such activities as having diminished value, as opposed to other individual or even group oral activities that would more clearly lead to the development of their reading and writing skills. This is because a warm-up that has nothing to do with the course content per se, but rather focuses on getting the students talking, may be perceived as irrelevant to the learning objectives of the course, while oral discussions that actively treat assigned readings in service of articulating original thoughts on those readings might be seen as highly relevant, and thus productive in terms of tapping into individual student motivation. When the lesson objectives are aligned with students' expectations and their educational motivations, they are more likely to feel engaged and personally invested in participating in classroom activities.

• Q3: Why do some of the strategies for participation management work well for some students but not for others?

Successful management of classroom participation involves a teacher's highly trained and attuned observation of the minute-by-minute interplay of dynamic variables within the classroom environment. Measured in terms of student participation, the success of any given lesson depends on the implementation of said lesson by taking into account the specific needs and characteristics of each individual within a group of students, including their cognitive abilities, learning styles, personality characteristics, willingness to communicate, and second language anxiety when managing student participation.

Grouping students with different cognitive abilities (for instance, aptitude, intelligence, memory, task completion strategies) may lead to more successful completion of tasks and overall participation. Any heterogeneous group of students will contain individuals with varying levels of cognitive abilities, and teachers should consider pairing or grouping students that have the potential to help each other to complete classroom tasks. Teachers in second or foreign language learning settings often use small group instruction as a strategy for delivering targeted, differentiated instruction to students at a similar level. Working in small groups has been shown to lead to better learning outcomes; while same-ability groups are simpler to implement and benefit high-achieving students, mixed-ability groups benefit all students, especially lower-achieving ones (Poole, 2008). More specifically, being grouped with peers who are more or less advanced can help students develop growth mindsets around learning as well as higher self-efficacy in their academic and nonacademic skills.

Identifying how students learn best and catering to those styles can have a dramatic effect on how they understand and connect with the different topics being taught, engage with the task at hand, and participate in activities. A learning style refers to a learner's preferred way of processing and dealing with new information, and it represents typical and consistent ways of responding to and using stimuli in the context of learning (Costa et al., 2020). From personality type assessments such as the Myers-Brigg model (Myers et al., 1998) to Kolb's (1984) work on experiential learning through a lens of learning cycles and learning styles, and Fleming and Mills' (1992) work on the modalities that people might prefer when learning (that is, the VARK model), the role of individual learning styles has consistently been shown to be of importance in educational settings. As Syofyan and Siwi (2018) assert in examining the impact of visual, auditory, and kinesthetic teaching strategies in economics education, "Accommodating teaching to learning styles improves students' overall learning results, increases both motivation and efficiency and enables a positive attitude towards the language being learned" (p. 648). For visual learners, teachers can use maps, flow charts, or color-coding to organize and relate learning materials; they can also prepare posters, PowerPoints, and image-laden handouts. For auditory learners, teachers can teach materials through audio recordings, or have students read materials aloud for peer listening, or identify pronunciation patterns in spoken discourse. Finally, for kinesthetic learners, teachers can write down material on slips of paper and ask students to move them around into proper sequence, use role play to dramatize concepts, fluency circles to allow students to move about the learning space while learning, and incorporate moments for board usage. Table 6.2 recaps some of the more accessible examples of these three preference types.

The next dimension of student individual variables that affect classroom participation pertains to their personality characteristics, some of which are

Table 6.2. Sample Activities for Visual, Auditory, and Kinesthetic Language Learners

Learning style	Sample activities
Visual	• Prepare posters, PowerPoints, and handouts for sharing. • Incorporate copyright-free images into readings and vocabulary activities. • Use maps, color-coding, and flowcharts to organize and relate materials.
Auditory	• Use audio recordings of teaching materials. • Have students read materials aloud so they can hear one another. • Identifying stress patterns in pronunciation exercises.
Kinesthetic	• Role-plays, reenactments, and dramatizations. • Sentence puzzles and cutout paragraph jumbles. • Fluency circles with changing partners. • Writing individual, pair, or group work on the board.

acceptance of personal risks, tolerance of ambiguity, a healthy self-esteem, and lack of inhibition. Students need to be willing to risk losing face by making mistakes in front of their peers and accept that it is OK to communicate with incomplete proficiency and comprehension. They also need to have a healthy self-esteem so that any corrective feedback they get from the teacher and from other students doesn't upset them. Finally, in order to increase classroom participation, students need to be willing to let go of some of their inhibitions. For example, extroverts and introverts may behave differently when choosing accuracy over speed, especially when they are under pressure to respond and required to perform publicly or extemporaneously. Raising students' awareness of these variables and giving them opportunity to prepare and rehearse in smaller groups can potentially help them become more confident to participate in front of a larger group.

Students' classroom participation can also be determined by their willingness to communicate (WTC), which is influenced by social, cognitive, and affective variables (Chen et al., 2022). This theoretical construct attempts to account for the reasons why students might choose to participate within and beyond the classroom. WTC posits that a number of internal (cognitive and affective) and external (sociocultural) variables will regulate a learner's communicative ability. Some examples of internal variables that correlate with students' WTC are second or foreign language self-confidence, perceived (in)competence, and desire to communicate with a specific person; examples of external variables that are more situational and social in nature are intergroup climate and social situations in all their forms, such as observing levels of politeness, turn-taking practices, and navigating situational registers. By being mindful of what can hinder students' willingness to communicate, teachers can ensure that the situational classroom environment is supportive and welcoming.

Finally, a student's anxiety might also affect their behavior in the classroom. Although some forms of anxiety are considered facilitative, some can become debilitative. In the latter case, learners might lose their ability to mentally focus during class. Horwitz (2010) argues that anxiety interferes with language learning and inhibits target language production because it can lead to disruptive behaviors like fidgeting, frequently falling asleep during class, or asking to be excused from class very often. Some causes of anxiety include culture shock, homesickness, impostor syndrome, negative impact of home life, microaggressions at school or at work, or trauma (Hardacre & Güvendir, 2020). The source of students' anxiety might be very context-specific. That is the case when students are otherwise relaxed and happy in the second or foreign language classroom, but may experience anxiety when they are put on the spot, when they are asked to speak in front of the class, when they are asked to participate in group or whole-class discussions by sharing their answers or opinions out loud, when they are not confident in their ability to use the target language with others, or when they feel like they are in competition with their classmates. Some strategies to lower students' anxiety in the classroom include the following: creating a safe space in the classroom where students can sit if they want or need to be left alone; recognizing that public speaking is not the only form of assessing students' oral proficiency and that teachers can, for example, allow students to turn in prerecorded videos of their oral performance, or assess them in private; using mindful meditation techniques at the beginning of the class; playing soothing music; and inserting mind-break activities throughout the class, among others (see Hardacre & Güvendir, 2020).

- *Q4: How do new teachers effectively navigate their students' personal beliefs and motivations, markers of identity, or home culture so that individual investment can be enhanced?*

New teachers cannot productively implement motivational and participatory practices without first acknowledging the role of the individual. Without great effort, instructors can develop a general sense of interest among their students, but ultimately each student is in a given classroom for any number of reasons. A logical starting point for new teachers to begin tackling these reasons—and classroom investment more generally—is to first get to know their students' personal characteristics on a deeper level while also showing equal investment on the educator's part. In this way, investment emerges as a two-way street that is achieved by both students and educators. For example, the easiest way in which a teacher can illustrate investment in their students is by learning their names (see Chapter 1 for a discussion of this). This may seem like it should go without saying, but in classroom observations of novice teachers, it is quite common to see teachers forget a person's name or betray that they have yet to actually learn it. This lack of respect towards students can create distance as it shows that the instructor is not replicating the type of investment they are asking of their students.

To truly get to the heart of classroom investment, teachers must in fact go well beyond mere names and delve substantively into the social constructs that make up the individual. Two of the more obvious constructs that can easily be examined are age and cultural/ethnic group. In terms of age, what might appeal to younger learners may be seen as infantilizing by adult learners. Through a moment-to-moment lens, this could be seen as an issue of engagement; however, when an instructor considers its impact over the span of a course, it becomes an issue of individual investment. For example, in terms of age, jazz chants and other forms of rote repetition might be better received by primary school learners, whereas real-world authenticity realized through advanced content subject matter might appeal more to learners in advanced college settings. In terms of culture or ethnicity, teachers might consider varying their course content by selecting authors of color when possible and avoiding the trap of seeing classroom minority students as spokespeople for their cultural/ethnic group. What both of these social constructs have in common is an attention to engagement that is grounded in investment as an overarching goal. By carefully curating classroom materials in this way, educators can create a playing field that is audience-driven and inclusive.

Many social constructs, such as sex, gender, and sexuality, however, can be less apparent and can require more interactional engagement between the teacher and the student. If teachers rely on a traditionalist's sense of conventional norms, then they may very well overlook the fact that these three terms are actually highly complex; indeed, personal identity can at times be overt/visible or covert/private, and these three constructs—sex, gender, and sexuality—are more and more frequently dissociated from traditionalist expectations. This is important because it implies that the approach educators use to address such delicate matters can in fact impact a student's classroom investment, especially given that the construction of certain activities may inadvertently reinforce or contradict individual social identities.

According to Norton Peirce (1995), a student's identity might conflict with their perception of a discussion topic or task, and this could impact their willingness to share their views with others. She argues that "[students'] decision to remain silent or to speak may both constitute forms of resistance to inequitable social forces" (p. 20). For example, in terms of familial relationships, for heteronormative, cisgender students who clearly identify in a traditional sense as male or female, identifying a romantic partner is exponentially less impactful than it is for, as an example, an LGBTQ-identifying student. In discussing family terms and connections within the language classroom, teachers may inadvertently ask their LGBTQ students to either out themselves or to lie in a public forum, and this can greatly dampen their willingness to invest through participatory sharing, especially in a class where peers could still be seen as potentially unwelcoming threats. This situation can be easily extended to the use of non-normative pronouns when discussing gender, or to the notion of biological sex, as females in some countries may not have the ability to speak freely in mixed-sex settings. If teachers want their students to invest in their courses, then they need to ensure that the lessons that they teach are not counterintuitive to students' lived experiences. This does not mean that the instructor should avoid things like familial terms or pronouns, as they are foundational aspects of common lived experience; rather, they should actively seek out strategies to render these areas less revealing by providing various pathways for reveals to be carried out, for instance, in private forums and submissions. And if teachers discuss these items whole-class, then they might consider making such reveals entirely voluntary so as to avoid awkwardness that might dissuade a student from wanting to participate. In this way, the teacher demonstrates respect for their learners by giving them a say in how they share their identity with others, allowing personal reveals to happen instead on the individual's terms.

Other constructs such as faith and socioeconomic status and class affiliation might be more visibly recognizable while remaining equally taboo in terms of navigating. As an example, a student who wears religious accessories might be shunned in certain participatory activities based on perceived differences that stem from incongruent belief systems to those of the other students. Likewise, students from the same country might be able to detect class-based differences based on attire or dialect, which in turn can impact the perception and treatment of one another based on preconceived notions. In such cases, instructors may have to actively educate students on the virtues of openness and acceptance in order to diminish exclusive practices that can harm student investment. The instructor must remember that social constructs are real and impactful, and it is their duty as an educator to ensure that no one student's beliefs, perspectives, or characteristics are more highly valued than those of other students, especially when such asymmetries can result in weakened learning outcomes for students who might be recipients of such prejudicial behavior.

What the aforementioned paragraphs outline is that biases are alive and active in all classroom aspects, and instructors have to work together as a community to ensure that these biases do not negatively impact the experiences of their students and their students' educational investment. Li (2020) recommends the use of multimodal pedagogical practices in order to include students' personal narratives within the lesson content. Politics represents a prime example of this argument. Each person may carry implicit biases based on their sociopolitical affiliations, and this could impact their interpersonal interactions. To promote a productive teaching and learning environment, educators have to be willing to acknowledge this fact. One way that they can prevent implicit biases in their teaching is to have peers observe them while they teach, or video-record their performance for later review. In doing this, the novice teacher gets to see aspects of their class that may not be readily accessible to them when they are in the midst of teaching. In doing such exercises, they might notice that they call on males more than females; similarly, they might find that some of their statements are insensitive to issues of diversity and require thoughtful introspection to ensure that the instructor can rectify any distancing or discriminatory behavior.

Some biases, however, can at times be thought of as counterintuitively positive. An example would be when a student's biases for learning in a particular way harmoniously interact with classroom practices. Gardner (2006) identifies an expansive set of intelligences—what he terms *multiple intelligences*—that impact how learners process educational materials. In Maftoon and Sarem's (2012) exploration of Gardner's intelligences, the authors identify pedagogical applications for nine intelligence types: verbal-linguistic; logical-mathematical; spatial-visual; musical; bodily-kinesthetic; interpersonal; intrapersonal; naturalistic; and existential. In the classroom, this might mean using music videos to explore modal verbs in the context of a song; where spatial-visual materials stimulate through their imagery; bodily-kinesthetic materials invoke movement in the video and the possibility of potentially recreating these movement in interactions; and musical materials explore the rhythm and cadence of the lyrics and beats. Close analysis of the lyrics might then promote verbal-linguistic learning, while ranking favorite lines taps into logical-mathematical skills that simultaneously appeal both to intrapersonal and interpersonal intelligences through comparative analysis and negotiation. Finally, naturalistic and existential classroom materials might examine authenticity in terms of the world around them and the music video's larger philosophical implications. The point here is that intelligence types are meaningful aspects of language learners' individual characteristics, and if teachers want to motivate their students to actively participate and engage as steps toward actively investing in their courses, then exploiting the full range of intelligence types within different classroom actions would not only help the students connect, but show them that educators are actively taking varied ways of learning into consideration in all that they do.

- *Q5: How do new teachers navigate the learning environment in ways that address participation challenges for the group, not just the individual?*

Contrary to the explorations in the previous question's response, motivation and participation are not solely tethered to the individual; rather, they are both intricately connected to the learner's environment and the collective culture that emerges within that environment. In truth, if new teachers want to motivate their students as a group, then they have to think beyond individual needs into what will be enticing for the larger classroom community.

A first step towards motivating the collective is in fostering a *good* learning experience. Teachers must acknowledge that a *perfect* learning experience is hard to come by; therefore, a *good* experience should be seen as a respectable goal given all of the variables that educators are constantly juggling. In adopting the idea of *good* as a goal, new teachers take on a healthier and more realistic stance that accepts that compromise is essential when treating individuals in collective spaces. Not all activities will speak to each student, and so perfection clearly represents a nonrealistic goal in many cases. Similarly, *poor* planning will lead to lackluster investment on the students' part because without strategic conceptualization teachers fail to attend to varied styles and approaches. *Poor* planning does not respect the individual, and it certainly does not respect the collective, as it implies a general lack of attention to learners' needs. Following this logic, the idea of a *good* learning experience emerges as something that should be attainable on a daily basis simply by intermittently varying classroom actions to address a wider swathe of learning styles.

One example of a technique that can foster motivation and participation with the aim of generating investment for the larger classroom community is through the use of an "in good faith" activity. This activity is one that is done the first day of class, where the teacher invites students to enter into a contract of participation that outlines pathways for success. Such contracts allow students to vocalize what engagement means to them and how it can be achieved. The "in good faith" activity then asks the students to describe the types of classroom actions that they find interesting, engaging, or enticing. By giving students an active voice, students feel heard, improving the likelihood that they will fully invest in the classroom community and its actions; the teacher also has the ability to fill in any gaps they deem essential, resulting in a collaborative pathway for investment that is both teacher and student informed.

Nevertheless, promoting active group participation is often complicated by various environmental factors. For instance, despite using placement exams, teachers may in fact find their student population to be varied in terms of overall proficiency. In such cases, the teacher may have to speak with a supervisor to understand what is possible in terms of rectifying the situation. However, if placement cannot be reevaluated, then the teacher will have a mixed ability class that will require accommodations. For instance, in this scenario a new teacher might apply various scaffolding strategies, such as mixing more proficient and less proficient students together in groups so that the less proficient learners can balance their struggles against the strengths of more proficient others. This can be highly motivating for less proficient students as it provides a safety net in which to work, shielding their lower proficiency until they are ready to join open class discussions. Likewise, it allows more proficient students a chance to demonstrate their linguistic command by explaining it to others. But new teachers must also remember that such actions can be demotivating for more proficient students if applied without proper meta-understanding, as they may see such grouping efforts as spaces in which they have to carry others.

Many other factors can negatively impact collective participation in the classroom, including the concept of interactional dynamics. First, new teachers might avoid pair work in favor of groups, as a group's composition naturally allows certain students to take on more of a leadership role and other students to listen and observe with less pressure. Teachers also have to consider the social fabric of the class in dealing with pair and group dynamics to ensure that personalities work well together. Second, teachers might set up ground rules in which everyone in class speaks on a daily basis, whereby dominant students cannot monopolize the class merely because they are faster. In this vein, the teacher might provide additional wait time for all questions in order to allow more processing time; they can also remind the class periodically that they want all voices to be heard so as to avoid demotivating more proficient students by overlooking their attempts to respond. Teachers can do this by directly calling on students, after adequate wait time and careful consideration of the impact of cold-calling. Third, new teachers can create a culture of responsibility, where any assigned tasks are fair game for open discussion, and so all are expected to be prepared; therefore, students would understand that class participation is in part achieved through individual preparation practices. Fourth, new teachers can physically move students around the class via random organizers such as by birthday, by alphabetizing favorite animal names, by selecting a number, for example. In doing this, they constantly challenge the individual in subtle ways by having them encounter new collective experiences and engagements. Fifth, new teachers can avoid pairings of a shared language that is not the target. In other words, if 90% of a given class speak Mandarin as a first language, and the remaining 10% speak different languages, instructors would want to keep classroom discourse in the target language to ensure that everyone is comfortable and has the same access to participatory actions. Lastly, new teachers can set up a culture in which individual students begin to see their peers as a source of overall enrichment, where the collective experience is given valuable prominence as a classroom resource for individual growth. As these points demonstrate, individuality is not necessarily at odds with collectivism, but it is up to instructors to ensure that neither is positioned as more or less valuable.

One final method of targeting collective investment is through defining the classroom as a safe interactional space removed from judgment. What this means is that teachers must situate the private interactions of the class as the property of the group, where the group protects its own for the sake of mutual advancement. In this way, fostering a sense of comradery becomes a core objective given its ability to bring diverse learners together in service of achieving common goals and benchmarks through increased whole-class participation, inclusive group dynamics, and supportive and engaging classroom atmosphere. In other words, teachers need to convey to students the importance of seeing themselves and the other students as teammates working equally to attain similar outcomes, and in so doing, the substance of the classroom interactions becomes sacred, something to be protected. Examples of how this might be implemented include games-based activities that promote team-mentality and lighthearted competition; community-building activities that invite the sharing of personal information in service of strengthening collegiality; comparative activities that invite students to engage in cultural comparison for the purpose of broadening interstudent understanding and acceptance; and potentially humor-based activities that allow for moments of levity and entertainment through common aesthetic orientations—though admittedly, humor has a subjective quality that requires careful curation of materials so as not to exclude or offend any one student.

Big Picture and Bottom Line

When it comes to fostering motivation and participation in the language classroom, there are seemingly endless pathways for success. If new teachers want to establish a productive learning environment, it begins with them knowing the terms as well as what they represent, not just in a definitional sense but also in a pragmatic sense. By grappling with these terms and targeting the ways in which they are realized, instructors can better ensure their consideration in all that they do.

Importantly, educators have to start seeing motivation and participation as simultaneously simple and complex, as culturally informed, as the domain of the individual and the collective, as teacher-driven and student-driven, and finally as somewhat predictable and somewhat obscure. Teachers will never be able to address all motivational and participatory needs, but in recognizing the many facets that make up these concepts, they can incrementally move their practices toward more productive outcomes.

Food for Thought

1. Revisit a syllabus that you or a peer have used in a class. After having reread the information it contains, create two Venn diagrams to help you assess the following:
   a. In the first Venn diagram, add one circle that reads *teacher-driven motivational aspects* and another that reads *student-driven motivational aspects*. Attempt to categorize the various components of the syllabus based on how well they fit.
   b. In the second Venn diagram, add one circle that reads *individual-driven motivational aspects* and another that reads *collective-driven motivational aspects*. Categorize the syllabus's components based on how well they fit.
2. In terms of participation, discuss with classmates or peers the techniques or practices that you have experienced as a learner that

left an impact on you. Be sure to offer examples for at least three of the following:

a. Ways in which you were made to feel heard.
b. Ways in which you were given agency.
c. Ways in which you were validated for your work.
d. Ways in which you were encouraged to offer more.
e. Ways in which you were acknowledged for your individuality.
f. Ways in which you were shut down.
g. Ways in which you were not given opportunities to shine.
h. Ways in which you were negatively sanctioned for incorrect responses.
i. Ways in which you were made to feel ashamed or different.
j. Ways in which you were rendered invisible in the classroom.

References

Chen, X., Dewaele, J.-M., & Zhang, T. (2022). Sustainable development of EFL/ESL learners' willingness to communicate: The effects of teachers and teaching styles. *Sustainability, 14*(1), Article 396. https://doi.org/10.3390/su14010396

Cirocki, A., Madyarov, I., & Baecher, L. (Eds.). (2019). *Current perspectives on the TESOL practicum: Cases from around the globe.* Springer.

Cook, L. S., Smagorinsky, P., Fry, P. G., Konopak, B., & Moore, C. (2002). Problems in developing a constructivist approach to teaching: One teacher's transition from teacher preparation to teaching. *The Elementary School Journal, 102*(5), 389–413.

Costa, R. D., Souza, G. F., Valentim, R. A. M., & Castro, T. B. (2020). The theory of learning styles applied to distance learning. *Cognitive Systems Research, 64*, 134–145. https://doi.org/10.1016/j.cogsys.2020.08.004

Dörnyei, Z. (2014). Motivation in second language learning. In M. Celce-Murcia, D. M. Brinton, & M.A. Snow (Eds.), *Teaching English as a second or foreign language* (4th ed., pp. 518–531). Heinle Cengage Learning.

Dörnyei, Z., & Ushioda, E. (2021). *Teaching and researching motivation* (3rd ed.). Routledge.

Fleming, N. D., & Mills, C. (1992). Not another inventory, rather a catalyst for reflection. *To Improve the Academy, 11*(1), 137–155. https://doi.org/10.1002/j.2334-4822.1992.tb00213.x

Gardner, H. (2006). *Multiple intelligences: New horizons in theory and practice* (Rev. ed.). Basic Books.

Hardacre, B., & Güvendir, E. (2020). Second language learning anxiety. In J. I. Liontas, TESOL International Association, & M. DelliCarpini (Eds.) *The TESOL encyclopedia of English language teaching* (2nd ed., pp. 1–7). Wiley-Blackwell. https://doi.org/10.1002/9781118784235.eelt0988

Horwitz, E. K. (2010). Foreign and second language anxiety. *Language Teaching, 43*(2), 154–167. http://dx.doi.org/10.1017/S026144480999036X

Kolb, D. A. (1984). *Experiential learning: Experience as the source of learning and development.* Prentice-Hall.

Li, M. (2020). Multimodal pedagogy in TESOL teacher education: Students' perspectives, *System, 94*, Article 102337. https://doi.org/10.1016/j.system.2020.102337.

Maftoon, P. & Sarem, S. N. (2012). The realization of Gardner's multiple intelligences (MI) theory in second language acquisition (SLA). *Journal of Language Teaching and Research, 3*(6), 1233–1241. https://doi.org/10.4304/jltr.3.6.1233-1241

Myers, I. B., McCaulley, M. H., Quenk, N. L., & Hammer, A. L. (1998). *MBTI® Manual: A guide to the development and use of the Myers-Briggs Type Indicator.* Consulting Psychologists Press.

Peirce, B. N. (1995). Social identity, investment, and language learning. *TESOL Quarterly, 29*(1), 9–31. https://doi.org/10.2307/3587803

Poole, D. (2008). Interactional differentiation in the mixed-ability group: A situated view of two struggling readers. *Reading Research Quarterly, 43*(3), 228–250. https://doi.org/10.1598/RRQ.43.3.2

Syofyan, R., & Siwi, M. K. (2018). The impact of visual, auditory, and kinesthetic learning styles on economics education teaching. *Proceedings of the First Padang International Conference on Economics Education, Economics, Business and Management, Accounting and Entrepreneurship (PICEEBA 2018)*, Advances in Economics, Business and Management Research, 57, 642–649. https://doi.org/10.2991/piceeba-18.2018.17

SECTION III

The Role of Assessment in the Language Classroom

CHAPTER 7

Understanding Classroom Assessment

Contextualization

This chapter situates the concept of assessment as a core classroom component that is often underestimated or in need of reflective thought. The chapter first establishes the general purpose of language assessment, followed by a discussion of what teachers can do when they would rather not use institutionalized methods of standardized testing. Next, it provides an overview of six important principles of language assessment (practicality, reliability, validity, authenticity, washback, and fairness) along with brief explanations of how they can boost the effectiveness of assessment instruments. Then, it discusses the role of standards in language assessment, the need for well-articulated student learning outcomes (SLOs), and the ways in which instructors can work to align both themselves and their classroom practices with the course/programmatic standards that frame SLO creation. Finally, this chapter discusses the purposes of formative and summative assessment to help the novice instructor make decisions about how and when and how to assess their students. The overall aim of this chapter is to aid instructors in learning to target learning outcomes in meaningful ways, rendering assessment a lesson design component that is most effective when it plays an active role in pedagogical action.

Case Study: Do I Really Have to Test My Students?

A teacher-in-training taking a language assessment class in an MA TESOL program shared with his teacher and classmates that he "didn't believe in testing." When asked to elaborate, he said that he felt that tests only make

126   Navigating the English Language Classroom

students feel anxious, and the time constraints and pressure undermine their ability to showcase their best performance. This student said that instead of spending time assessing their students, teachers should focus more on teaching (and less on testing) as oftentimes the washback effects of formal testing can have a negative impact on the ESL curriculum. These are undoubtedly valid points.

Well, this teacher-in-training was also starting a new job as an ESL tutor. So at the end of the semester, when the teacher asked her students to reflect on the usefulness of the course and whether they thought they had learned something they could apply to their future jobs in real life, this student offered the comment that after having been through the experience of tutoring an ESL student, he realized that he had to think about how to assess his student—albeit at an informal manner and for formative purposes—in order to gauge his tutee's progress and his own teaching effectiveness.

The novice teacher portrayed in this case study came to understand that it is possible to assess students without necessarily testing them all the time. Even though teachers don't always have to *test* their students, they still have to *assess* their performance and progress, and they have to report this information in a manner that others would understand and apply when making decisions about placement, moving students to the next level, admitting them to a university in a country that speaks the target language, or hiring them to work at an international company where they will likely be required to use the target language. Therefore, this assessment information must be translatable by all relevant stakeholders such as other teachers, school administrators, parents, and most importantly, the student, which is typically accomplished via grades or some other reporting system that makes reference to SLOs and proficiency level objectives.

Common Concerns

The following questions represent some of the most common concerns and questions that novice teachers typically have related to classroom assessment and testing.

- *Q1. When a teacher prefers not to test their students all the time, what can they do in order to avoid testing or decrease the number of tests they give their students?*
- *Q2. Should a teacher assess everything their students do? If not, what should they assess?*

- *Q3. What are the general "best practices" of language assessment that a teacher should try to keep in mind when choosing an existing test or designing one from scratch?*
- *Q4. Why should a teacher consider (inter)national standards and institutional SLOs when developing assessments for their class?*
- *Q5. What are the main differences between formative and summative assessment, and are teachers required to do both?*

Effective Practices for Classroom Assessment

- **Q1. When a teacher prefers not to test their students all the time, what can they do in order to avoid testing or decrease the number of tests they give their students?**

It's true that testing students and preparing them for tests shouldn't be front and center in a language classroom. Excessive testing can be overbearing and counterproductive. Nevertheless, this decision is not always up to the teacher. So even if a teacher does not agree with their program or department's testing philosophy regarding the number of tests required per term, or with the rigidity of the grading distribution, they still need to consider the school's take on testing and beyond-the-classroom evaluations tied to such tests (Martínez Marín & Mejía Vélez, 2021). For example, they can ask their program coordinator if students are to be held back when they don't meet the SLOs or course objectives. Students' progression through the school's pipeline often relies on their achieving course-specific learning objectives. Teachers should also ask their school about students' expectations of receiving preparation for standardized language proficiency tests taken at the end of the program. Finally, teachers should also try to find out whether students' performance on their summative tests will be used as a measure of teaching quality and efficacy. The bottom line here is that if this decision is not up to the teacher, they will have to decide whether they will abide by the school rules or look for a different job.

On the other hand, sometimes the instructor of record does have a say on the number of tests their students will take. When that is the case, teachers have to make decisions on the manner and frequency of student assessment. Frequent testing like daily pop quizzes is not necessarily productive or a good use of classroom time. But not *testing* students all the time does not entail not *assessing* them frequently. Teachers should explore informal methods of summative assessment if there is room in the grading distribution or when tests are not required, as well as strategies for formative assessment. Some examples of informal activities that are task-based and helpful in providing opportunities for assessment are portfolios, project-based assessments (PBAs), group tasks, oral presentations, debates, role-plays, media development (short videos, vlogs), incorporating websites (English Central, Kahoot), exit tickets, observation of students' performance in solo activities or in pair or group work, journals, and more (Güvendir & Hardacre, 2020). Regular classwork and homework can be used as formative assessment to gauge students' progress and the need for adjustments in instruction and classroom content. Varying the types of activities in order to cater for different learning styles and participation preferences may provide students ample opportunities to demonstrate their skills. Making the best use of alternative and informal forms of summative and formative assessment can be a suitable replacement for formal quizzes and tests.

Another important consideration related to the selection of assessment methods has to do with reporting students' progress. Teachers should find out if numerical grades are required by the school at the end of a term, or if they are allowed to use a different grading system, such as holistic letter grades and pass/non-pass or credit/noncredit. For example, *noncredit* ESL classes at community colleges in the United States often use a pass/non-pass system because it is usually the case that the grade from a noncredit class does not count toward a student's degree. Not having to report numerical or letter grades at the end of a term removes the need for formal tests. Students typically have to obtain a C (which is usually 70% of the total score) in order to get a passing grade at the end of the course, and the grade distribution is often based on informal assessment activities like projects and homework assignments. On the other hand, *credit* ESL classes at community colleges do require that teachers report a final numerical score based on formal (and informal) tests, which is converted into a final letter grade before it gets reported to the registrar's office. These letter grades do count toward students' degree requirements, and therefore they can affect students' grade point average (GPA).

Finally, teachers must be prepared for the possibility that midterms and finals might be required by the school where they are hired to work. When starting on a new teaching position, it is important to speak to the program coordinator about the institution's assessment philosophy and try to come to an understanding of their role as a facilitator, and to best comply with these norms. Teachers should find out what the institutional constraints are when it comes to testing as well as important information such as whether or not tests are completely preset, or whether teachers would be able to negotiate some compromise.

• Q2. Should a teacher assess everything their students do? If not, what should they assess?

A number of factors should be gathered and evaluated before making a decision regarding what and how often to assess students. The first thing to consider is whether or not students have taken a placement test before they were assigned to a class. Placement tests are somewhat helpful to group students by range of proficiency; however, placement tests are not always accurate, either because the school is using a test that was not designed for placement, or because the placement test is very limited in terms of assessing the wide range of skills needed for students to succeed in the level they were placed. Nevertheless, regardless of how students were placed in a class, teachers should give them a diagnostic test on the first day of the term. A diagnostic test is typically meant to help teachers gauge the range of pre-existing language knowledge and skills that students may already have prior to the start of a new term. This information can sometimes be used to create additional support classes, to reclassify students' levels when a placement test failed to do so, to guide the scaffolding of lesson activities, and to provide accommodations for students who need additional support. Teachers can use a diagnostic test to collect information about students, and they can use it to provide students with formative feedback; but it should not be used for grading purposes. Tests and activities created for the purpose of offering formative feedback are typically ungraded and provide low-stakes opportunities to promote and measure student knowledge and skills. When the pressure and stress are removed from the assessment process, students can perform to the best of their ability, giving teachers a good picture of the skill-level distribution across a group of students.

The number of tests and assessment activities that teachers should plan for their classes mostly depends on the type of class. Not everything students do needs to be assessed, but taking note of their performance even when it's not being assessed for a grade will help teachers get a more comprehensive picture of their linguistic competence and development. A students' competence can only be assessed indirectly via performative activities. Competence is often defined as the complete extent of knowledge and skills that students have already acquired up to that point; thus, measuring students' competence via performance is an irrefutable challenge because one single task or activity cannot assess it comprehensively. It is like trying to gauge the vast amount of information that is in a student's brain just by asking a few questions—it can't be done, unfortunately. Therefore, every oral and written classroom and homework activity should be treated as an opportunity to assess students' listening, speaking, reading, and writing abilities formally and informally, formatively and summatively.

When it comes to deciding which language skills to test, teachers need to consider the purpose of the course they are teaching. If the course is supposed to cover all four skills (listening, speaking, reading, and writing), then teachers need to assess them all. But if it is a conversation class, then they need only assess students' oral skills and not reading or writing. Teachers should also consider the context where they are teaching in order to prioritize certain language skills that need more opportunities for assessment and reinforcement. For example, EFL students typically have better reading and writing skills than listening and speaking due to the type of input and practice they typically get, whereas ESL students might have more acute listening skills given their exposure to English on a daily basis. Heritage learners, on the other hand, typically have better oral skills than reading, writing, and grammar if they interact with relatives who speak the target language, and adult learners may have better grammar and worse pronunciation than younger learners, with the latter typically finding it easier to develop better pronunciation.

- *Q3. What are the general "best practices" of language assessment that a teacher should try to keep in mind when choosing an existing test or designing one from scratch?*

When creating tests and assessment activities, teachers must consider the following six *best-practice* assessment principles: authenticity, validity, reliability, practicality, washback, and fairness. A brief explanation of each of these principles is given below, and an assessment instrument evaluation checklist is provided in Table 7.1. These principles describe the ideal best practices for assessment, but teachers will need to consider the constraints imposed by the setting where they teach (for example, school, predetermined and mandatory tests, geographical location, access to resources, time available, and so on).

The first best-practice principle is *authenticity*. It requires that teachers create assignments to assess students' performance in realistic or true-to-life scenarios, relevant to the purpose of the class and students' learning needs and goals. The closer the assessment instrument is to a real-life situation, the more useful and meaningful it will be to both the teacher and their students. For example, if students are adults taking a business English class because they work in business, assessment activities should make use of typical business scenarios in their design. The results of their performance on such assessments would give students feedback that is directly relevant to their professional needs. If the school asks teachers to use predetermined tests that are not very authentic, other forms of classroom activities that make use of authenticity could be incorporated so that students can still get this kind of feedback.

The second principle, *validity*, adds the importance of creating an assessment instrument that measures only what was covered in class and what is within the scope of the course and its learning objectives. As Brown and Abeywickrama (2019) put it, "[a] valid test of reading ability actually measures reading ability—not 20/20 vision, or previous knowledge of a subject" (p. 32). Another example of applying test validity is creating a quiz to test students' ability to use the simple present to talk about their daily habits; this quiz should only make use of daily habit language covered in class, ask students to use only the simple present (and not other verb tenses), and not ask students talk about content they are not familiar with, like whether or not they follow American pop culture. Besides invalidating the quiz, it would also make it culturally biased. If the school requires that teachers use a test that has validity problems, teachers can try to talk to the school administration about improving some of the test questions to make it a bit more valid. Teachers can also create informal classroom assessment activities that provide a little more validity to the assessment and to the results obtained from them.

The third principle, *reliability*, requires that the measurement results be consistent regardless of when the test is given or who grades it. In order to be reliable, a test must have consistent conditions across its administration, so it has to contain clear instructions for scoring, and it must include tasks that are unambiguous to the test-taker (Brown & Abeywickrama, 2019). On the other hand, teachers might rate the same test differently on different days if they are not relying on a grading rubric, leading to a loss of intra-rater reliability. In addition, when it comes to more subjective open-ended questions, two raters grading the same test might have different opinions about what constitutes an acceptable answer when they don't rely on a grading rubric, leading to decreased inter-rater reliability. Finally, the environmental conditions surrounding the test can impact test administration reliability. For example, in the case of a listening test, the conditions of the audio player, the quality or loudness of the speakers, and environmental noise will impact students' ability to hear the test's audio tracks.

The fourth principle is *practicality*, which requires that teachers consider the required conditions for the test administration. Important considerations to evaluate a test's practicality are the following: the test fits into their or the school's budget; it can be completed within the amount of time available; it takes into account the resources available at the school site such as media players, speakers, photocopiers, projectors, computers, books, and seating arrangements; the teacher is allowed sufficient time to grade the test and possesses the scoring guides required for grading it. Perhaps the most difficult consideration for a novice teacher to gauge—and potentially a little out of their control—is the amount of time their students will require to complete the test. One solution is to take the test themselves (or ask a colleague to take it), making sure to answer all questions at a reasonable pace (not very quickly given that a teacher is obviously more proficient than their students), and then double or triple that time. Teachers must remember that their students may want to read instructions and examples repeatedly in order to make sure that they fully understand what they are being asked to do, or that they might need additional time to think about what to say or how to answer a question. For example, if it is a writing assignment, make sure to include ample time for planning and outlining.

The fifth principle, *washback*, urges teachers to consider what kind of implications that a particular test might have on their instructional practices, both before and after the test. Washback can refer to both promotion and inhibition of learning (Messick, 1996). Although negative washback may be a point of contention, especially when it comes to the role of excessive standardized testing and the pressure on the teacher to help their students succeed on such tests, washback can actually have a positive consequential validity on teaching and learning. In order to promote learning, assessment activities must positively influence what and how teachers teach, and what and how students learn (Brown & Abeywickrama, 2019). One way to generate more positive washback for students is to give students enough time to prepare for assessment activities and offer timely and constructive feedback afterwards so that they can improve their language development.

The sixth principle that teachers should keep in mind when planning classroom assessment is test *fairness*. Teachers must do their best to avoid unintended personal and cultural biases when creating assessment assignments. Fairness has been broadly defined as the equitable treatment of all test-takers during the testing process, absence of measurement bias, equitable access to the constructs being measured, and justifiable validity of test score interpretation for the intended purpose(s) (American Educational Research Association et al., 2014). A biased test will include aspects of cultural knowledge, personal experience, or worldviews that are not within the scope of the course, rendering the test content invalid. Test bias creates an error in the measurement due to the inclusion of construct-irrelevant components that result in systematically higher or lower scores on the measurement depending on the group under examination (Kunnan, 2013). In order to improve test fairness and avoid test bias, teachers can ask a variety of people with diverse perspectives to review their assessment instruments. Teachers can also increase test fairness by creating assessment assignments with crystal clear instructions, by providing equitable conditions for all students to perform to their best ability, and by making interpretations and using test scores only to assess the learning objectives they were originally meant to assess. However, if the school requires that teachers use predetermined tests that contain unfair elements, they can talk to the school administrator and ask for permission to make improvements to the test, or they can create other forms of fair classroom assessment that counterbalance the unfairness found in the mandatory tests.

Table 7.1 provides a checklist with questions a teacher may wish to consider when creating assessments. They can be used as an initial instrument to help reflect on those assessment principles and, with time and practice, teachers can expand this checklist based on personal experience.

During the discussion of the best practices for language assessment, the use of predetermined or preexisting tests selected by school administrators (and not the teacher) was mentioned several times. This is because having to use tests that were created by others to assess our students is fairly common. Some of these tests may at first seem to be good choices because they were created either by program coordinators, who typically have a lot of teaching experience and familiarity with the school population, or by reputable English language teaching (ELT) publishers, who have been in the field for decades and hire editors with a lot of experience to design testing materials, and they pair those materials with their textbooks, workbooks, audio files, and so on. There is also the temptation to adopt testing materials that were created by teachers from all over the world who have graciously shared their work on the internet. So when deciding to go with one of these many existing materials, teachers need to make sure that the tests selected meet all the assessment principles: that is, that they are authentic, valid, reliable, practical, bias-free, and fair. If they aren't, then teachers must make the necessary modifications to those tests in order to improve their efficiency, observing all the best-practice principles. In fact, sometimes it can be more difficult to improve or adapt an existing test to suit their assessment goals than it would be to create a test from scratch to obtain one that would meet the needed assessment objectives. One example of a misuse of a preexisting test is when an language school uses a test meant to assess students' chances of success at an American university (for example, ETS TOEFL/GRE, IELTS)—which will contain academic topics (content found in college-level courses, for

134   Navigating the English Language Classroom

Table 7.1. Assessment Instrument Evaluation Checklist

Assessment instrument evaluation checklist	
Authenticity	• I make use or real-life materials. • My materials resemble real-life scenarios.
Validity	• My assessment materials only include language and tasks that are part of the curriculum or syllabus. • All my assessment materials have been covered in class beforehand. • My assessment materials are limited to what I am trying to assess.
Reliability	• I have created a scoring rubric or checklist. • If I'm asking my peers to help me grade the assessment materials, we all have a common understanding of how to use the rubrics to produce similar grading scores or decisions. • I am very clear on how to use my grading rubric so that I can grade my students consistently regardless of the day, time, or order I grade their work. • The tasks in the assessment materials are clear enough that students can perform to the best of their ability.
Practicality	• I have access to all resources I need. • I have allocated sufficient time for my students to work on the assessment. • The location where my students will work on their assessment is suitable and secure.
Washback	• I have considered the effects the assessment materials will have on my teaching. • I have considered the effects the assessment materials will have on my students' future classroom performance.
Fairness	• My assessment instrument ensures equitable treatment of all test-takers during the testing process. • My assessment instrument is absent of measurement bias. • My students understand what is being assessed and how they will be graded. • I will be able to justify grades based on rubrics, checklists, or performance descriptors.

instance), be at a high intermediate level and in a highly academic format—
as their *placement* test. It would be preferable for placement tests to contain
topics relevant to the scope and purpose of the courses in that school, as
well as questions ranging from beginning level to advanced in order to place
students based on their score. Another example of an inappropriate use of
an existing test is to adopt a standardized English *proficiency* test (like those

from Cambridge Assessment, or Michigan Language Assessment) and use them instead of a course-tailored test, based on the erroneous assumption that because both the course and assessment instrument fall under the same stated ability level (such as high beginners, or low intermediate), that the proficiency test must cover the same content as the course. This practice violates the principle of validity, as the test won't cover the content taught, and the other best-practice assessment principles would have to be examined due to the high likelihood that they were also violated.

Finally, teachers should also consider the test design. A test can come in several forms: it can be oral, written, a mixture of both, and questions can prompt answers through multiple-choice items, multiple matching, short answers, or long answers. When designing questions, teachers should consider placing the easier questions first and harder questions last: multiple choice and short answer questions should be presented first, and the longer answer questions should go last; the wording of a questions (and answer alternatives if required) should be unambiguous and in clear English at a level that students would understand; when possible, each type of question should show an example of how to respond to the question so that the example can supplement the instructions in case it was not fully understood by the student. Teachers must remember that the purpose of any assessment instrument is to give students their best chance to produce a suitable response, so try not to ask trick questions or cause students to doubt themselves.

• Q4. Why should a teacher consider (inter)national standards and institutional SLOs when developing assessments for their class?

There are several reasons why teachers should consider at least familiarizing themselves with an international proficiency standard such as the Common European Framework of Reference for Languages (CEFR) (Noijons et al., 2011) or some of the TESOL standards (see Bright et al., 2015; Hubbard, 2021). The most important reasons would be that most ELT materials produced by major ELT publishers are aligned with one or more standard(s), and novice teachers would benefit from having a good awareness of how students' proficiency levels are expected to evolve from the entry level to the highest proficiency level. So, while certain courses might not need to be aligned with an international standard at all—as, for example, casual conversation classes or private pronunciation tutoring lessons, in which teachers typically create their own teaching and assessment materials—most language programs adopt textbook series from publishers that do align with an international standard. Another reason to be aware of the teaching and assessment objectives prescribed by international language proficiency standards is that they provide a frame of reference that is translatable to other schools and programs anywhere else in the world, as well as professional colleagues presenting at international conferences, such as the yearly TESOL international conventions.

However, more important than being familiar with international language proficiency standards and frameworks, teachers should be well informed about the SLOs of their own institutions and programs and have their own expectations about achieving those goals (Turner & Windle, 2019). SLOs are statements that specify what students will know or be able to do or demonstrate when they have completed a course or program, and achieving them depends on a number of factors, from teaching materials to classroom interactions. SLOs specify an action by the student that must be observable, measurable, and able to be demonstrated, and it is up to the teacher to help students demonstrate what their students can do in the target language. A course's SLOs should inform every aspect of a lesson plan and of assessment activities so that by the end of a course, students will be able to move on to higher proficiency courses and achieve their own learning and academic or professional goals.

• *Q5. What are the main differences between formative and summative assessment, and are teachers required to do both?*

Instructors should target assessment outcomes in meaningful ways, rendering assessment a course component that is most effective when it plays an active role in pedagogical action (Hardacre & Güvendir, 2018). As content is taught within a course, teachers should evaluate how well the information is absorbed and retained. Two essential components of classroom assessment are formative assessment and summative assessment.

The first type of classroom assessment, *formative* assessment (also known as formative evaluation, formative feedback, or assessment for learning) includes a range of formal and informal assessment procedures conducted by teachers during the learning process in order to modify teaching and learning activities to improve student attainment (see Table 7.2). Formative assessment refers to a wide variety of methods that teachers use to conduct in-process evaluations of student comprehension, learning needs, and academic progress during a lesson, unit, or course (see Hewagodage, 2020). Formative assessments help teachers identify concepts that students are struggling to understand, skills they are having difficulty acquiring, or learning standards they have not yet achieved so that adjustments can be made to lessons, instructional techniques, and academic support (Gan & Leung, 2020). The general goal of formative assessment is to collect detailed information that can be used to improve instruction and student learning while it's happening. What makes an assessment "formative" is not the design of a test, technique, or self-evaluation, per se, but the way it is used—that is, to inform in-process teaching and learning modifications.

The second type of classroom assessment, known as *summative* assessment, is used to evaluate student learning progress and achievement—what students have learned—at the conclusion of a specific instructional period, usually at the end of a project, unit, course, semester, program, or school year (see Table 7.3). By assessing students at the end of an instructional period,

Table 7.2. Examples of Formative Assessment Strategies

Name of activity	Definition/explanation
Teacher's questions	Questions teachers pose to individual students and groups of students during the learning process to determine what specific concepts or skills they may be having trouble with. A wide variety of intentional questioning strategies may be employed, such as phrasing questions in specific ways to elicit more useful responses.
Teacher's feedback	Specific, detailed, and constructive feedback that teachers provide on student work such as journal entries, essays, worksheets, research papers, projects, ungraded quizzes, lab results, or works of art, design, and performance. The feedback may be used to revise or improve a work product, for example.
Exit tickets	"Exit tickets" quickly collect student responses to a teacher's questions at the end of a lesson or class period. Based on what the responses indicate, the teacher can then modify the next lesson to address concepts that students have failed to comprehend or skills they may be struggling with. "Admit slips" are a similar strategy used at the beginning of a class or lesson to determine what students have retained from previous learning experiences.
Self-assessments	Self-assessments ask students to think about their own learning process, to reflect on what they do well or struggle with, and to articulate what they have learned or still need to learn to meet course expectations or learning standards.
Peer-assessments	Peer assessments allow students to use one another as learning resources. For example, workshopping a piece of writing with classmates is one common form of peer assessment, particularly if students follow a rubric or guidelines provided by a teacher.

Table 7.3. Examples of Summative Assessment Strategies

Name of activity	Definition/explanation
End-of-unit or chapter quizzes or tests	Formal tests or quizzes that cover content taught in a unit of chapter. They can vary in length and question types.
End-of-term tests	Formal tests or quizzes that cover content taught throughout the entire term. They can vary in length and question types.
Standardized tests	Standardized tests used for the purposes of school accountability, college admissions (e.g., the SAT or ACT), or end-of-course evaluation (e.g., Advanced Placement or International Baccalaureate exams).
Performance assessment	Culminating demonstrations of learning.
Portfolios	A type of performance assessment that is collected over time and evaluated by teachers at the end of a course or term.
Capstone projects	Capstone projects that students work on over extended periods of time and that they present and defend at the conclusion of a school year or course.

summative assessments provide teachers insight into how well their students have mastered the delivered content and whether or not they are ready to move on (Siepmann, 2023). Because they are typically assigned grades that get reported not only to students but also to administrators and other stakeholders as a documented measure of students' progress and achievement, summative assessments are typically considered more high stakes than formative assessments (Mahshanian et al., 2019).

Monitoring incremental assessment activities can inform next directions of future lesson plans. For example, short summative assessment can serve as a student achievement check at closure points, while formative assessments can provide immediate feedback not only to the teacher but also to the students. Teachers should keep in mind that assessment is both local and global, which means that it should help the teacher facilitate progression from task to task, while also allowing the teacher to collect comprehensive evidence (from different sources) of student progress, performance, and linguistic development that align with the desired learning outcomes.

Tables 7.2 and 7.3 provide some examples of assignments that could be used for the purpose of formative and summative assessment respectively.

Big Picture and Bottom Line

Classroom assessment is undoubtedly an enormous responsibility, one that has immediate effects on the quality of teaching and students' learning experience, as well as several other consequences for all the stakeholders involved. It is important to stay well informed on the research behind all assessment best practices so that assessment can be treated with the seriousness it deserves. A good teacher will not only invest a good amount of time preparing their lessons, but also observing how those lessons impact their students' learning and development.

Food for Thought

1. Imagine you were assigned a CEFR level A1 (intro level, beginners) to teach at a private EFL school in a non-English-speaking country.
   a. Try to find out what the CEFR framework suggests should be the student learning outcomes for this level. Then, think of one four-hour session lesson that you would teach to this group of A1 learners. What language content would you cover?
   b. Think of at least three strategies you can use for the purpose of formative assessment, and discuss why you think these strategies would work well with the A1 group of learners and for the lesson you chose to teach in 1a.
   c. Create a summative assessment quiz to be used at the end of this lesson. Discuss:
      i. What grading system and distribution will you use for this quiz?
      ii. How will you provide feedback to your students about their performance on this quiz?
      iii. What measures will you take to make sure that your quiz complies with the best assessment practices (authenticity, validity, reliability, practicality, positive washback, and fairness)?
2. Now imagine that this is another year and that you were assigned another class, which is a CEFR B1 (lower intermediate) level class. This would be a group of adult students taking an intensive ESL course in an English-speaking country. This course meets every day (Monday through Friday), six hours a day, for twenty-four

weeks. Try to find out what the CEFR framework suggests should be the student learning outcomes for this course, and plan how you will assess your students daily and throughout the term. The program coordinator gave you complete freedom to design your own tests and assignments. So you need to decide how often you will assess your students, what kind of assignments you will ask them to do, how you will grade them, and how you will report your students' performance to them.

References

American Educational Research Association, American Psychological Association, & National Council on Measurement in Education (2014). *Standards for educational and psychological testing.* American Educational Research Association.

Bright, A., Hansen-Thomas, H., & de Oliveira, L. (Eds.) (2015). *The Common Core State Standards in English Language Arts for English language learners: Grade 6–12.* TESOL Press.

Brown, H. D., & Abeywickrama, P. (2019). *Language assessment: Principles and classroom practices* (3rd ed.). Pearson.

Gan, Z., Leung, C. (2020). Illustrating formative assessment in task-based language teaching. *ELT Journal, 74*(1), 10–19. https://doi.org/10.1093/elt/ccz048

Güvendir, E., & Hardacre, B. (2020). Task-based language teaching and grammar. In J. I. Liontas, TESOL International Association, & M. DelliCarpini (Eds.) The TESOL encyclopedia of English language teaching (2nd ed., pp. 1–6). Wiley-Blackwell. https://doi.org/10.1002/9781118784235.eelt0989

Hardacre, B., & Guvendir, E., (2018). Cognitive perspectives in teaching speaking. In J. I. Liontas, TESOL International Association, & M. DelliCarpini (Eds.) The TESOL encyclopedia of English language teaching (pp. 1–7). Wiley-Blackwell. https://doi.org/10.1002/9781118784235.eelt0232

Hewagodage, V. (2020). Utilizing internet resources in TESOL: The design of English language learning and formative assessment practices. In C. E. Dann, & S. O'Neill (Eds.), *Technology-enhanced formative assessment practices in higher education* (pp. 60–86). IGI Global. https://doi.org/10.4018/978-1-7998-0426-0.ch004

Hubbard, P. (2021). Revisiting the TESOL technology standards for teachers: Integration and adaptation. *CALICO Journal, 38*(3), 319–337. https://doi.org/10.1558/cj.20068

Kunnan, A. J. (2013). Fairness and justice in language assessment. In A. J. Kunnan (Ed.) *The companion to language assessment* (pp. 1098–1114). Wiley. https://doi.org/10.1002/9781118411360.wbcla144

Mahshanian, A., Shoghi, R., Bahrami, M. (2019). Investigating the differential effects of formative and summative assessment on EFL learners' end-of-term achievement. *Journal of Language Teaching and Research, 10*(5), 1055–1066. http://dx.doi.org/10.17507/jltr.1005.19

Martínez Marín, J. D., & Mejía Vélez, M. C. (2021). Master of TESOL students' conceptions of assessment: Questioning beliefs. *Revista Actualidades Investigativas en Educacion, 21*(2). http://dx.doi.org/10.15517/aie.v21i2.46782

Messick, S. (1996). Validity and washback in language testing. *Language Testing, 13*(3), 241–256. https://doi.org/10.1177/026553229601300302

Noijons, J., Bérešová, J., Breton, G., & Szabó, G. (2011). *Relating language examinations to the Common European Framework of Reference for Languages: Learning, teaching, assessment (CEFR). Highlights from the Manual.* Council of Europe Publishing.

Siepmann, P. (2023). The literary portfolio: Summative assessment of literary competences in autonomous learning environments. *TESOL Journal, 14*(2), Article e702. https://doi.org/10.1002/tesj.702

Turner, M., & Windle, J. (2019). Exploring the positioning of teacher expertise in TESOL-related curriculum standards. *TESOL Quarterly, 53*(4), 939–959. https://doi.org/10.1002/tesq.527

CHAPTER 8

Implementing Assessment Expectations and Outcomes

Contextualization

The purpose of this chapter is to discuss the important role of classroom expectations when it comes to assessment of students' performance. Because the language learning process involves the activation of myriad skills which often vary considerably, instructors must demonstrate foresight in all actions to prevent unfair or ill-conceived assessment materials development. For example, one area that is often troublesome for new instructors is the act of writing task instructions. Task instructions are paramount to establishing the correct expectations of what students are being asked to do, and yet it is possible to find so many examples out there of poorly crafted task instructions. This chapter presents best practices that can enhance student buy-in and engagement with classroom assessment activities. It also provides instructors with methods for encouraging student investment in course activities through the practice of targeted goal-sharing, where students are overtly educated on the larger plan for learning objectives, training them to see the purpose behind tasks. Please note that in this chapter, the terms *testing* and *assessment* refer to the basic process of designing assignments that will help the teacher draw inferences about students' language ability or performance from sampled behaviors.

Case Study: Trust without Trusting

The case study used in this chapter is a cautionary tale for those who blindly trust that the assessment packet they get as part of a textbook series perfectly matches the content covered in class. The following example happened in a community college in Southern California. The teacher in this story was teaching a lower intermediate writing skills course. The textbook adopted for this course came with an accompanying CD-ROM with a preloaded bank of test questions, and all the teacher had to do was tell the program which textbook unit they wanted to create a test for, and what kind of activities they wanted: included from it is listening, reading, writing, vocabulary, and grammar test item banks. The program pulled questions from its preloaded bank and a test and answer key were generated, at which point all the teacher had to do was hit "Print" and then make thirty copies of the test to distribute to the students in class. Well, after the test was over, a group of students approached the teacher to complain that some of the questions were not covered in class. And they were right—the teacher came to realize that a lot of the vocabulary questions were about the right topic, but they were making use of words that were new to the students and had not been taught in class. The teacher in this case saw no alternative but to cancel those questions and regrade all tests. Students were satisfied with the solution, but unfortunate events like this one undermine students' confidence in the validity of future assessments created by this teacher. Or, had the teacher refused to correct the situation, it could have hurt their rapport entirely. Students expect assessment instruments to cover only what was taught in class, and they want to be treated fairly. If they feel like they have been cheated or tricked, they will complain to the teacher or to their superior, and they have every right to do so. So the moral of this real-life story is, even when using publisher-endorsed assessment packets, go through the material carefully to make sure the questions are well-crafted and that they have content validity.

Common Concerns

Below are questions that are commonly asked by novice teachers and teachers-in-training about navigating classroom expectations when creating their own assessment materials (tests, quizzes, classroom tasks, home assignments, and so on).

- *Q1. What do teachers need to think about when creating assessment activities that will meet their students' expectations?*
- *Q2. How can rubrics help teachers convey the performance expectations for a given activity?*
- *Q3. How can teachers improve student receptivity to assessable tasks and assignments while simultaneously predicting and eliminating problems before they arise?*

- *Q4. When the assessment outcome doesn't meet students' expectations, what are some strategies that teachers can implement to address their students' questions and concerns?*
- *Q5. How can teachers make sure their students' performance reflects their competence?*

Effective Practices for Implementing Assessment Expectations and Outcomes

- **Q1. What do teachers need to think about when creating assessment activities that will meet their students' expectations?**

When creating assessment materials, teachers should consider the factors that make them suitable for the purpose of their class and students. There are five basic principles that should always guide the creation of assessment materials, namely: content validity, reliability, authenticity, practicality, and washback (Brown & Abeywickrama, 2018). In other words, teachers need to think if the assessment material they are creating does indeed cover—and is limited to—important content that was covered in class, that their test is capable of generating similar results across repeated administrations when conditions are similar, that it resembles tasks that may occur in real life and that are relevant to students, that they will have the necessary resources to administer it and grade it, and that it has the potential to positively inform instruction with formative feedback, among several other relevant test characteristics (see Chapter 7). Teachers should also make sure that the assessment material is free of cultural and personal biases which might affect students' understanding of what they are being asked to do.

Another important factor is the purpose of the assessment material. What the teacher is trying to evaluate must guide the format of the test and its content. A language assessment instrument can be used for the purpose of diagnostics, placement, comprehension check, progress check, culminating achievement, and proficiency assessment, and it can help teachers make decisions about retaining or promoting a student, about moving on to new topics or reinforcing certain lessons, about the efficacy of group dynamics, and about the effectiveness of instructional materials. The type of assessment teachers decide to use should reflect the type of outcome desired and the evaluation required from it.

Implementing Assessment Expectations and Outcomes 145

The ideal time to plan assessment procedures, including frequency and grading distribution, is before the term starts. An assessment plan for a course should include a few higher-stakes assignments (that is, worth more points) to be distributed throughout the term, and some more frequent and lower-stakes assignments (worth fewer points), such as daily practices activities and homework assignments. Teachers can also consider creating assessment activities that are not for grade, but more for practice and formative feedback (see Chapter 7). Teachers also need to decide which assignments will assess each of the student learning outcomes and when to schedule them, keeping in mind that content related to specific learning outcomes need to be covered in class before it is assessed.

Tasks can be completed in class or at home, and each has their own advantages. First, in-class assessments can be impromptu (that is, without warning, on the spot), or scheduled on the course calendar so that students have ample notice to prepare. It really depends on what the teacher is trying to assess. Impromptu tasks and pop quizzes give students no time to prepare, so teachers may get a more raw snapshot of students' current understanding or ability, which could be useful in case they are trying to gauge if the lesson they just taught was effective or if students will need reinforcement practice activities; it is possible that a pop-up quiz will catch students unprepared, before they have a chance to fully grasp a concept or master the particular ability the teacher is trying to assess. When scheduling tests and quizzes, teachers should allow students a chance to study and prepare for them. Because it might require a certain amount of time for students to fully grasp certain concepts and/or master certain skills, being allowed time to study and prepare for a test or quiz can help students get where they need to get—that is, the achievement of the particular student learning outcome that is going to be assessed.

Students can be asked to showcase what they know and what they can do, and they can either do so by themselves or via collaboration with a partner or a group. For example, if teachers want to assess students' language use skills, they can ask them to complete reading and writing tasks that require the use of those particular language items, or they can ask them to talk with a partner about a topic that would elicit that particular kind of language (*language* here refers to both vocabulary and grammar). But in the first option, the teacher would also be able to assess their reading and writing skills, whereas in the second case, they would be able to assess their listening and speaking skills. During class, a lot of the work students will be involved with is going to be collaborative, and teachers should make use of those opportunities to assess their students' learning and progress.

- **Q2. How can rubrics help teachers convey the performance expectations for a given activity?**

Very often students are not clear on what they are supposed to do to receive the highest grade on an assignment. In order to prevent this, there are three supporting steps that teachers can use in conjunction, which are to provide 1) very clear guidelines to help students prepare for the assignment; 2) very clear and detailed instructions, including samples and examples when possible; and 3) clear rubrics that lay out exactly what they expect students to do in order to get an A (or the highest grade) in that assignment. Rubrics can be time-consuming to create, but they make grading much faster, fairer, and more efficient, and they can always refer to a rubric when students come to see them to ask why they received a particular grade (Li, 2020). Figure 8.1 summarizes the main advantages of using rubrics when it comes to helping students prepare for assignments and help teachers stay fair and focused when grading the assignment.

Rubrics are especially important to maintain grading reliability and ensure fairness (Smith & Paige, 2019). By making sure that a rubric addresses the SLOs that need to be assessed by a particular task or assignment, teachers must show restraint from grading beyond the student ability level (Poehner & Yu, 2022), or beyond the intended purpose of the assessment

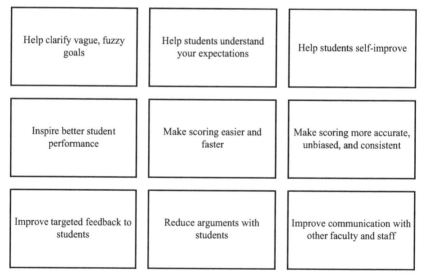

Figure 8.1. Advantages of using a rubric.

(Hardacre, 2023). If the proficiency level of students would make reading the rubric a little challenging, teachers should consider creating a simplified version, maybe in the form of a simple checklist, that teachers can distribute to their students prior to the task.

The purpose of the assessment material should guide the choice of rubric (see Ellis, 2017). Rubrics can be holistic, analytic, or focused on a primary trait. Holistic rubrics typically contain general descriptions of the performance expected for each ability range, say, A, B, or C; for example, in a holistic rubric for a final paper, a teacher would provide a general description of the desired characteristics of an A paper, a B paper, and a C paper. Analytic rubrics break down each ability range into more specific categories of areas the teacher would like to assess separately; for example, if their students are writing a final paper, more specific analytic categories for a paper would include descriptions of required formatting, content, organization, and mechanics (to name a few popular ones) (Ferris, 2010). A primary trait rubric, on the other hand, would have one major category that would receive most of the grade's weight, but the instructor can still consider other variables in the final grade (see Appendices 8.1, 8.2, and 8.3 for different examples of rubrics).

All rubrics should be carefully tailored to a specific assignment. This means using language and specific examples of performance or inclusion criteria that make reference to the task at hand. Teachers should avoid using generic templates that won't be as efficient in guiding their students in what to include or leave out of a graded assignment.

One of the least helpful characteristics of generic rubrics that teachers should avoid is the use of vague gradation of key terms that differentiate across distinct performance domains. For example: category descriptor for an A performance in a pronunciation test: "Student's pronunciation is not very distracting"; category descriptor for a B performance: "Student's pronunciation is somewhat distracting"; for a C performance: "Student's pronunciation is severely distracting." The words "very," "somewhat," and "severely" in this example could mean different things to different people as they are not very precise or quantifiable terms. They don't specify what kind of pronunciation issues are to be expected in each grade range, and they leave grading open to personal interpretation and bias. So imprecise descriptors and vague adjectives are to be avoided at all costs when designing rubrics that will guide not only the teacher during grading, but also will help students prepare for assignments and manage their expectations.

148   Navigating the English Language Classroom

- ***Q3. How can teachers improve student receptivity to assessable tasks and assignments while simultaneously predicting and eliminating problems before they arise?***

It is important to provide very clear and unambiguous information about assessment procedures and grading from the beginning of the course in order to manage students' expectations and avoid possible misunderstandings. Students need to understand right away what will be expected of them and what they need to do to succeed in the course. There are three main ways to make this happen. One way is to have a very detailed syllabus where the teacher lays out all the assignments and tests students will have throughout the term, along with very clear dates, instructions, examples or samples, and so on. The second way is to design tasks and assignments with crystal clear instructions and create a space for clarification questions. And the third way is to give students copies of the grading rubrics, or at least simplified checklists describing the expected performance thresholds and their grading distribution. The following are additional examples of things teachers can do to improve the clarity of course expectations that may improve student receptivity to assignments and that can potentially eliminate grading issues and grievances later on: provide students with a checklist of areas to be assessed in their performance; give examples or samples of the performance they are looking for; have extra models and examples at the ready to illustrate or animate the method of assessment in meaningful ways; share rubrics with students ahead of time; post the rubric ahead of time on the course management system; write grading expectations on their syllabus; and share with students the policy on late work and on plagiarism.

Another important consideration is whether or not an assignment needs to be graded. Not all assessments carried out in or outside the classroom need to be assigned a numerical or letter grade. Teachers sometimes fear that if an activity is not graded, students will not be invested in doing them. But it is important to help students see the value in practicing their language skills when it's not for grade so they are ready to perform at their best when it is.

When it comes to grading, it is important to acknowledge other forms of grading systems like contract grading. In traditional grading, educators determine assignments, exams, and projects before the course begins. Students are expected to follow the syllabus, attend class, complete the assignments required, and reach the student learning outcomes by the end of the term. The grade the student receives is a reflection of how well they achieved the proficiency standards set in the curriculum and the student learning outcomes for that particular course. On the other hand, the contract grading system allows each student to devise their own grading outcome for the

Implementing Assessment Expectations and Outcomes 149

class by picking and choosing which assignments or projects they intend to complete—that is, how much labor they are willing to put into their grade (Inoue, 2019). Grades are assigned on the basis of an agreement between the student and the professor of what comprises the labor required to get an A, a B, or a C in the class (Frank & Scharff, 2013). Although the student has a say in what is to be accomplished throughout the course, both the student and professor must negotiate what seems to be fair and come to a mutual agreement (Danielewicz & Elbow, 2009). Teachers must consider the flexibility they have within the institution they work and the purpose of the course they are teaching when they are deciding between traditional grading and contract grading. Contract grading focuses on *processes*, whereas conventional grading focuses on *products*, *outcomes*, and *results* (Danielewicz & Elbow, 2009, p. 260). But for a focus on the process to work, teachers must engage students in frequent critical self-revision and peer review (Vuogan & Li, 2022) and offer plenty of ongoing feedback (Kang & Han, 2015) and speedy grading, so that students know where they stand and whether they are making any real progress in the course. With the flexibility of contracts, teachers can highlight the processes that are crucial for students' learning, but contract grading may be inadequate and inefficient if the contract is used simply as a checklist of the work that students need to turn in before the end of the term, without a focus on the developmental process of the work to be produced. What's more, ESL education is typically shaped around international proficiency standards based on incremental performance outcomes (that is, the can-do abilities that students need to master within the period of a course) and as such, it is more easily paired with traditional grading.

- **Q4. When the assessment outcome doesn't meet students' expectations, what are some strategies that teachers can implement to address their students' questions and concerns?**

It is possible that some of the students will come to a teacher when they are concerned about having been unfairly assessed, whereas others might not have the courage to approach their teacher because they might think it is not their place to question their teacher. But it doesn't mean they won't continue to be dissatisfied if they think a test or assignment was unfair or if they feel they were asked a trick or ambiguous question. So even when the test is as valid, reliable, and fair as it can be, teachers should still have a review session during which students are allowed to ask for clarification on issues related to ambiguous test or assignment instructions, or about unclear or misleading prompts. In fact, teachers should allow for questions before (e.g., clarification questions) and after the assignment in questions (e.g., related to the students' performance on the test) and to allow students to voice their concerns, understand how they can improve, and stay engaged in the assessment process, including valuing the teacher's feedback (Hyland, 2003).

Especially when teaching English to speakers of other languages, teachers might have students from several different cultures. Classroom dynamics such as teacher–student relationships can vary based on culture, influencing students' willingness to approach the teacher. Therefore, it is very important to write on the syllabus and to constantly remind students how and when teachers want to be approached when they have questions or concerns. Teachers have the responsibility to educate their students about how to advocate for themselves in formal settings, how to interact with their teachers, and how to voice their concerns and complaints. In addition, if they feel comfortable approaching the teacher first, they will be less likely to go straight to their teacher's superior with a complaint, and teachers can attempt to diffuse the situation and preserve their relationship with that student and with their superiors.

Sometimes teachers may not be at fault for an ill-designed assessment. That would be the case when they were not involved in the creation of tests and assignments, so it might not be directly their fault if it turns out the tests are not entirely valid, are unfair, had trick questions, or were biased. One way to minimize problems when teachers are not involved in the creation of the test is to go over the test beforehand to try to spot problem areas. Teachers can also go over the test questions in class to create a space in which students can ask for clarifications on what they are being asked to do. If it turns out that the teacher or the students have concerns about the validity or fairness of the test, the teacher could try to seek out a superior to resolve the issue, at which point they can ask about the possibility of canceling or substituting certain questions, modifying them, or replacing them with revised or better-crafted questions.

An area of students' expectations that is extremely hard to navigate is the culture of grade inflation. A grades should be attainable with hard work, and they should not be a given expectation for all students. But if students don't get an early warning of an impending B or C by getting their grades early in the semester, they will feel that they were robbed of the chance to try to get an A. Another scenario would be when students believe that work of performance in the B or C range deserves an A simply because that is the grade they have always gotten from previous teachers. So how can this trend be correct and students' perceptions of their own performance and their grade expectations be adjusted? First, teachers need to grade things quickly so students know where they stand in the course. Second, teachers should have clear rubrics for all graded assignments with descriptions of A, B, C, D, and F performances that they can share with their students to improve grading transparency. Third, teachers should provide samples of students' A/B/C/D/F performance on written and spoken assignments along with matching rubrics delineating the exact explanation of why that sample received that grade. Lastly, teachers should go over these materials in class with their students before the assignment is due, to allow students to ask clarification questions and for them to adjust their perceptions.

Another grade expectation management that teachers might have to navigate is when a student is perfectly happy receiving a C when it would be preferable that they strived for an A. Any teacher should hope to motivate their students to give their best, but sometimes students are happy to just "barely pass" or "get by." If a teacher notices this behavior in one of their students, they should talk to them, as sometimes they have their plates full with several jobs and family commitments, so the C performance could actually be the best they can offer at that moment. But if they are just bored and lacking the motivation to do better, then the teacher can ask them what course improvements would change their attitude. Sometimes just showing them that they actually care, value their input, and that they are willing to accommodate them can help students improve their attitudes and correct their behavior.

Sometimes students will compare their grades with one another and will come to their teacher and complain that their friend got a higher grade than them, that they think they deserve the same grade because in their minds they have put in the same amount of work into the course. In this case, the teacher should invite the student to their office hours and ask them to bring the work(s) they are complaining about, and that they have the scoring sheet or rubric, instructions, and performance samples with them when they come to their office hours, so that they can patiently show the student why they received the score they did. Every time a teacher grades assignments, they should be careful and attentive to how they are interpreting students' answers, and how the performance fits the rubrics and matches the SLOs because they might be asked to defend that grade—to the student, to their parent(s), or to their superior. When teachers are fair and transparent, they have nothing to fear. But if they did not use a rubric, or boosted the grade of one student only, or if they let any other type of unfairness or bias influence their grades, then they will sooner or later be called to answer for this misjudgment.

• Q5. How can teachers make sure their students' performance reflects their competence?

This question requires that the terms *competence* and *performance* be defined and differentiated. Chomsky (1965) was the first to differentiate linguistic competence from linguistic performance, and he described *competence* as an idealized capacity that is located as a psychological or mental property or function, and *performance* as the production of actual utterances. In other words, a second language learner's linguistic competence encompasses their complete breadth of knowledge of the linguistic system and their ability to understand sentences in that language, whereas linguistic performance of a second language learner is limited to the language more readily and promptly available to use during their written or spoken production. It is the latter that students make use of when speaking in class or writing an essay.

But teachers are often concerned about getting authentic samples of students' unaltered performance, especially when students are allowed to work at home, unsupervised. After all, it might be tempting to look for answers on the internet, to elicit help from friends or tutors, or use resources like dictionaries and grammar checkers. So teachers may wonder if their students' work is original. Well, there are ways to check. There are several plagiarism-checking services like Turnitin, Unicheck, PlagiarismChecker. com, Grammarly, among many others.

When trying to prevent plagiarism, it is important to have a policy about it that is clearly stated on the course syllabus and that is explained on the first day of class. Teachers should include information about when students will be allowed to use linguistic support resources when being assessed, whether tests will be open or closed book, which assignments will make use of a dictionary or a computer, whether the use of grammar checkers like Grammarly is acceptable for work done at home, or whether they can use supplemental language-focused apps.

Many teachers still think that allowing students to use such support resources is like allowing them to cheat, and that it defeats the purpose of the assessment. That can be true if the purpose of the assessment is to gauge students' level for placement purposes, if it is a diagnostic test of their performance level, or if students' achievement at the end of a semester is being assessed. But the purpose of an assessment instrument might also be to reinforce taught materials, or to push their performance boundaries. In such cases, it is perfectly acceptable to allow students to use language support resources as long as they are doing the work themselves, because in the process of using language apps, dictionaries, spelling, grammar, and plagiarism checkers they are encountering new language forms and are consolidating what they know.

Big Picture and Bottom Line

Setting up a positive tone toward classroom assessment and navigating students' expectations can be quite challenging. It helps when students see personal value in the information obtained from assessments. Activities that are authentic and meaningful have better chances of enlisting students' interest (Hardacre & Güvendir, 2018). Certain approaches to teaching and assessment, such as task-based language testing, have allowed assessment materials to evaluate students' capability to use language in real-life situations, interactively, with other people, to accomplish meaningful goals (Brindley, 1994). Authenticity and meaningfulness are not sufficient, however. It is crucial that teachers strive to show transparency and professionalism when it comes to grading practices by explaining policies, sharing rubrics, and providing samples when applicable; it is also equally important that assessment instruments are well designed so that students have a clear understanding of what the performance expectations are.

Food for Thought

1. Find a rubric that your institution uses, or one from the internet. Discuss in pairs how they address the scope of the activity they are meant to help grade, and what their strengths and weaknesses are. In respect to the weaknesses, how would you improve them?
2. The syllabus is typically the go-to place for important information about a course, which includes student learning outcomes, graded assignments, and grading procedures. It is important to be thorough there so that students can manage their expectations. But besides the syllabus, what are some other visible places where you can post instructions, rubrics, and samples for your students' easy access?
3. In small groups, discuss how plagiarism has been treated by different institutions you have attended or teachers you have had. In light of your experience and teaching philosophy, how do you think you would treat it in your own classroom?

References

Brindley, G. (1994). Task-centred assessment in language learning: The promise and the challenge. In N. Bird, P. Falvey, A. B. M. Tsui, D. M. Allison, & A. McNeill (Eds.), *Language and learning: Papers presented at the Annual International Language in Education Conference (Hong Kong, 1993)* (pp. 73–94). Hong Kong Education Department.

Brown, H. D., & Abeywickrama, P. (2018). *Language assessment: Principles and classroom practices* (3rd ed.). Pearson.

Chomsky, N. (1965). *Aspects of the theory of syntax*. MIT Press.

Danielewicz, J., & Elbow, P. (2009). A unilateral grading contract to improve learning and teaching. *College Composition and Communication, 61*(2), 244–268. http://www.jstor.org/stable/40593442

Ellis, R. (2017). Oral corrective feedback in L2 classrooms: What we know so far. In H. Nassaji & E. Kartchava (Eds.), *Corrective feedback in second language teaching and learning: Research, theory, applications, implications* (pp. 3–18). Taylor & Francis.

Ferris, D. R. (2010). Second language writing research and written corrective feedback in SLA: Intersections and practical applications. *Studies in Second Language Acquisition, 32*(2), 181–201. https://doi.org/10.1017/S0272263109990490

Frank, T., & Scharff, L. F. V. (2013). Learning contracts in undergraduate courses: Impacts on student behaviors and academic performance. *Journal of the Scholarship of Teaching and Learning, 13*(4), 36–53.

Hardacre, B. (2023). Assessing university students' writing development and performance during remote instruction. In K. Sadeghi (Ed.), *Technology-assisted language development in diverse contexts: Lessons from the transition to online testing during COVID-19* (pp. 131–147). Routledge.

Hardacre, B., & Güvendir, E., (2018). Cognitive perspectives in teaching speaking. In J. I. Liontas, TESOL International Association, & M. DelliCarpini (Eds.), *The TESOL encyclopedia of English language teaching* (pp. 1–7). Wiley-Blackwell. https://doi.org/10.1002/9781118784235.eelt0232

Hyland, F. (2003). Focusing on form: Student engagement with teacher feedback. *System, 31*(2), 217–230. https://doi.org/10.1016/S0346-251X(03)00021-6

Inoue, A. B. (2019). *Labor-based grading contracts: Building equity and inclusion in the compassionate writing classroom*. The WAC Clearinghouse; University Press of Colorado.

Kang, E., & Han, Z. (2015). The efficacy of written corrective feedback in improving L2 written accuracy: A meta-analysis. *The Modern Language Journal, 99*(1), 1–18. https://doi.org/10.1111/modl.12189

Li, M. (2020). Multimodal pedagogy in TESOL teacher education: Students' perspectives. *System, 94*, Article 102337. https://doi.org/10.1016/j.system.2020.102337

Poehner, M. E., & Yu, L. (2022). Dynamic assessment of L2 writing: Exploring the potential of rubrics as mediation in diagnosing learner emerging abilities. *TESOL Quarterly, 56*(4), 1191–1217. https://doi.org/10.1002/tesq.3098

Smith, G. S., & Paige, D. D. (2019). A study of reliability across multiple raters when using the NAEP and MDFS rubrics to measure oral reading fluency. *Reading Psychology*, *40*(1), 34–69. https://doi.org/10.1080/02702711.2018.1555361

Vuogan, A., & Li, S. (2022). Examining the effectiveness of peer feedback in second language writing: A meta-analysis. *TESOL Quarterly*, *57*(4), 1115–1138. https://doi.org/10.1002/tesq.3178

Appendix 8.1

Graduate-Level Final Research Paper Analytic Rubric

Criteria/points	4	3	2	1
Introduction	Exceptional introduction that grabs interest of reader and states topic.	Proficient introduction that is interesting and states topic.	Basic introduction that states topic but lacks interest.	Weak or no introduction of topic. Paper's purpose is unclear
Thesis statement	Thesis is exceptionally clear, arguable, well-developed, and a definitive statement.	Thesis is somewhat clear and an arguable statement of position.	Thesis is unclear or somewhat vague or ambiguous.	Thesis is very weak, not arguable, or missing.
Quality of literature review and information and evidence provided	Paper is exceptionally researched, extremely detailed, and historically accurate. Information and evidence provided clearly relates to the thesis.	Paper is well-researched and uses information from a variety of sources. Information and evidence provided relates to the main topic.	Information relates to the main topic, but few details or examples are given. Shows a limited variety of sources.	Information has little or nothing to do with the topic. Evidence is weak or not connected to the thesis.
Quality of analysis	Exceptionally critical, relevant, and consistent connections made between evidence and thesis. Excellent analysis.	Consistent connections made between evidence and thesis Good analysis.	Some connections made between evidence and thesis. Some analysis.	Limited or no connections made between evidence and thesis. Lack of analysis.

(continued)

Appendix 8.1 (Cont.)

Criteria/points	4	3	2	1
Organization and flow	Exceptionally clear, logical, mature, and thorough development of thesis with excellent transitions between and within paragraphs. All body paragraphs have a topic sentence that relates to the thesis. Paragraphs are organized in a logical manner, and contain smooth transitions.	Clear and logical order that supports thesis with good transitions between and within paragraphs. Body paragraphs have clear topic sentences. Paragraphs are organized in a logical manner.	Somewhat clear and logical development with basic transitions between and within paragraphs. Not all body paragraphs have topic sentences.	Lacks development of ideas with weak or no transitions between and within paragraphs. No topic sentences.
Conclusion	Excellent summary of topic with concluding ideas that impact reader. Introduces no new information.	Good summary of topic with clear concluding ideas. Introduces no new information.	Basic summary of topic with some final concluding ideas. Introduces new information. Summary might sound a little repetitive.	No conclusion, or lack of summary of essay's topic.
Style/voice	Style and voice are not only appropriate to the given audience and purpose, but also show originality and creativity. Word choice is specific, purposeful, dynamic, and varied.	Style and voice appropriate to the given audience and purpose. Word choice is specific and purposeful, and somewhat varied throughout.	Style and voice somewhat appropriate to given audience and purpose. Word choice is often unspecific, generic, redundant, and clichéd.	Style and voice are inappropriate or do not address given audience, purpose. Word choice is excessively redundant, clichéd, and unspecific.

Appendix 8.1 (Cont.)

Criteria/points	4	3	2	1
	Sentences are clear and to the point.	Sentences are mostly clear and to the point.	Sentences are somewhat unclear and vague.	Sentences are very unclear and vague.
Grammar, usage, mechanics	Excellent control of grammar, usage, and mechanics. Entirely free of spelling, punctuation, and grammatical errors.	May contain a few spelling, punctuation, and grammar errors. Almost entirely free of spelling, punctuation, and grammatical errors.	Contains several spelling, punctuation, and grammar errors which detract from the paper's readability.	Contains so many spelling, punctuation, and grammar errors that the paper cannot be easily understood.
In-text citation format	In-text citations use APA style flawlessly.	In-text citations uses APA style with minor mistakes.	Frequent errors in APA in-text citations.	Paper does not use APA style for in-text citations, or evidence of plagiarism.
Use of APA Style latest edition to format paper	Paper's formatting in APA style is flawless (title page, page number, running head, font, font size, double-spaced, heading levels, references, etc.).	Paper's formatting in APA style is mostly correct with some errors (title page, page number, running head, font, font size, double-spaced, heading levels, references, etc.).	Frequent errors in APA format.	Lack of APA format, or numerous errors.

Appendix 8.2

Upper Intermediate Composition Holistic Rubric

A = Excellent (Superior Performance)

Content: A-level work uses an assignment as the occasion for a piece of writing compelling enough to engage readers on its own terms. It presents individual insight or viewpoints with enough fullness and cogency to command readers' respect, if not their assent. It complements its fresh thought by creating a distinctive voice through aptly chosen writing that is believable and theoretically sophisticated.

Language: The grammar standard for A level is characterized as language that rarely impedes the flow of reading. There is structural and lexical diversity in A-level grammar that approximates the language command of a native speaker of the language. Words are not misspelled, and are used according to context and definitional sense. Punctuation and capitalization are used appropriately. There is a sophistication to overall structures that is advanced yet not overly convoluted. Proper weighting of subordination. Paragraphs are strong and cohesive.

(Numerical values: A+ = 98.5; A = 94.5; A- = 91)

A grade of A+ is earned based on writing that is well beyond expectations (rare, in essence it is a stellar piece of writing).

A grade of A is earned based on writing that meets the parameters listed in the A-grade scale above.

A grade of A- is earned based on writing that is better than good, but slightly insufficient based on A-grade scale parameters.

B = Above Average (Good Performance)

Content: B-level work meets all of an assignment's expectations with clear competence. Usually lacking A work's fresh thought and approach or its compelling development, B work nevertheless demonstrates its author's ability to respond intelligently to an assignment's demands, to structure and focus ideas clearly through writing, to select significant details and examples and to organize them effectively, and express these ideas with a nice sense of flow.

Language: The grammar standard for B level is characterized as language that infrequently impedes the flow of reading. There is structural and lexical diversity in B-level grammar that closely resembles the language command of a native speaker of the language. Words are sometimes misspelled, but the sense behind choice and usage is clear. Punctuation and capitalization could be improved, but are relatively error free. There is a movement towards sophistication where advanced thought is shown, but sometimes through fragmented or convoluted structures. Subordination and coordination are properly achieved, though they could use some improvement. Paragraphs could benefit from some revision.

Implementing Assessment Expectations and Outcomes 159

(Numerical values: B+ = 88; B = 84.5; B- = 81)

A grade of B+ is earned based on writing that is slightly above, but not superior to, the parameters listed in the B-grade scale.

A grade of B is earned based on writing that meets the parameters listed in the B-grade scale above.

A grade of B- is earned based on writing that is better than fair, but slightly insufficient based on B-grade scale parameters.

C = Average (Fair Performance)

Content: C work is entirely adequate but nothing more. C work meets the assignment's specifications, has a serviceable structure, and provides enough elaboration with examples and analysis to make its intent understandable. The ideas are discernable, but the overall expression of those ideas takes additional energy on the reader's part. C work, comparatively speaking, lacks the sharp focus, full and purposeful development, and stylistic awareness necessary for an above average characterization.

Language: The grammar standard for C level is characterized as language that impedes the flow of reading to varying degrees. There is less structural and lexical diversity in C-level grammar, and it frequently strays away from language models of native speakers of the language. Words are misspelled, and context and definitional sense are not appropriately applied in constructing thoughts. Punctuation and capitalization are in need of revision. There is a lack of sophistication in the overall structure of sentences that reflects an underdeveloped sense of academic language. Subordination and coordination are not used in a manner that enhances the writing. Paragraphs need work.

(Numerical values: C+ = 78; C = 74.5; C- = 71)

A grade of C+ is earned based on writing that is slightly above average, but which does not merit above average recognition.

A grade of C is earned based on writing that meets the parameters listed in the C-grade scale above (minimum passing grade).

A grade of C- is earned based on writing that is better than poor, but insufficient for a C (C- is considered non-pass grade).

D = Poor (Below Average Performance)

Content: D work is clearly inadequate in at least one or more ways. Although D work may demonstrate competence in some facets, its strengths will be outweighed by apparent pervasive weaknesses that constrain the value of the writing from coming forth: failure to meaningfully engage an important aspect of the writing task or to maintain a focus; skimpy or illogical development; significant negligence towards language and stylistic expression; persistent lack of subordination. The readability of the piece is extraordinarily low, causing the reader to stop frequently to try to parse meaning from the writing.

Language: The grammar standard for D level is characterized as language that unacceptably impedes the flow of reading. There is a general absence of structural and lexical diversity in D-level grammar, and the language does not emulate language models of native speakers of the language. Spelling is careless, and the context and definitional sense of words and phrases is generally disregarded and left up to the reader to decipher. Punctuation and capitalization show no clear application of rules. The language is more or less void of sophistication and subpar when compared to academic expectations for this course. Overall, the language is not at the standard for 2i.

(Numerical values: D+ = 68; D = 64.5; D- = 61)

> *A grade of D+ is earned based on writing that is below average, but with high potential for average status (non-pass grade).*

> *A grade of D is earned based on poor writing that meets the parameters listed in the D-grade scale (non-pass grade).*

> *A grade of D- is earned based on poor writing that has some potential, but is currently insufficient for a C (non-pass grade).*

F = Fail (Failing Performance)

Content and Language: F work fails to respond acceptably to an assignment. F work may misunderstand or disregard the assignment's intent, lack any pattern of organization, or make enough errors in standard English sentence structure to make it nearly impossible for a reader to follow the author's thoughts. F should not be understood simply as a penalty grade for unsubmitted or incomplete work; it is given to any work that fails to meet an assignment's demands or to meet the minimum standards of university discourse, and in cases where failure to submit significantly impacts course activities (such as peer review).

(Numerical values: 59 and below, all considered non-pass grades)

Appendix 8.3

Rubric for a Final Oral Presentation of a Film Class

Student name(s): _____

Presentation title: _____

Check marks:

Presentation (50 points)

_____/25 The presentation addressed the points necessary

§ _____ Film title and release year

§ _____ Basic plot/storyline

§ _____ Comedic genre/type

§ _____ American cultural theme

§ _____ Student opinion of film

§ _____ Recommendation of film

_____/5 The presentation used appropriate film clips (if used)

_____/5 The presentation related to the course content

_____/10 The presenters were knowledgeable about the film

_____/5 The presenters did not just read slides/notes

Language (40 points)

_____/5 Strong voice quality and clarity (loud, clear voice)

_____/15 Appropriate language use (word choice, grammar, phrasing, pronunciation)

_____/15 Good flow/pace (transitions, meaning, pauses)

_____/5 Eye contact with audience was well achieved

Time (10 points)

_____/5 Did the presentation use the time allotment well?

_____/5 Did it not meet or exceed the time limit?

Culture notes:

_____

_____

Humor notes:

_____

_____

Q&A notes:

_____

Final score: _____

CHAPTER 9

Managing Feedback

Contextualization

This chapter addresses the concerns that new instructors face in terms of providing meaningful and effective feedback on students' linguistic performance. Because there are a host of feedback-related issues that plague novice language teachers, this chapter will explore several core pragmatic concerns that can assist in navigating the steep learning curve of providing such feedback in a timely and productive manner. This chapter also briefly explores the various types of written and spoken feedback that are typical of the language classroom and how they can be treated with greater efficacy within varied classroom settings.

Case Study: When the Feedback Process Fuels Burnout

A recent graduate student teaching assistant (TA) in a writing intensive program indicated that he had spent roughly one hour per paper while grading the first draft of a multiple iteration assignment. With twenty students, this round of grading tallied up to approximately twenty hours of feedback work for this draft alone. In addition, the program he was working for strongly encouraged one-on-one TA–student conferences to discuss the feedback being provided and to ensure more productive reception by students, adding approximately twenty additional minutes of time per student and causing him another 6 hours and 40 minutes of work once all was said and done. The TA ended up at a total time dedication of approximately 26 hours and 40 minutes for this single task, a number that is certainly not tenable when considering the fact that the final version of this paper would soon go through the same timely feedback process (minus the conferencing), and the draft for the course's second paper was quickly approaching, which in turn meant the process would repeat itself anew. Compound this with the fact that his course was taking place in a ten-week quarter system, thus rushing its pace a bit more than a semester system, and also the fact that there were three major papers in total, which meant there would be a third iteration to his feedback cycle—and the end result was a recipe for extreme burnout. The TA, rightfully so, expressed great concern about his ability to thrive in this type of teaching environment due to his constant fatigue and perceived ineffectiveness, and it ultimately resulted in him seeking future employment elsewhere on campus in programs where simple-to-grade tests were the norm.

The concerns expressed in this TA's story are not uncommon for new teachers. In fact, when speaking to seasoned language instructors, feedback management can remain an issue long into one's career. Because instructors are consistently pressed for time, learning to navigate this terrain becomes an essential component in improving their overall effectiveness as educators. That doesn't mean that there is a right way or a wrong way to provide feedback, nor does it mean that such a method can be applied to all teaching situations. What it does mean, however, is that there are ways of measuring effectiveness in a given scenario and applying best practices that will adequately contribute to more productive feedback cycles and outcomes.

Common Concerns

The questions below on managing feedback reflect some of the general concerns that are consistently raised by new language instructors once they are in their own classrooms. Though the list is not exhaustive, it presents dilemmas that are common across the teachers whom the authors of this book have worked with. Each question is first presented here, but they will be addressed in turn throughout the remainder of this chapter.

- *Q1. Where do novice teachers even begin in giving feedback on student performance?*
- *Q2. How much time is too much time to spend giving feedback?*
- *Q3. How can novice teachers make the feedback process more productive in terms of their general approach?*
- *Q4. How does feedback translate into actual grades?*
- *Q5. Students make mistakes when speaking in class, and it isn't always good to interrupt them every time they are trying to speak. But how else can teachers address their issues?*

Effective Practices for Managing Feedback

- **Q1. Where do novice teachers even begin in giving feedback on student performance?**

When new teachers attempt to provide feedback on student performance, it can be difficult to know what or what not to treat. This is exacerbated by the fact that each student comes with their own learning style and individual proficiency. Given that there is no blanket approach that will work in all situations and with all students, the first step toward giving feedback resides in the realization that every scenario requires its own assessment approach and treatment plan, both of which can be exceedingly time-consuming to hammer out. Nevertheless, there are some general strategies that can help educators reduce the impact of idiosyncrasies within the feedback process and relieve the burden of multistudent or multiproject workloads. In other words, with a tool kit of strategies, an instructor is better equipped to decide what to explicitly attend to and what to leave for student discovery.

One variable that should be considered from the onset is the distinction between global and local errors (Burt & Kiparsky, 1974; Celce-Murcia et al., 2014). Local errors (that is, mechanics-focused errors) have less impact on overall comprehension, making them less relevant when prioritizing feedback in higher-order assignments such as papers or presentations. Conversely, global errors (that is, meaning-focused errors) impact comprehension, making them a more productive starting place for improving meaning and promoting audience receptivity.

As instructors, it can be tempting to want to treat all errors, but this can in fact be counterproductive. For language teachers, addressing all errors, and particularly all local errors, means devoting time to issues that are not necessarily going to result in productive outcomes for the assignment, which can result in a lack of meaningful improvement in performance. To paraphrase, during a subsequent reading of a student's work after focusing on local-level revisions, the instructor might not see meaningful improvements, despite the fact that the language could truly be in a better place. For students, a focus on local errors can lead to cognitive shutdown when the feedback presents as overly excessive or convoluted; this shutdown emerges because micromarking language can quickly venture into superfluous extremes, where the student cannot readily identify the major issues due to sensory overload.

When instructors overmark granular concerns that are local—or mechanics-focused—in nature, students often perceive the feedback as lacking in terms of focus. The result is that students end up applying much needed cognitive energy and resources to inconsequential aspects instead of homing in on message-oriented, global items (meaning-related items) that will ultimately have a greater impact on quality. In essence, when feedback is not focused on the most meaningful items, it can result in diminished returns for both parties. Prioritizing global issues is thus a more effective starting point when managing feedback. Ordering feedback in this way makes sense when we consider the fact that the language used in student work will inevitably change drastically if the general message presents as unclear or off target. But to start with global issues, teachers must first embrace the fact that abstaining from excessive local feedback does not mean that they are relinquishing their duties as teachers. They will inevitably provide some degree of local language feedback, but by prioritizing global language feedback first, revision to language will be more secure, as the students' ideas will be more developed.

According to Bitchener and Knoch (2009), there is also the issue of focused feedback versus unfocused feedback. The former refers to a specific subset of items that the setting aims to target, whereas the latter refers to all potential issues that a teacher can identify within a piece. Though unfocused feedback does treat very real errors, it does not typically result in students experiencing more significant improvements. To illustrate, unfocused feedback on mechanics can lead to overload that is in many ways debilitating, especially when it appears that virtually all language effort is in error. Similarly, unfocused feedback on meaning, such as when a teacher aims to apply an idiosyncratic preference where an otherwise clear and effective point is made, might lead to a sense of confusion among students, and rightfully so if the structures they used actually accomplish the objective. While it may feel more comprehensive to the teacher to offer unfocused feedback that spans all aspects, it can frequently result in issues of fairness. The unfair angle stems from the fact that the instructor has likely not had enough opportunity to review all of the possible errors that unfocused feedback would encompass.

As a result of the nebulous nature of unfocused feedback, focused feedback, by contrast, presents as firmly grounded within the scope of the course material. Take, for instance, focused feedback on mechanics, where the items identified by the instructor typically fall within the larger umbrella of items that have been covered. For example, if the present perfect tense was covered, then it is fair game in terms of feedback and assessment. In a similar vein, focused feedback on meaning aims to remain within the scope of what has been discussed or taught to students. As an illustration, if an instructor

166   Navigating the English Language Classroom

didn't teach about a specific subcause associated with an effect, then it likely should not factor into feedback on the cause–effect relationship in the student's work; instead, the feedback should stick to items that were in fact overtly explored. With this logic, it is not surprising that focused feedback better allows instructors to target key issues in a manner that is more easily and readily digestible for students. It also allows teachers to streamline their feedback, channeling their energy into overall more productive outcomes.

When considering where to begin with feedback, teachers' assessment goals must always remain in focus; however, students can also inform how feedback will be shaped. The criteria associated with student performance are often documented in guide sheets and rubrics, making any deviations seem tricky and potentially subjective. Nevertheless, when students see certain language points as crucial to their development, it is equally good practice to attend to some of these pronouncements, as they can promote student investment over time. A productive path might therefore be to allow space for a few items that might otherwise go unattended if based solely on the instructor's parameters. This does not mean that the rubric itself has to change, especially since many programs restrict such actions; however, it does imply that the teacher may be able to request from students one or two additional items that will speak directly to the students' self-perception of need. For example, when students submit their work, instructors can ask students to include two grammar or content points they would like specific feedback on. These items would not be scored; rather, they would simply allow the instructor to speak to something the student sees as important. Instructors would, of course, need to teach students how to provide such focused requests, but allowing this kind of input accommodates the students' personal ideas about their own needs, a valuable action when seeking to attain student feedback receptivity. Knowing this can be helpful for new teachers because it prioritizes a student-centered window of interpretation, in turn allowing students to more actively engage with guide sheets and rubrics as documents that are at least partially tailored for each learner as an individual. Table 9.1 shows examples of the forms rubric-centric versus student-centric feedback might take in such collaborations.

Instructors should also keep in mind that feedback is more complex than simply correcting overt mechanics and meaning. The issue alluded to here is one of effort versus competency. All instructors cherish thoughtful effort on the student's part, but effort itself is not an indicator of successful language acquisition. Effort should certainly be situated for students as a necessary step in achieving competency, and instructors can incorporate it into rubrics through strategic language choices (using verbs that denote

Managing Feedback 167

Table 9.1. Examples of Rubric-Centric versus Student-Centric
Feedback Benchmarks

Feedback category	Feedback source	
	Rubric-centric	Student-centric
e.g. Organization	"Paragraphs are clearly organized with topic sentences that are then developed with an effective body and culminating thought."	"Is it possible to point out places where a new paragraph is not required but would improve the readability of my work?"
e.g. Diction	"Word choice selections have been thoroughly reviewed throughout the essay to minimize any lexical meaning-related issues and improve the overall argument and messaging."	"I feel like I am using the correct words, but I also feel like I could vary them more to make the meaning more expressive. What feedback might you offer to improve my vocabulary range?"
e.g. Grammar	"Verb tenses and aspects have been applied in meaningful ways that reflect each verb's intended prescriptive use as well as its associated rhetorical effects."	"Would it be possible to indicate places where nouns might be more effective in place of a verb tense/aspect that accomplishes a similar rhetorical goal?"

precision, refinement, and advancement, for example). Nevertheless, students commonly equate time spent with better performance, and fostering the idea that effort and competency are equals can lead to a false sense of achievement.

Below are three sample strategies for minimizing the false equivalency between effort and competency in an essay writing assignment. The purpose of these three strategies is to showcase how effort might and might not be accounted for within assessment protocols.

Sample Strategy 1

Instructors can take an analytic rubric that uses tiered categorizations of competency (e.g., A-level content, organization, or language use versus B, C, and D-level content, organization, and language use) and reformulate the overall criteria with a separate category that focuses exclusively on effort. Instructors should pay close attention to

(continued)

168 Navigating the English Language Classroom

(Cont.)

the category percentages, weighting each accordingly. Instructors can then determine what A-level effort looks like in relation to B, C, or D-level effort. For example, A-level effort might include language that speaks to students seeking out supplemental instructor conferencing or writing-center assistance when possible; C-level effort might include language that speaks to a general lack of attention to detail, specifically when it applies to items that have been pinpointed in classroom discussions, outlined in teacher draft feedback, or emphasized in classroom materials.

Sample Strategy 2

Instructors who use a required, non-adaptable holistic rubric that includes minimal or less specific language on effort in the revision process might be able to develop a supplemental reflective protocol that showcases how effort was applied. To illustrate, students might be asked to include an annotated version of their paper which uses text comments to indicate major revisions and how they were considered and then implemented. Because holistic rubrics typically provide a general blurb for a given level (e.g., A-level—without detailed categorical gradations on individual components), their language can at times be difficult for students—and teachers—to navigate with specificity (they are general blurbs, after all). Reflective additions such as these do not deviate from the required rubric; rather, they provide additional tangible measurements through which vague language on effort can be effectively operationalized. Instructors might also ask students to write a process summary describing their overall revision approach.

Sample Strategy 3

Instructors can educate students on what the rubric entails by reviewing it in class. In doing this, the instructor can shape the parameters of effort, if it is included, through student input. Collaborative exercises such as this can increase understanding as well as buy-in on how effort, as a concept, will be considered. These teacher–student generated understandings, for any such component, can then be posted alongside the rubric, where students always have a sense of what individual graded components mean and how they will be treated. By soliciting student input in this manner, effort becomes a term with identifiable substance, not an arbitrary item that can be applied at will. Such articulations provide agreement that extensive work alone does not equate to gained competency.

These three strategies imply that simply trying hard is not a strong indicator of learned language features; they also ensure that the concept of effort has identifiable parameters. Applying such tactics speaks to the concern that passing students based on an ill-defined sense of effort is in many ways doing them a potential disservice. The danger stems from the fact that they may not be ready for subsequent levels and content, where passing under the guise of effort alone may result in insufficient performance in subsequent settings. Instructors should always keep in mind that unless an entire program places equal value on effort as an assessable feature, rogue valuations might result in grade asymmetries that can mislead students into thinking they are further along than they actually are. With this understanding, effort-based scoring should really only factor into assessment if it is overtly captured in the scoring protocol. If not, students may come to see the assessment as an exercise in subjectivity.

Given the extensive range of terms presented in this subquestion, it is useful at this point to recap each to ensure their overall clarity. Table 9.2 reaffirms the core key terms explored in this section to ensure that they are readily accessible for teachers who are trying to gauge their approach to feedback and struggling with the nomenclature that envelops the feedback process.

Table 9.2. Key Feedback Terms and Dichotomies to Consider

Key feedback dichotomies for novice instructors to consider	
Local errors	Micro-level issues that do not impact the overall message or comprehensibility of a text's larger meaning.
Global errors	Macro-level issues that do impact the overall message or comprehensibility of a text's overall message and meaning.
Focused feedback	Smaller, more manageable sets of issues that can be effectively treated. Other issues may exist but be treated at other times as needed.
Unfocused feedback	Larger, less manageable sets of issues that treat all errors without discrimination between the most and least important.
Effort	Energy a student puts into their work in order to achieve high performance standards.
Competency	Language results that a student exhibits through collective effort and thoughtful performance.

• *Q2. How much time is too much time to spend giving feedback?*

When asking language teachers how much time they spend on individual feedback sessions, the results vary wildly. Whether it's ten minutes or an hour on a given student's work, the number is always connected to the assignment's core parameters and general intensity. This means that the type of assignment (for example, listening/speaking, reading/writing, drills, group, pair, individual, first iteration or second iteration, graded, or simply participatory) greatly influences the time that will be spent on an assignment's review and the feedback provided.

One technique that language teachers can incorporate to reduce time spent on assignments is to weigh the assignment's place along a learning continuum. For example, if students are working on the first draft of an essay, it might be counterproductive to focus heavily on grammatical aspects at this point since the ideas themselves will typically require a great deal of refinement. Providing excessive feedback on grammatical structures during this early phase could lead to students feeling overwhelmed and teachers spending time on items that might inevitably disappear as the ideas become clearer. A more productive approach might be to use the early stages of an assignment's continuum as the time for negotiation of ideas and meaning, saving specific language structures for a moment when they will be more meaningful to the student's output. The same can be said for listening/speaking activities. By providing in-class workshopping time to hone a student's ideas, for example in a pre-speaking phase, teachers can help students walk through their ideas before being critiqued on the language that they use. This provides learners with space to perfect their ideas before attempting to produce them accurately, which serves to support more developed language grounded in strong context, while also easing the feedback load of the instructor through scaffolded prioritization.

When instructors are unable to incorporate multistep assignments (such as drafted papers) within their course, in-the-moment recalibrations of focus might be warranted to maximize the effectiveness of the instructor's time. Grammar-focused drills can shed light on this statement. Typical drills are presented in a one-and-done type format, where students attempt tasks and receive immediate feedback. Depending on the degree of difficulty of the assignment, this feedback can range from a single word to a complete rewrite of a sentence or paragraph. What is important to keep in mind is that the design of the activity plays a role in how much time and feedback instructors should provide. For instance, if an activity involves reading a sentence and filling in a blank with the correct verb conjugation, teachers would certainly need to consider how that verb form interacts with the words and larger context surrounding it. This may require educators to explain a temporal relationship in which one clause clearly happens at a point in the past before another clause's verb in the past (that is, the past perfect/past relationship). Without greater context, it would be hard to distinguish which tense or aspect is most effective in this case, and so the feedback really could become quite complex. That stated, most drill activities require a straightforward response that merits less intensive feedback, especially when correction triggers the correct response in the student's mind. Such students may need no more than the right answer to understand (for example, match a term with a definition). In such cases, less feedback might be warranted. Recognizing when to delve into intensive detail and when to keep it simple can thus be a useful tool for instructors who are already strapped for time and think they have to give all that they have in every instance. In short, feedback in grammar-focused drills may simply be an issue of reading the signs and responding accordingly.

When instructors lack the time and resources to offer multistep assignments to their students, or when they are teaching lower levels focused on structures over larger swathes of context, granular language feedback becomes an inevitable aspect instructors must face. It is important to remember, however, that it is not the instructor's job to eradicate all language errors. If particular grammar items are yet to be taught in a given course, then it stands to reason that holding the student accountable for those items at an earlier stage in the learning process could lead to students seeing feedback as unfair. Teachers need to pick and choose their battles, and one way of doing this is to provide feedback on items that have been treated or that must be in place for advancement between levels. Providing feedback on all of the items covered to date may also be ineffective, as it can again lead to a lack of focus. Teachers do have to give granular feedback, but what this exploration implies is that even granular feedback has its limitations and understanding how to navigate those limitations can help teachers better address learning outcomes.

Lastly, instructors need to keep in mind that written feedback and spoken feedback (which will be addressed in more depth later in this chapter) often take on significantly different forms. Outside of formal graded presentation-style assignments, feedback on speaking skills is typically relegated to in-the-moment activities where it takes on a corrective identity. What this means is that oral feedback often consists of short corrections in the form of recasts (reformulations of student language using correct forms). Written assignments often result in comments that must be broken down and digested in solitude, where the student is then responsible for following up with the instructor if more explanation is needed. In this way, spoken feedback emerges as potentially much more intrusive, while written feedback emerges as much more elusive due to its typical asynchronous reception and interpretation. To navigate these two assertions, teachers should keep in mind that spoken language is not only about accuracy but fluency, and achieving fluency means knowing when to let errors go in favor of continued language production. If we interrupt our students' speaking with corrections for all errors, we will ultimately stifle their ability to speak in continuously fluent stretches. Likewise, written comments on student work should be carefully constructed in ways that make them transparent to students. Avoiding terms such as *awkward* or *incorrect grammar*, in favor or more telling feedback can improve written feedback. For instance, the teacher might write that a given verb conjugation does not capture the time and aspect of a given context, where there is an event in the past that precedes another event in the past (the past perfect). Here, the teacher doesn't name the tense but rather explains the function, and in this way pushes the student to discover the answer based on a previously addressed rule. This takes additional crafting time for the teacher, but is arguably more productive for the teacher and the student as it will eliminate obscurity through precision, which ultimately cuts down on ambiguity. Equally important in written feedback is knowing when to take a lighter touch when addressing errors, as surface-level error attention can, at times, hamper attempts at student fluency in writing-focused activities and projects. In such moments, surface-level attention is not ideal because it can have a counterproductive impact on the amount of writing students produce (Chandler, 2003). In this way, knowing when to pull back (that is, refraining from adding feedback for the sake of fluency) can actually improve the amount of writing produced by students, and this should not be seen as slacking on the part of the teacher; rather, it is a reaction to the goals of the task. Table 9.3 recaps a few of the example tips explored above.

In short, instructors must always keep in mind that the type of activity plays a role in feedback production, as does the weighting of the activity and its position along a continuum of learning. Each scenario will have its own parameters, and if instructors wish to improve their management of feedback, factoring in continuum positioning as well as a given activity's intrinsic skill constraints can promote more effective pedagogical moves.

Managing Feedback   173

Table 9.3. Examples of Feedback Burden in Relation to Time

Activity	Examples of feedback-time connections
General writing skills	Avoid vague terms such as *awkward* or *tense/aspect* that lack precision. Use language that points students in the right direction without revealing the desired outcome, while also providing enough clues to get them started. Allow students to discover correct outcomes through focused guidance.
	Consider spending less time on grammar in early drafts and more time on ideas and meaning, especially when fluency is key. Language will change as ideas grow, making language feedback in late stages potentially more meaningful.
General speaking skills	Focus on items that have been covered in class or that represent key learning outcomes for the course/level. Minimize the urge to give feedback on all grammar items, as this can lead to highly unfocused reception by students.
	Aim to allow students to speak with less feedback interruption when fluency outweighs accuracy in an activity. Instead, let them focus on getting their message across. Only interject when feedback ensures comprehension.
	Vary feedback styles so as to make the feedback more appropriate according to need. When fluency and accuracy are both important, taking notes and circling back after can be less intrusive, though more time-consuming.

- ### *Q3. How can novice teachers make the feedback process more productive in terms of their general approach?*

Good teachers are always concerned with improving their classroom techniques and strategies to better address the needs of their students, and though this usually pertains to lesson planning, activity design, materials development, and general student–teacher interactions, it also pertains to the less glamorous process of providing feedback. But the approach that educators adopt can have a significant impact on how feedback translates into improvements for students.

One common aspect of the feedback process that causes sleepless nights for many instructors is the overall interplay between feedback and grades. Some teachers advocate for grades on early iterations of work because they allow students to clearly see where they stand in terms of performance, in addition to being a way to hold students accountable for the quality of their work. Unfortunately, this idea adds a punitive element to developmental stages where students are really still refining their ideas. Other teachers advocate for less punitive measures in the early stages, as this is seen as promoting freedom of thought and experimentation in output, both of which are qualities that demonstrate a student's productive interaction with the target language.

Instructors should always keep in mind that grades are not the same as feedback. Grades are product-oriented, meaning they are less prone to fluidity or change. Feedback is process-oriented, meaning that, when applied productively, it is more aligned with the idea of incremental improvements to performance over time. By realizing the differences between the two, novice instructors can more effectively design assignments to match learning outcomes. For instance, a quiz, which is typically more summative in design, is most likely better conceptualized as a grade-focused task, especially when the goal is to simply determine whether target knowledge was actually acquired. This type of focus might, by its very nature, exclude more intensive and in-depth forms of feedback, and this is perfectly fine if the goal is merely meant to hold students accountable for demonstrating knowledge on specific language deliverables. Conversely, intricate assignments, tasks, or projects that require more formative input over longer periods of time might be seen as better situated for a feedback-focused approach, particularly when instructors consider that the goal is sustained improvement over time. In such formative scenarios, instructors will want to invest in the feedback process, as it is necessary in achieving better assessment outcomes. This formative approach is still connected to the eventual grades that students will receive, but it allows the students to realize their grade through gradual processes of experimentation. Importantly, the categorical division between summative and formative assessment explored in this section should not be received as a value judgment for one being *good* and the other *bad*; there is often productive interplay between the two, where both can contribute to overall learning outcomes (Lau, 2016). In short, thoughtful recognition of variables related to how grades and feedback are realized can lead to more productive engagement when needed and less time investment when the task does not merit it.

When feedback is required as a part of an assignment, it can be focused with greater precision through the use of rubrics, which, by nature, constrain the assessment of student work to predetermined, measurable outcomes (McGriff, 2006). Rubrics should capture the key learning outcomes of an assignment while also providing a means of remaining consistent across students. By thoughtfully constructing rubrics in a manner that accurately captures the essence of the assignment, instructors render feedback that is more focused and less prone to excess. Thoughtful rubric design also lends itself to increases in speed when providing feedback. For instance, if a rubric has an entire section that focuses on word choice, then the feedback an instructor produces could possibly target academic register, tone, and precision with greater emphasis. If that same rubric mentions punctuation only lightly, in passing, where it is treated as secondary to other issues, then excessive feedback on commas, periods, colons, and semicolons might seem less focused to a learner who reviewed the rubric and tried to channel their energy on outcomes clearly defined by the instructor. That does not mean that punctuation is less important, but it does mean that it is presented as less important in this particular assignment. Teachers need to realize that rubric design is, in a way, a contract between an educator and a learner, and that breaching this contract can result in students seeing feedback as less effective and unfair. At the same time, teachers might see feedback as difficult to pin down, time-consuming, and ineffective in the greater scheme of teaching and learning. By using rubrics thoughtfully and adhering to defined deliverables, instructors can increase student buy-in and reduce time spent on items that were never meant to be heavily weighted in the feedback process.

One additional strategy that instructors can make use of in improving the feedback process is by varying their feedback style. As an example, some programs may require face-to-face conferencing between students and teachers, especially in writing projects. In conferencing, the instructor can discuss feedback as opposed to writing it and having it deciphered by a student devoid of guidance. This type of feedback is more time-consuming given that it could potentially mean ten, twenty or more minutes of time with an individual student. In a K-12 environment, this is certainly not feasible for teachers who are already overworked and in the classroom with students throughout their entire day. For these instructors, peer review and in-class workshopping can help to recreate this type of oral feedback, but it will most likely not be enough to supplement written feedback from instructors. In K-12 environments, conferencing might be realized as short interactional feedback moments within the classroom, most likely in stages before a graded iteration.

For community college instructors and teachers in university settings, however, course loads may lend themselves well to both peer review and student conferencing, as instructors typically have more freedom in how they structure their class meetings. This freedom means that if an action such as peer review is valued, there is usually a way to work it into their course design given the activity planning freedom these instructors more frequently enjoy. In terms of conferencing, it is important to note a common concern expressed by many of the novice community college and university teachers the authors have worked with: they simply do not have the time to read papers at home and then conference with students in addition to this. But in many cases, by simply adding an additional ten minutes to the conferencing time, teachers can read student work on the spot and provide in-the-moment oral feedback, where students take notes in real-time, reducing the overall amount of time spent writing comments. Such practices can more effectively focus feedback on items that teachers are reacting to in real-time, where emotional affect can provide better clarity on what is meant or intended. In this way, conferencing has the potential to better maximize an instructor's time and in turn produce better receptivity for students as they are able to ensure their comprehension through interaction. It should be noted, however, that in-the-moment reading places a great time burden on instructors. Until teachers feel comfortable with the pace of conferencing and reading on the spot, they should build in ample breaks so as to allow catch-up time if needed.

One final method for improving feedback is to more effectively apply the level of feedback at a teacher's disposal. As Figures 9.1 and 9.2 insinuate, each level of feedback carries with it a time burden, with direct feedback (that is, micro-marking and correcting errors) requiring more substantial teacher effort than holistic feedback (reading comprehensively with a culminating set of feedback ideas; see Ferris, 2011, for a more in-depth exploration of feedback types and their implications). This does not mean that holistic feedback is easier to produce; in fact, it can be extremely difficult to summarize the entirety of one's feedback into paragraph form in a way that is productive. However, holistic feedback refocuses the burden of revision from the teacher to the student, where general statements are positioned as guides for students to then do the actual work of locating and remedying valid concerns. Holistic shifts allow students to make discoveries for themselves—through noticing—that will be more meaningful in the greater scheme of their language-acquisition process. Direct marking, by contrast, typically keeps instructors from seeing the bigger picture because they are focused on microlevel concerns. This can result in a perceived overall diminishment in quality because such microlevel attention often causes teachers to overlook good ideas owing to poor articulation. Nevertheless, there may be instances in which such microlevel feedback is needed, especially when it pertains to extremely difficult concepts or idiosyncratic concerns that are

Managing Feedback 177

Direct Feedback: *The instructor directly interacts with a student text in a manner that suggests, rephrases, alters, or overtly corrects the student's writing.*

Whether aliens exist or not is a question asked [that has been] by all but yet to be definitively answered [many, yet it remains to be...]. In XXXXXXXXX's article, the author is contemplating upon [contemplates] the question whether life [of] exists beyond the Earth or not. Even though the author carefully observes and considers all the technological advancements that have been made in the past in quest for [the] extraterrestrial life, he was [is?] unable to express the true situation [convincingly state his case???]. XXXXX's portrayal of possibility of life ...

Semi-Direct Feedback: *The instructor directly interacts with a student text in a manner that uses a limited set of codes to indicate the type and location of language problems.*

Whether aliens exist or not is a question asked [clarity and flow] by all but yet to be definitively answered [w/c; punctuation; transition; phrasing/precision]. In XXXXXXXXX's article, the author is contemplating [verb tense] upon [collocation] the question whether life [preposition] exists beyond the [article] Earth or not [delete (wordy)]. Even though the author carefully observes and considers all the technological advancements that have been made in the past in quest for [article] extraterrestrial life, he was [verb tense?] unable to express the true situation [meaning / specificity]. XXXXX's portrayal of possibility of life ...

Indirect Feedback: *The instructor interacts with a student text by simply highlighting, circling, or underlining (etc.) problematic language aspects, without actually indicating a grammatical category or correction.*

Whether aliens exist or not is a question asked by all but yet to be definitively answered. In XXXXXXXXX's article, the author is contemplating upon the question whether life exists beyond the Earth or not. Even though the author carefully observes and considers all the technological advancements that have been made in the past in quest for extraterrestrial life, he was unable to express the true situation. XXXXX's portrayal of possibility of life ...

Figure 9.1. Examples of direct, indirect, and semi-direct feedback.

devoid of standard explanations. By better understanding the level of feedback and the burden each level places on the various stakeholders in this process, teachers can more effectively make use of feedback design while also incrementally increasing student ownership of their work through strategic increases in their learning burden.

178   Navigating the English Language Classroom

Marginal Feedback: The instructor interacts with a student text by adding notations in the form of ongoing comments, often in the margins and near the problematic language aspects.

Whether aliens exist or not is a question asked by all but yet to be definitively answered. In XXXXX's article, the author is contemplating upon the question whether life exists beyond the Earth or not. Even though the author carefully observes and considers all the technological advancements that have been made in the past in quest for extraterrestrial life, he was unable to express the true situation. XXXXX's portrayal of possibility of life ...	The opening sentence is not grammatically correct, making the meaning less precise and harder to comprehend. Pay closer attention to your verb tenses; examine the prepositions and articles in this area. Also, you might want to think about reducing wordiness. Check your article usage in this area. What do you mean by *true situation*? I feel like I know what you want to say, but the way that you are saying it is not coming across clearly for the reader. Can you use more specific terminology that guides the reader more precisely?

Holistic Feedback: The instructor interacts with a student text by adding a qualitative summary of praise and/or critique, often located at the end of the student's writing.

Whether aliens exist or not is a question asked by all but yet to be definitively answered. In Ethan XXXXX's article, the author is contemplating upon the question whether life exists beyond the Earth or not. Even though the author carefully observes and considers all the technological advancements that have been made in the past in quest for extraterrestrial life, he was unable to express the true situation. XXXXX's portrayal of possibility of life ...

Dear Student: My first set of comments deal with your paper's content, while the second set addresses language-focused aspects of your paper. Please note that these two sets of ideas are often interconnected, however, and alterations to one set often affects the other.
- Content: In terms of how you treated the content of the original piece, I think that you have some great ideas and that they are explained well, overall. The examples that you chose for the body show... With regard to your analyses, I feel that you should focus on...
- Language: First drafts represent a space in which the ideas are still in development, so I don't want to go into too much detail now, as the language will ultimately change. That stated, I can offer a few grammatical items that you might want to pay attention to. For instance, you might review your use of articles, especially when... You might also look at verb tense and aspect, for instance when...

Figure 9.2. Examples of marginal and holistic feedback.

• *Q4. How does feedback translate into actual grades?*

The program an instructor teaches in is always of concern when considering feedback, especially since the feedback teachers provide eventually translates into actual grades. Programs commonly have their own grading ethos, and a teacher's ability to navigate this ethos can be tricky, especially for new instructors who are still determining their own philosophical approach.

One major feedback/grade concern stems from the fact that new instructors might find it difficult to translate feedback into an actual number or letter because student performance can sometimes teeter between grade brackets. Borderline grades can be seen as less clear for the instructor and potentially render the grade translation less fair in the eyes of the student. But this translation process is a necessary step given the current educational system in which most programs function. In today's system, a final tally is needed to represent student success in terms of learning outcomes, and this can cause anxiety in novice teachers who are more comfortable with praise and less comfortable with critique.

To mitigate grade stress, there are a few useful techniques that can be applied. Novice teachers should seek out advice early on from colleagues who have been teaching in their program for a longer period of time. New instructors can also perform mapping exercises that allow them to better understand the definition of an A versus a B. This means that they can map out, for lack of better terminology, the constituent parts that make up an A- or a B+. In reality, the difference between these two is slight, but most instructors still know an A paper when they see it. The implication is that grading schemas may need more complexity than a simple A = this or B = that formula. If an instructor is unsure of how to do this or feels that their ability to explain their grading measures is lacking (be it through a lack of experience or through having to use a rubric that was supplied to them), the instructor should have a concerted discussion with program leaders or more experienced colleagues. Such engagements can improve a new teacher's understanding and help bring them into programmatic alignment. The new instructor will also need to ensure that they have clear understandings of what constitutes an A or a B, not just through descriptions or blurbs, but through tangible language and content items that can be identified and explained to students with ease. Through mapping and understanding programmatic expectations, teachers can more easily make the leap from feedback to grades.

- *Q5. Students make mistakes when speaking in class, and it isn't always good to interrupt them every time they are trying to speak. But how else can teachers address their issues?*

Oral feedback is often easy to envision but difficult to put into practice. This conundrum emerges because oral feedback is typically interwoven with real-time student performance, making it more invasive to student language use when offered in context. Similar to written feedback, oral feedback can range from direct to holistic in nature, but it is important to understand what these variations mean when dealing with learners in real time, as spoken feedback can easily become jolting to learners who are still experimenting with the language.

The first consideration that new instructors need to keep in mind when deciding when to give oral feedback is that spoken performance is highly connected to the accuracy–fluency continuum (Pallotti, 2009). In other words, when speech is more accurate, it is typically slower and more deliberate, which reduces—or at least gives the impression of a reduction in—fluency. Conversely, when speech is more fluent, it is typically more conversational in its speed and presents as less concerned with granular detail, which positions linguistic accuracy as less important than the delivery of overall communicative message. Both accuracy and fluency are equally important, but depending on the objectives of the task at hand, one might need to take precedence over the other. For example, in an activity that is not focused on reading skills but does involve reading aloud, it may in fact be counterproductive and invasive to correct every pronunciation concern. In such a situation, it might be better to allow the student to read with ease, only interjecting when pronunciation is leading to comprehension issues that could lead to incorrect learning outcomes. Such restraint can be difficult for new instructors who feel a sense of responsibility to attend to all issues; however, it is essential that new instructors understand that attending to all errors essentially robs students of productive moments of noticing and discovery that they could have on their own.

By overcorrecting, which has been positioned as harmful in various forms of student production (Alrabai, 2016), students come to rely on the teacher as the primary authority of language information, which can reduce motivation for self-investigation and self-regulation. Similarly, teachers who never or rarely correct can be seen as disengaged, especially when other students step in to provide input. To avoid students filling uncomfortable gaps by providing their own feedback, new teachers can set ground rules early on in the classroom where, from day one, students understand why feedback might be withheld. For example, an instructor can actually explain the merits of in-the-moment feedback and post-reflective feedback, helping the students see that there are sound pedagogical reasons behind the actions being taken. In truth, the accuracy–fluency continuum is a difficult relationship to master, but with forethought into how scenarios may play out, new instructors can make better choices and can help students understand that all actions, even those that seem to be nonactions, are being carried out for specific reasons.

The question of accuracy versus fluency is also productive when educators consider the role of feedback in terms of fostering participation through autonomous action. When students feel they are not being scrutinized for every aspect of their speech, they tend to speak in more fluent—but not always more accurate—ways. Language instructors ultimately want their students to practice with the language, trying out new forms as they learn them and refining other forms in which trouble persists. In this way, reserving oral feedback can actually promote more healthy forms of fluency-focused participation in the classroom that can in turn lead to more autonomous language use. And as Little (2022) asserts, students who claim target language agency "gradually develop a proficiency that is reflective as well as communicative," where "the target language becomes a fully integrated part of their plurilingual repertoire and identity" (p. 64).

Take for example the dynamics in small group work that eventually lead to larger classroom discussions. Research has shown that language learners perform negotiations of meaning more effectively in groups than when working with teachers (Rulon & McCreary, 1986; Doughty & Pica, 1986; Foster, 1998). It thus stands to reason that when working in groups, it is important to allow students the time to negotiate what they want to say. This allows students to test out ideas on copresent interlocutors, often in a less intimidating interactional format, so that they can work out problems on their own or with the assistance of peers. Frequent interjections on the part of the instructor can break this negotiation of meaning and reposition the instructor as the sole authority when in fact students often offer a great deal of value in helping their peers realize accuracy. That is not to say, however, that in-the-moment feedback is unwarranted. As Littlewood et al. (1996) contest, if spoken "feedback is done with great sensitivity to students' self-esteem in a trusting and supportive environment, it should enhance their confidence and proficiency rather than inhibit their desire to speak English" (p. 83). But this can be difficult to implement, even for more experienced teachers. In this way, it might be more productive to state that taking a less invasive stance in terms of feedback, at specific times and for specific purposes or outcomes, can allow teachers to strategically place emphasis back on student knowledge and allow the process of student interactional communication to be the first act in sorting out responses. Indeed, research has shown that peer-initiated feedback, in terms of pronunciation error, can be more productive than teacher-initiated feedback (Ahangari, 2014). But if peer-initiated feedback fails or presents as inadequate in achieving outcomes, instructors are then primed to offer their thoughts and to steer students into more productive uses of the language. This essentially maximizes student interactional time and places the students themselves at the heart of their responses and the feedback process, promoting healthy participation through autonomous group work. In following this line of reasoning, one of the most important aspects to remember is that instructors are constantly making decisions on when, where, and how to offer advice to students. Sometimes it is perfectly fine to simply take a back seat with feedback, and other times it is in the students' best interest to hear directly from their instructor. New teachers should not feel obligated to offer feedback just because they are in charge; experimentation between students can be equally effective in improving language use.

When deciding on productive errors to treat, it is essential that new instructors weigh the importance of accuracy versus fluency, and it is important to keep in mind that some errors are just more productive than others in terms of feedback, implying the need for choice on the teacher's part (McMartin-Miller, 2014). In saying this, the ideas in this chapter posit that new instructors should be selective, focusing on errors that can be treated in meaningful ways that will lead to improved language performance. This is where the distinction between errors and mistakes is useful. A mistake implies that the student knows the proper form but produces a form that is not representative of acceptable grammar. In such instances, students should be able to self-correct if given time to realize the ramifications of their language use. An error, on the other hand, implies that the student did not know the proper form and is unable to self-correct. Errors are a sign that instructors may need to provide additional instruction rather than intrusive correction in the moment. For example, in a recently recorded training observation of an ESL TA at a Los Angeles university, the TA attempted to correct a student's incorrect use of verb tense, where, in that particular context, the student was using the simple past *wrote* in place of the more appropriate *have written*. Though the TAs correction was accurate, it was obvious that the student could not distinguish the difference between the two forms, rendering the instructor's feedback less effective because it was overlooking the fact that the student lacked the appropriate verb tense knowledge needed to decipher the feedback. In short, the TA had perceived the error as a mistake and had taken actions to treat it accordingly, with little additional input. The student simply smiled and repeated the feedback; but she kept going with her contribution as if the feedback meant nothing to her. The image this conveyed was that the student had not truly processed the verb tense information, especially since she made a similar error in the sentence that followed. In this case, the incorrect usage made by the student emerges as a more productive issue to address through an in-depth lesson, not on-the-spot correction. Understanding errors and mistakes can help new instructors prioritize feedback in ways that will truly benefit their students. After understanding this, the logical next step is thus one of deciding which errors, as opposed to mistakes, should then be prioritized over other errors. As a general rule of thumb, if an error is causing issues of comprehensibility, then it is something that should be prioritized. Knowing this can allow less experienced teachers to see that they cannot address everything, but with a little finesse they can fine-tune their feedback to result in better outcomes.

Big Picture and Bottom Line

Two of the most effective actions that new instructors can take, in terms of managing feedback, is to investigate and experiment. The investigation component comes from knowing the school, knowing the program and its expectations, and ultimately knowing the student population. When new instructors take the time to learn the landscape, they learn the framework within which individual innovation can occur. This innovation should always keep larger programmatic goals and expectations in mind, but once the boundaries are defined, experimentation can be promoted. The experimentation component then comes from knowing how far teachers can push things, as well as from listening to others and keeping abreast of new practices as they emerge within the field. Language instructors have a duty to remain in tune with new techniques and insights as they develop, especially if they want to remain in tune with best practices within the field. Doing so can greatly improve experimental attempts in that they will consistently be grounded in best disciplinary practices. Reflecting on and making use of these two actions—investigation and experimentation—thus helps new teachers by providing them with tools to productively tackle the feedback dilemma.

Finally, it is also worth remembering that instructors should not feel as though they are tethered to their classroom. Education professionals become teachers because they want to help students learn, and this should not translate into a teacher being seen to be on call in terms of feedback. New teachers need to realize that it is OK to set feedback boundaries. It is not their job to respond to emails seeking feedback at all hours of the day and across weekends. A 24-hour window on feedback is a reasonable boundary for email requests (as long as they can actually be answered by email), and drafted papers may take longer to return than a student might expect. Teachers are busy with many tasks, and personal life should not be

184 Navigating the English Language Classroom

sacrificed for the sake of feedback management. By following some of the practices above, new teachers should be able to set reasonable work schedules for themselves while also remaining effective in terms of providing feedback to their students.

Food for Thought

1. Pull a student paper that was particularly troublesome in terms of giving feedback.
   a. Identify at least three of the six items listed below:
      i. Feedback that was overly wordy or confusing.
      ii. Feedback that was vague or unclear.
      iii. Feedback that resulted in you simply correcting the student's work by offering a correct form/response.
      iv. Feedback that was repetitive.
      v. Feedback that was, in retrospect, beyond the scope of instructed items.
      vi. Feedback that addressed an issue that no time was spent on in class.
   b. After reflecting on the items you have identified, how could you conceivably adjust your approach to giving feedback to make it more productive for students? Please keep the individual student in mind, as this will inevitably impact the effectiveness of different practices.
2. Reflect on a feedback practice that is common for you as an instructor when orally interacting with your students. Contemplate a short-term strategy for making that feedback more productive in terms of promoting autonomous language learners. Use the following questions to help you focus your response:
   a. What could you do differently when giving individual oral feedback on projects or assignments in a one-on-one teacher–student scenario?
   b. How could you better use your already limited time when openly addressing one student's needs in a context where there are a range of diverse needs being presented each and every moment by many students?
   c. How do you know when enough feedback has been provided and you can move on with your lesson? You cannot stop every

minute, as the class would essentially become an exercise in treating errors, so how can you manage class stops and starts to improve your interactions with students?

d. To what extent should you minimize oral correction in favor of student discovery and noticing? How can you promote the idea of noticing through self-monitoring to improve students' ability to diagnose and treat their own developmental needs?

e. Given the limited time you have with students on a given day, how can you choose corrective measures that address issues that cannot be overlooked in the classroom for fear of them leading to misinterpreted information?

References

Ahangari, S. (2014). The effect of self, peer and teacher correction on the pronunciation improvement of Iranian EFL learners. *Advances in Language and Literary Studies, 5*(1), 81–88.

Alrabai, F. (2016). Factors underlying low achievement of Saudi EFL learners. *International Journal of English Linguistics, 6*(3), 21–37. https://doi.org/10.5539/ijel.v6n3p21

Bitchener, J., & Knoch, U. (2009). The value of a focused approach to written corrective feedback. *ELT Journal, 63*(3), 204–211. https://doi.org/10.1093/elt/ccn043

Burt, M., & Kiparsky, C. (1974). Global and local mistakes. In J. H. Schumann, & N. Stenson (Eds.), *New frontiers in second language learning* (pp. 71–79). Newbury House.

Celce-Murcia, M., Brinton, D. M., & Snow, M. A. (Eds.). (2014). *Teaching English as a second or foreign language* (4th ed.). Heinle Cengage Learning.

Chandler, J. (2003). The efficacy of various kinds of error feedback for improvement in the accuracy and fluency of L2 student writing. *Journal of Second Language Writing, 12*(3), 267–296. https://doi.org/10.1016/S1060-3743(03)00038-9

Doughty, C., & Pica, T. (1986). "Information gap" tasks: Do they facilitate second language acquisition? *TESOL Quarterly, 20*(2), 305–325. https://doi.org/10.2307/3586546

Ferris, D. R. (2011). *Treatment of error in second language student writing* (2nd ed.). University of Michigan Press.

Foster, P. (1998). A classroom perspective on the negotiation of meaning. *Applied Linguistics, 19*(1), 1–23. https://doi.org/10.1093/applin/19.1.1

Lau, A. M. S. (2016). "Formative good, summative bad?" – A review of the dichotomy in assessment literature. *Journal of Further and Higher Education, 40*(4), 509–525. https://doi.org/10.1080/0309877X.2014.984600

Little, D. (2022). Language learner autonomy: Rethinking language teaching. *Language Teaching, 55*(1), 64–73. http://doi.org/10.1017/S0261444820000488

Littlewood, W., Liu, N.-F., & Yu, C. (1996). Hong Kong tertiary students' attitudes and proficiency in spoken English. *RELC Journal, 27*(1), 70–88. https://doi.org/10.1177/003368829602700104

McGriff, S. J. (2006). Assessing what really matters: Rubrics can improve student achievement [Paper presentation]. *29th Annual Proceedings*, Annual Convention of the Association for Educational Communications and Technology, Dallas, Texas, pp. 307–312. https://citeseerx.ist.psu.edu/document?repid=rep1&type=pdf&doi=8c4f34898ebe8c0f1b3724dca73c716311b72753#page=318

McMartin-Miller, C. (2014). How much feedback is enough?: Instructor practices and student attitudes toward error treatment in second language writing. *Assessing Writing, 19*, 24–35. https://doi.org/10.1016/j.asw.2013.11.003

Pallotti, G. (2009). CAF: Defining, refining and differentiating constructs. *Applied Linguistics, 30*(4), 590–601. https://doi.org/10.1093/applin/amp045

Rulon, K. A., & McCreary, J. (1986). Negotiation of content: Teacher-fronted and small group interaction. In R. R. Day, (Ed.), *Talking to learn: Conversation in second language acquistion* (pp. 182–189). Newbury House.

SECTION IV

The Integration of Technology in the Language Classroom

CHAPTER 10

Using Corpora as a Resource

Contextualization

This chapter aims to explore the use of English text corpora as a resource for English language instructors.[1] Corpus linguistics has emerged to serve as one of many technological platforms that can aid in the development of "practical, innovative, and sustainable solutions that are responsive to the challenges of language teaching and learning in our increasingly networked, technologized, and mobile worlds [...]" (The Douglas Fir Group, 2016, p. 20). Though English text corpora have become a frequently used resource in the development of English language teaching (ELT) materials by professional textbook authors and publishers, many teachers still underutilize them due to a lack of familiarity, apprehensions about their seemingly complex interface, or misconceptions about their practicality. Thus, this chapter seeks to help novice instructors understand the basic functions of English text corpora (Flowerdew, 2015) and to translate these functions into accessible tools for developing authentic materials (Golonka et al., 2014) to illustrate and teach authentic register variation, discipline-specific differences in language use, collocations, phraseology, vocabulary use in context, meaning of grammatical forms and their usage in context (Ellis et al., 2016; Tyler & Ortega, 2018), and to help students develop autonomy and improve their self-editing skills (Chen et al., 2015).

---

1. A text corpus is a language resource consisting of a large and structured set of texts.

Case Study: Time Constraints and Lack of Resources

An instructor of a lower intermediate (equivalent to the Common European Framework of Reference for Languages [CEFR] B1 level) summer English as a second language (ESL) class at a higher education institution in the southwest of the United States reported feeling discouraged from using corpora with her students during class because she believed that training her students to use it would require allocating a certain amount of learner training time, which her already very tight schedule could not afford. Summer classes at that particular educational setting were only six weeks long, and within that timeframe she had to cover several curricular topics and work with students on a number of writing assignments. She had a feeling that her students would come to see using corpora as a useful resource, especially while working on their writing assignments, but she didn't think that she had enough in-class time to conduct a workshop and teach students how to use them.

But this teacher remembered attending a talk at a TESOL conference a few years before and hearing about using text corpora in the ESL/English as a foreign language (EFL) classroom to improve learner autonomy. However, when it came to incorporating that newly learned concept into her own teaching, she wasn't sure how feasible or practical this idea was. Besides not thinking she had enough time to teach her students how to use it, she believed that another challenge would be availability of computers and reliable Wi-Fi internet access in the classroom. Her classroom did not have computers or tablets for students to use during class, and not all students had a personal laptop or tablet that they could bring to class. In addition, asking students to use their own phones and cellular data in case the school Wi-Fi was not working could be perceived by students as unfair or inequitable. So the lack of easily available hardware equipment paired with an unreliable internet access to allow students to interface with an online corpus engine during class time rendered using a text corpus in that class impractical, in that teacher's point of view.

In addition to the challenges that she would face related to her students' access to computers and the internet, she added that preparing materials based on English corpora was very time-consuming because she was not very familiar with such search engine tools. She wasn't sure that spending her time searching through a text corpus in order to create language teaching materials was worth the effort. Therefore, with a sense of shame and defeat, she concluded that it was easier to just keep using the textbook and ready-to-print worksheets downloaded from websites with free teacher resources.

This teacher's challenges and concerns are extremely common; in fact, they probably resonate with a good number of teachers reading this chapter who struggle with the demands of tight and rigid curricula, with reduced access to computers and internet in their classrooms, and with limited free time to create ELT materials on top of their busy schedules due to a heavy teaching load, large groups of students, and continuous grading. These struggles are very real and can't be overlooked. For this reason, the purpose of this chapter is to offer a few suggestions on how to overcome these challenges, how to use a text corpus for lesson planning and materials development, and how to teach students to use it independently.

Common Concerns

The following five questions reflect some of the most common concerns expressed by language teachers who are unfamiliar with or are reluctant to adopt an English corpus for the preparation of authentic and contextualized teaching and assessment materials:

- *Q1. Not all teachers are familiar with text corpora, so what are they, and where should teachers start?*
- *Q2. How can teachers use an English corpus to prepare good language teaching materials?*
- *Q3. How can students benefit from learning to use a corpus?*
- *Q4. If a teacher is already strapped for time having to teach a busy curriculum, how do they make the time to incorporate the use of corpora in their class?*
- *Q5. How can teachers increase students' access to a corpus inside and outside of the classroom?*

The scope of concerns and questions that novice teachers might have in regards to the use of English corpora may not have been entirely represented in these five questions, but they certainly represent some of the wider issues that might prevent a teacher from using a corpus as a teaching (Braun, 2005; Boulton & Cobb, 2017; Vyatkina & Boulton, 2017) and assessment resource (Crossley & McNamara, 2013). In the following section, each of these five questions will be discussed, and suggestions of potential solutions will be presented.

Effective Practices for Using Corpora

- **Q1. Not all teachers are familiar with text corpora, so what are they, and where should teachers start?**

This question requires that the term *text corpus* be defined first. In the same way that the word *corpus* in human anatomy refers to the main body or mass of an organic structure, in linguistics a *text corpus* refers to a body of a structured collection of written texts. The systematic study of language use in various text *corpora* (the latter is the plural form of this Latin-origin noun) is the basis of corpus linguistics. Research using corpus linguistics utilizes large amounts of authentic text from a selection of sources of similar discourse types or genres to study the semantic, syntactic, and pragmatic properties of a word or a phrase. The main goal of corpus linguistics is to conduct reliable language form, meaning, and use analysis based on its natural context and with the least possible amount of artificial interference. Text corpora exist in several mainstream languages, and they are often based on vast collections of discourse-specific or genre-specific sources. Despite the increasing popularity and availability of corpus tools and resources, and their increasing use in teachers' pedagogy and research (Hardacre & Snow, 2020; Le Foll, 2021), their use in English language teaching is not as widespread as it could be, possibly due to a lack of teacher training to use them (Callies, 2019) or lack of teacher investment and contribution to its normalization (Chambers & Bax, 2006; Pérez-Paredes, 2022).

The very first step in adopting a text corpus is selecting one (Chang, 2014). There is a very large number of English corpora available on the internet, more than it would be reasonable to list in this chapter (see Table 10.1 for an abbreviated list). It is also possible that some of the corpora listed here may become obsolete within a decade or so, or others not included here might emerge and become mainstream. Notwithstanding, having acknowledged these caveats that might date this book in a matter of a few years, the corpora listed are among the more widely known for now, and seem to be used very often in current ELT materials, more specifically in English for academic purposes, and English for specific purposes presentations and publications.

Although it is true that there are many options of English text corpora available on the internet, language teachers need to consider the type of English they represent and whether they are useful to create classroom materials (Hubbard, 2013). In addition, many are not free of charge, or the type of access that is free has restrictions and limitations. Therefore, when choosing

Table 10.1. Some Well-Known English Corpora with Their Size and Text Sources

Corpus name	Abbrev. / acronym	Focus and strengths[2]
Intelligent Web Corpus	iWeb	14 billion words, taken from about 100,000 of the most widely used websites in the world.
Collins Birmingham University International Language Database (Collins Corpus)	COBUILD	4.5 billion words. It contains written material from websites, newspapers, magazines, and books published around the world, and spoken material from radio, TV, and everyday conversations. New data is fed into the corpus every month, to help the Collins dictionary editors identify new words and meanings from the moment they are first used. (Source: https://blog.collinsdictionary.com/the-history-of-cobuild/)
News on the Web Corpus	NOW Corpus	18.3 billion words from a wide range of online newspapers and magazines (technology, entertainment, sports, politics, etc.)
Oxford English Corpus	OEC	2.1 billion words. It includes language from the UK, the United States, Ireland, Australia, New Zealand, the Caribbean, Canada, India, Singapore, and South Africa. The text is mainly collected from websites; some printed texts, such as academic journals, have been collected to supplement particular subject areas. (Source: https://en.wikipedia.org/wiki/Oxford_English_Corpus)
Global Web-Based English	GloWbE	2 billion words from global websites in English. About 60% blogs (informal). Useful to compare varieties of English: American, British, Australian, etc.
Corpus of English Wikipedia		1.9 billion words. Texts are lemmatized and morphologically analyzed.
Corpus of Contemporary American English	COCA	1 billion words. Best coverage of all types of genres (informal to formal): TV/movie subtitles, blogs, web pages, spoken, fiction, magazines, newspapers, and academic.

(continued)

---

2. The descriptions of the corpora are drawn from their respective sources and english-corpora.org.

Table 10.1. (Cont.)

Corpus name	Abbrev. / acronym	Focus and strengths
Bank of English	BoE	650 million words from written English, collected from websites, newspapers, magazines, and books; there is also a large component of spoken data using material from radio, TV, and informal conversations. It is a subset of COBUILD.
Google Ngram Viewer		200 billion words from 8 million books. This is a search engine that charts word frequencies from a large corpus of books and thereby allows for the examination of cultural change as it is reflected in books. It is made up of scanned books available in Google Books.
British National Corpus	BNC	100 million words. Contains samples of written and spoken language from a wide range of sources, designed to represent a wide cross-section of British English, both spoken and written, from the late 20th century.
Corpus of Historical American English	COHA	475 million words, from 1810–2000. The largest corpus of historical American English. Useful to examine historical linguistic change.
TV Corpus		325 million words of data from 75,000 TV episodes from the 1950s to the present day. All of the 75,000 episodes are tied to their IMDB entries (which serve as metadata). Extremely informal language. Can also be used to compare dialects and changes since the 1950s.
Movie Corpus		200 million words of data in more than 25,000 movies from the 1930s to the present day. Informal language.
Corpus of American Soap Operas	SOAP	100 million words of data from 22,000 transcripts from American soap operas from the early 2000s; informal language.
TIME Magazine Corpus	TIME	100 million words. It is a corpus of American English from about 275,000 TIME magazine articles from 1923–2006. Serves as a great resource to examine changes in American English during this time. Part of the BYU corpora.
The Strathy Corpus of Canadian English		50 million words. It is a corpus of Canadian English. The corpus contains more than 1,100 spoken, fiction, magazines, newspapers, and academic texts.

Table 10.1. (Cont.)

Corpus name	Abbrev. / acronym	Focus and strengths
American National Corpus	ANC	22 million words of written and spoken data produced since 1990. It includes a range of genres, including emerging genres such as email, tweets, and web data.
British Academic Written English Corpus	BAWE	6.5 million words from proficient university-level student writing from the early 21st century. It contains just under 3,000 good-standard student assignments, evenly distributed across four broad disciplinary areas (arts and humanities, social sciences, life sciences, and physical sciences) and across various levels of study (undergraduate years and masters level). (Source: https://www.coventry.ac.uk/research/ research-directories/current-projects/2015/ british-academic-written-english-corpus-bawe/)
Michigan Corpus of Upper-Level Student Papers	MICUSP	2.6 million words. Composed of A papers written by undergraduate and early graduate students at the University of Michigan. This searchable database makes it possible to see disciplinary differences in academic writing, to observe the various ways that a particular word or phrase is used, and to pull out features of particular papers. (Source: https://eresources.eli.lsa.umich.edu/ micusp-corpus-of-written-academic-papers/)
Michigan Corpus of Academic Spoken English	MICASE	1.7 million words (nearly 200 hours) of spoken language. It focuses on contemporary university speech. Speakers represented in the corpus include faculty, staff, and all levels of students, and native, near-native, and non-native speakers. (Source: https://ca.talkbank.org/access/0docs/ MICASE.pdf)
TED Corpus Search Engine	TCSE	The first TED-LIUM corpus (2011) was composed of 118 hours of speech. The latest version now comprises 452 hours of audio. TCSE (created by Yoichiro Hasebe in 2015) now contains over 5,000 talks.
Santa Barbara Corpus of Spoken American English	SBCSAE	249,000 words. The Santa Barbara Corpus includes transcriptions, audio, and timestamps which correlate transcription and audio at the level of individual intonation units. (Source: https://www.linguistics.ucsb.edu/ research/santa-barbara-corpus)

which corpus to use to create teaching materials, the first thing teachers will need to do is decide what language characteristics they are looking for in the corpus and whether they will be able to access it (Huang, 2011). For example, some corpora collect texts from only spoken language (speech is transcribed into text), like the Michigan Corpus of Academic Spoken English (MICASE) and the Santa Barbara Corpus of Spoken Academic English (SBCSAE), while others only include written language, like the Michigan Corpus of Upper-Level Student Papers (MICUSP) and the Google Books Ngram Corpus. Some corpora only include American English, like the Corpus of Contemporary American English (COCA), while others include only British English, like the British National Corpus (BNC) and the British Academic Written English Corpus (BAWE); examples of other English varieties are the Scottish Corpus of Texts and Speech, the Strathy Corpus of Canadian English, and the Australian National Corpus. Some corpora are age-specific, like the Bergen Corpus of London Teenage Language (COLT); and some are restricted to a specific professional field, like the Corpus of Historical American English, and the Hansard Corpus, which contains nearly every speech given in the British Parliament from 1803–2005 (with about 1.6 billion words total).

Therefore, once a teacher decides on the characteristics that their target collection of English texts needs to have, they should be able to narrow down the list significantly. The next step would be to choose among the remaining options of corpora. One way to decide is to look at how big the remaining corpora are and pick the largest one. Large corpora will provide more flexibility in terms of results and contexts of language use, and they also increase the likelihood of an expression or linguistic term occurring in the samples of text that comprise the corpus. Some corpora have about 100 million words (for example, the British National Corpus), while others contain a staggering amount of 14 billion words (the iWeb corpus). The larger the corpus, the more likely it would be to find examples of the concordances they are looking for, and the more reliable the information about frequencies and occurrences would be.[3]

After a teacher has determined which corpus they want to work with, they should invest the time to become familiar with it (Kilgarriff, 2012). One thing they can do early on is to read the documentation on the corpus's

---

3. A concordance is a list of the words in a text or group of texts, with information about where in the text each word occurs and how often it occurs. The sentences each word occurs in are often given.

website as most of them do actually provide guidelines on how to use their system (see Figure 10.1). The original creators of a corpus often publish articles showing examples and guidelines of how to use it. There are also hundreds of videos on YouTube teaching how to use some of the better known corpora; if they are lucky, maybe teachers will find some videos for the corpus they chose. Because watching video tutorials is such an important way to learn how to do things these days, the availability of tutorial videos on YouTube or other educational content video streaming (LinkedIn Learning, for instance) could also be a selection criterion for their choice of a text corpus.

At first, the corpus web-based interface may seem confusing, too busy, or not user-friendly, but some search interfaces are more intuitive than others. LexTutor, WordAndPhrase, Voyant Tools, and AntConc are examples of web-based interfaces that help their users retrieve, analyze, and visualize information from a corpus or other text sources. For example, the LexTutor interface (https://www.lextutor.ca/conc/eng/) helps users search for concordances on the iWeb corpus in a more intuitive design than iWeb's native

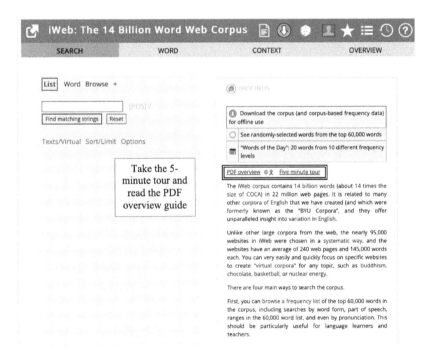

Figure 10.1. Getting familiar with the iWeb Corpus.

search engine. WordAndPhrase (https://www.wordandphrase.info/wap_c oca.pdf) is another search tool that scans COCA's database (see Figure 10.2). However, if a teacher wants to get more nuanced information from a corpus, it is better to use the corpus's native search engine, which gives them more control of search parameters.

Figure 10.2. Find WordAndPhrase's icon on the COCA page.

Finally, educators should take the time to look around, click on hyperlinks that lead to tutorials, guides, and examples to get more information about the collection of texts the corpus has, how the results are displayed, and if it can be further narrowed down with additional search parameters (see Figure 10.3). Tutorials and examples can be very helpful, but the only way a teacher can be certain that they know how a corpus works is to try it out for themselves.

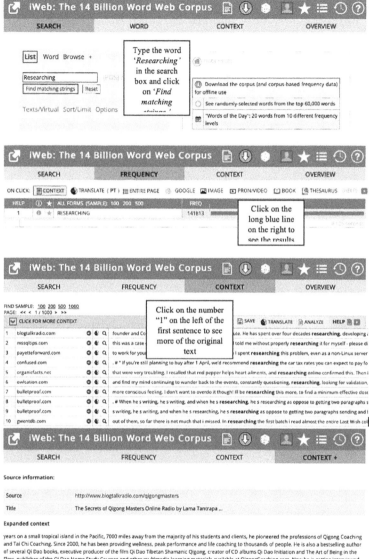

Figure 10.3. Practice using iWeb with the word "researching."

The web-based interface with this particular corpus illustrated in Figure 10.3 can yield a lot of information, which teachers will find out as soon as they try it out. For example, results can be narrowed down to retrieve only a fraction of the existing tokens. Figure 10.4 shows results obtained by restricting results to verbs only, and Figure 10.5 produces the high-frequency verbs that follow the word typed, organized by frequency of occurrence.

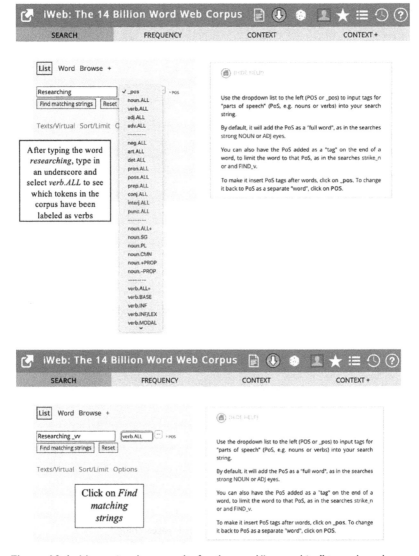

Figure 10.4. Narrowing down results for the word "researching" to verbs only.

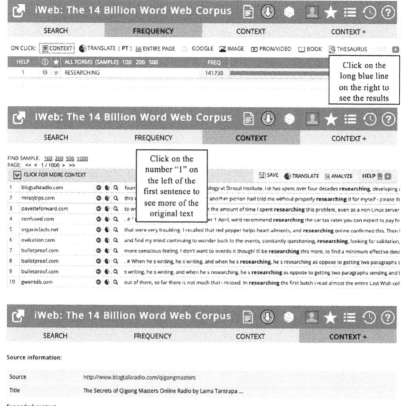

Figure 10.4. (Cont.)

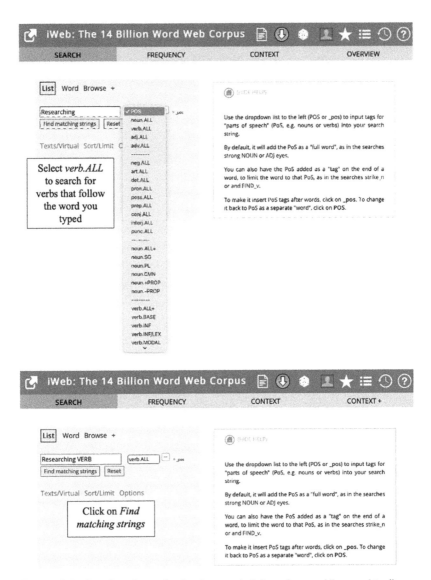

Figure 10.5. Searching for verbs that frequently follow the word "researching."

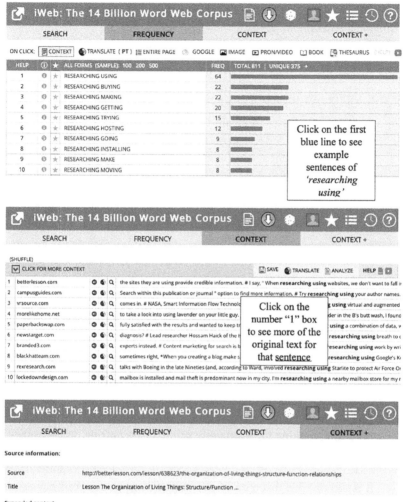

Figure 10.5. (Cont.)

• *Q2. How can teachers use an English corpus to prepare good language teaching materials?*

Some teachers have the privilege to work with wonderfully crafted ELT textbooks whose authors have done a thorough job of researching suitable authentic audio materials from podcasts, TV shows, radio shows, and news broadcasts; and print materials from magazines, newspapers, websites, and text corpora in order to create reading, writing, speaking, and listening activities. Some ELT publishers even offer an accompanying assessment generator tool also loaded with additional authentic materials related to the textbook lessons so that teachers can create tests for their students. For those lucky teachers who have been able to make use of a carefully designed textbook that is not only current and authentic but is also relevant to the age group they are teaching, appropriate for the level of their students, and suitable for the purpose of the course or program, learning to use a corpus only for the sake of creating additional materials is perhaps unnecessary. Nevertheless, it can still be argued that even those teachers would benefit from using a corpus when they see the need to create scaffolding materials for students who need additional support, or, maybe every once in a while, to swap a text from the textbook with something potentially "more interesting" for their students.

But the truth is, many teachers work at schools that require instructors to create their own teaching and assessment materials in hopes of reducing costs for their students. Other instructional locations might have a program or level coordinator (or a school administrator) who makes the textbook selections for all classes without asking for instructors' input, often making decisions based on price or convenience. In such cases, a textbook may sometimes not match students' true proficiency level, or their background characteristics and learning goals. It is also possible that a textbook was published several years before and is now outdated and obsolete. Even when a textbook makes use of authentic texts, they are very often linked to current affairs, which become outdated very quickly. When a teacher feels like any of these scenarios describes their situation, they should adopt an English text corpus. Having access to free and searchable authentic excerpts of language from which they can pull examples will make their job of creating teaching and assessment materials much easier.

Finally, when creating classroom activities from a corpus, students can be involved in the process. Given that it is important for students to also become familiar with a genre-appropriate text corpus, teachers can simply create a guided activity containing questions that can only be answered if students consult a text corpus (see Gilquin, 2021). Figure 10.6 is an example

In-class Activity
(Pair Work) Use iWeb to explore the word *suggest*. Try to answer the following questions: 1. Which form of the word *suggest* is more common, the noun form *suggestion,* or the verb for *suggest?* Where can you find this information on the iWeb screen?   2. Search for collocations with the word *suggest*, and identify the most common noun, verb, and adjective that collocates with this word.   3. Using the medium cluster, what are the top two three-word clusters that the word *suggest* appears in?   4. What are three synonyms for *suggest* in terms of meaning *recommend?*   5. What are five topics that commonly appear with the word *suggest?*

Figure 10.6. A sample activity with the word "suggest" using the iWeb Corpus.

of a simple activity making use of the iWeb corpus to ask students to explore the linguistic properties of the word *suggest.* This word has peculiar syntactic constraints, such as having to take the subjunctive mood when used in a complex sentence that requires a noun clause (*The doctor suggested that he stay in bed*), but it can also be followed simply by a noun or noun phrase (*The doctor suggests rest*; or *The doctor suggests resting for a week*). Presenting students with a guided activity asking specific questions that correlate with the types of information a corpus can yield is a good way to train students to rely on a corpus to learn more about the typical forms, meanings, and uses in context of various words and phrases in English.

• *Q3. How can students benefit from learning to use a corpus?*

Besides the fact that a corpus can help teachers create teaching and assessment materials based on authentic and contextualized genre-specific texts, teachers should also consider the benefits that a corpus can offer to EFL/ESL students (Lee et al., 2018; Warren, 2016).[4] Students can learn to use a corpus to check for collocations and phraseology, to learn about the different uses and meanings of words, to study how grammatical forms are used in context, to perform genre analysis, to analyze register conventions, and to explore disciplinary styles and conventions.

An instrumental part of the process of learning a second or foreign language involves gradually increasing one's knowledge of the target language's lexicon (Csomay & Prades, 2018; Dang, 2019), which includes not only a

---

4. Open educational resource for training teachers to create corpus-informed English language teaching materials: https://pressbooks.pub/elenlefoll/

word's denotation and connotation, but also its phonological and morphological features, its grammatical rules, such as its semantic and syntactic constraints, and its usage and pragmatics (Ellis et al., 2016). For example, a student can use a corpus to find out which argument placement is more common for the ditransitive verb *give*; in other words, is the placement of the direct object in front of the indirect object more common (*subject + give + something + to someone*) or does the indirect object occur more frequently in the first object position (*subject + give + someone + something*)?

Using a corpus can help students explore the dimensions of linguistic knowledge beyond the scope of a textbook. It can also help students prioritize which words to learn, favoring high-frequency words and phrases. For example, a student can look for high adjective–noun co-occurrences, like adjectives that are frequently used with the noun *butter*, such as *unsalted butter* or *rancid butter*. Learning to use the more frequently co-occurring phrases (for example, word–word collocations) may help language learners sound more fluent in the target language. In agreement with this view of prioritization of language items that are more commonly used in English, Webb and Nation (2017) explain that efficient language learners must figure out which words in English are used more frequently, and then prioritize the learning of those. They argue that it is incredibly difficult for a language learner to ever know as many words as a native speaker, which may lead to the frustration of long-time learners who fail to communicate with native speakers of their target language.

Having access to an English text corpus can do just that; it can help learners decide which words, collocations, phraseologies, and word forms to focus on based on their usefulness, context, purpose, and frequency of occurrence in authentic texts, as opposed to attempting to acquire a vast assortment of words that are not part of day-to-day use. Many students bring to class their pocket dictionaries, or sometimes electronic dictionaries, which have the added benefit (depending on how the teacher sees it) of providing translations in their native languages. Some dictionaries have accumulated a massive collection of words in English. For example, Webster's *Third New International Dictionary, Unabridged* contains about 470,000 entries; the *Oxford English Dictionary, Second Edition* reports that it includes a similar number. But typically, native speakers only know about 15,000 to 20,000 lemmas in their own language.[5] So how should

---

5. Lemmas are word families; i.e., a root word and all its derivational and inflectional affixes. For example: *eat, eats, ate, eaten, eating.* Another example is *cold, colder, coldest, coldish.*

learners pick 15,000 words out of the very large number of words found in English? Naturally, they should pick the high-frequency words, the ones used most often in the media, in the news, or at work. Common dictionaries do not provide that information, but text corpora do. Students can use an English text corpus to find out how common a word they came across is, and how likely it is that this word would be used in day-to-day interactions. For example, they can compare the use frequency of the words *house* and *abode*, or compare the number of occurrences of the words *perhaps* and *peradventure* and then decide which of them they should strive to use more instead.

- **Q4. If a teacher is already strapped for time having to teach a busy curriculum, how do they make the time to incorporate the use of corpora in their class?**

There is a common expression that goes, "Don't teach the book. Teach the students!" (author unknown, n.d.). Well, most EFL/ESL schools hand novice teachers a packed course syllabus with several course objectives and student learning outcomes that should be met by the end of one quarter or one semester. So having to deal with a busy curriculum comes with the teaching territory. But one important solution is to simply not use every single suggested activity in the textbook. It is in fact advisable to carefully select those activities that a teacher thinks would work best for their students, and to skip, replace, or adapt those that might be too long, too boring, too hard, or less relevant for their students. If a teacher has determined that certain activities need to be axed or replaced in order to better cater for their students, then they certainly will need a tool to help them quickly find other more suitable texts. This is where an appropriate preselected English text corpus comes in. Some teachers spend too much time looking for supplemental materials online; using a corpus the teacher is already familiar with will prove to be a plentiful resource that provides better control of authentic and contextualized language phrases and collocations to match various lesson objectives.

Another advantage of using a corpus when teachers have a busy curriculum to follow is that a lot of the search work can be transferred to the students. Having students perform guided searches enables a more student-focused environment. In addition, students will become more autonomous and less dependent on the teacher to check the accurateness of their work. They can look for phrasal collocations or grammatical form appropriateness, and with that information they can edit their own work. For example, they can check what preposition follows a certain verb (for example, they can check when [context] they should use *arrive in* and when to use *arrive at*), or whether a certain noun typically takes the definite article (as in, *I go to ___ school at UCLA*). If students are already familiar with a corpus, (the teacher has already used the corpus in class a few times, perhaps, and provided guided tutorials, and so on), or, alternatively, they know how to conduct refined searches on Google, this acquired ability will enable students to work independently from the teacher. By learning to quickly and easily check the accuracy of their language use, and using that information to revise their own work, the quality of student work can be potentially better, which in turn may reduce the amount of time a teacher will spend grading (that is, time spent on teacher feedback on items that students could have checked on their own and self-edited—or peer edited, if working in pairs—prior to turning in their work).

• Q5. How can teachers increase students' access to a corpus inside and outside of the classroom?

This is a very valid concern. There might be technical issues that would hinder the use of an online corpus during class or outside of the classroom. Using an online corpus inside a classroom and during class would require access to smartphones, tablets, laptops, or computers, along with reliable access to the internet in that classroom. If a teacher's classroom has internet access but no hardware, they can check how many students have internet-enabled devices and ask students to login to the school's Wi-Fi in order to use a corpus during class. If not everyone has a smart device but some do, then teachers can have students work in groups. But if a teacher's school does not offer internet connectivity, then they would have to check with their students first how comfortable they would be with using their own data plans. For example, teachers can ask students to fill out an anonymous survey at the beginning of the course asking if they have a smart device they can use in class, and if they would be willing to use their provider's data quota to perform certain pedagogical activities online—which does not have to be limited to corpus searches, of course, as there are many other fantastic pedagogical tools that teachers can use online with their students. If students give the teacher the green light, the teacher is all set; but if a teacher learns that their students would rather not use their cellular data on pedagogical activities, then their last resort is to create corpus-based activity worksheets and hand out hard copies in class for students to take home and bring to class the next day.

An important time-saving recommendation is to ask students to preregister and create their own accounts before they come to class. Some corpora require that users create an account before being given access. To make sure that students will be able to create their accounts without a teacher's assistance, teachers should create a worksheet with step-by-step instructions, and ask students to go over it at home or at the school's computer lab. Creating a detailed step-by-step guideline worksheet with screenshots, circles, and arrows is highly recommended so that students can follow those steps independently in order to create their own accounts without requiring in-class assistance from the teacher.

Another issue to consider is potential cost to the school, the teacher, or the student. Most linguistic corpora are free of charge, but some may limit either teachers' access or the number of searches they can make at a time; and a few more specialized corpora might charge to grant access. Therefore, if they would rather choose a free, unlimited, and no-registration-required tool, teachers should keep in mind that internet search engines (such as Google) can be also used as corpora for more limited and quick searches. For example, when searching for an exact match of word combinations on Google, teachers can use double quotation marks (" ") around a phrase to look at its occurrences in the results (see Figure 10.7). Double quotes are used to force Google to search for the exact words or phrases used within the quotes. For example, the phrase "jump squats" will prioritize the results that contain this exact phrase. Following results with exact matches, Google also offers combinations with synonyms of the words within the quotes to offer additional results; using the same example, it would also suggest results for "jump lunges," "reverse squats," among others. In addition, if they want to look for high-frequency words that follow a certain word, they could add an asterisk after that word. The same can be done to look for words that precede their target word. This is often called the "wild card" search (see Figure 10.7). To search for an unknown word that follows a known word, they would write the following combination in the Google search box: *word* *. For example, if a teacher types in the search box "*happy* *" they might get the following results: *happy birthday*, *happy place*, and *happy to contribute to [. . .]*. There are several other symbols that a teacher could use in Google searches, and if they want to learn more, just Google "refine web searches."

Finally, a lot of the corpus search work done by students can be carried out outside of the classroom. But teachers must make sure that their students have access to a computer at home, at school, at work, or at local libraries, among other possible and reasonable places. But because having to access a computer outside of their homes or class requires additional free

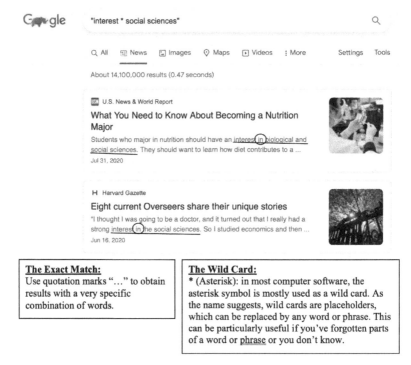

Figure 10.7. Two useful search parameters for Google: "the exact match" and the "wild card."

time, instructors should give them enough time to plan accordingly. The advantage of assigning some of this work to be done as homework is that 1) it takes less of a teacher's potentially limited class time; 2) it teaches students a valuable independent skill; and 3) it increases students' amount of language practice with and exposure to authentic language. The disadvantage, however, is that teachers would not be with them to offer support when they are still learning how to use it. To prevent such difficulties, it is recommended that they create handouts or tutorials teaching students how to use a certain corpus for homework assignments.

Big Picture and Bottom Line

Learning to use a new tool for the first time always involves some investment of time, depending on their preexisting familiarity with similar tools: in this case in particular, search engines. But learning to use a text corpus has so many potential benefits that it is worth taking the time to learn how to use it. For teachers, text corpora can provide a valuable source of authentic texts from various genres that also represent contextualized language use, while reducing the pressure of finding good teaching and assessment materials at short notice. Text corpora can be used in the language classroom to illustrate and teach authentic register variation, discipline-specific differences, collocations, phraseology and vocabulary use, and descriptive grammar, among other applications. For students, using a text corpus will help them become independent learners and autonomous editors.

Food for Thought

1. Based on the discussions in this chapter, find a sample of student writing that could benefit from using a corpus that contains texts from academic sources. Discuss:
   a. What features of this student's writing could be improved by using a text corpus.
   b. How you would help students use this corpus in order to self-edit their own writing.
2. Use iWeb to create an activity in which students are asked to search for the form, meaning, and use of the word *evidence* and discuss their findings. Create a number of specific questions that will guide their search for specific linguistic features of the word, like collocations, parts of speech, semantic and syntactic constraints, contextual use, etc.

References

Boulton, A., & Cobb, T. (2017). Corpus use in language learning: A meta-analysis. *Language Learning, 67*(2), 348–393. https://doi.org/10.1111/lang.12224

Braun, S. (2005). From pedagogically relevant corpora to authentic language learning contents. *ReCALL, 17*(1), 47–64. https://doi.org/10.1017/S0958344005000510

Callies, M. (2019). Integrating corpus literacy into language teacher education: The case of learner corpora. In J. Mukherjee, & S. Götz (Eds.), *Learner corpora and language teaching* (pp. 245–264). John Benjamins.

Chambers, A., & Bax, S. (2006). Making CALL work: Towards normalisation. *System, 34*(4), 465–479. https://doi.org/10.1016/j.system.2006.08.001

Chang, J.-Y. (2014). The use of general and specialized corpora as reference sources for academic English writing: A case study. *ReCALL, 26*(2), 243–259. https://doi.org/10.1017/S0958344014000056

Chen, M.-H., Huang, S.-T., Chang, J. S., & Liou, H.-C. (2015). Developing a corpus-based paraphrase tool to improve EFL learners' writing skills. *Computer Assisted Language Learning, 28*(1), 22–40. https://doi.org/10.1080/09588 221.2013.783873

Crossley, S., & McNamara, D. (2013). Applications of text analysis tools for spoken response grading. *Language Learning & Technology, 17*(2), 171–192. http://dx.doi.org/10125/44329

Csomay, E., & Prades, A. (2018). Academic vocabulary in ESL student papers: A corpus-based study. *Journal of English for Academic Purposes, 33,* 100–118. https://doi.org/10.1016/j.jeap.2018.02.003

Dang, T. N. Y. (2019). Corpus-based word lists in second language vocabulary research, learning, and teaching. In S. Webb (Ed.), *The Routledge handbook of vocabulary studies* (pp. 288–303). Routledge.

The Douglas Fir Group (Atkinson, D., Byrnes, H., Doran, M., Duff, P., Ellis, N. C., Hall, J. K., Johnson, K. E., Lantolf, J. P., Larsen–Freeman, D., Negueruela, E., Norton, B., Ortega, L., Schumann, J., Swain, M., & Tarone, E.) (2016). A transdisciplinary framework for SLA in a multilingual world. *The Modern Language Journal, 100*(Suppl. 2016), 19–47. https://doi.org/10.1111/modl.12301

Ellis, N. C., Römer, U., & O'Donnell, M. B. (2016). Constructions and usage-based approaches to language acquisition. *Language Learning, 66*(Suppl. 1), 23–44. https://doi.org/10.1111/lang.1_12177

Flowerdew, L. (2015). Data-driven learning and language learning theories. In A. Leńko-Szymańska, & A. Boulton (Eds.), *Multiple affordances of language corpora for data-driven learning* (pp. 15–36). John Benjamins.

Gilquin, G. (2021). Using corpora to foster L2 construction learning: A data-driven learning experiment. *International Journal of Applied Linguistics, 31*(2), 229–247. https://doi.org/10.1111/ijal.12317

Golonka, E. M., Bowles, A. R., Frank, V. M., Richardson, D. L., & Freynik, S. (2014). Technologies for foreign language learning: A review of technology types and their effectiveness. *Computer Assisted Language Learning, 27*(1), 70–105. https://doi.org/10.1080/09588221.2012.700315

Hardacre, B., & Snow, M. A. (2020). Teaching pedagogical grammar in English language teacher education. In D. L. Banegas (Ed.), *Content knowledge in English language teacher education: International experiences* (pp. 65–80). Bloomsbury. https://doi.org/10.5040/9781350084650.0010

Huang, L.-S. (2011). Corpus-aided language learning. *ELT Journal, 65*(4), 481–484. https://doi.org/10.1093/elt/ccr031

Hubbard, P. (2013). Making a case for learner training in technology enhanced language learning environments. *CALICO Journal, 30*(2), 163–178. https://doi.org/10.11139/cj.30.2.163-178

Kilgarriff, A. (2012). Getting to know your corpus [Paper presentation]. In P. Sojka, A. Horák, I. Kopeček, & K. Pala (Eds.), *Text, speech and dialogue,* 15th international conference, TSD 2012, Brno, Czech Republic, Proceedings (pp. 3–15). Springer. https://doi.org/10.1007/978-3-642-32790-2_1

Le Foll, E. (Ed.). (2021). *Creating corpus-informed materials for the English as a foreign language classroom: A step-by-step guide for (trainee) teachers using online resources.* Pressbooks. https://pressbooks.pub/elenlefoll/

Lee, H., Warschauer, M., & Lee, J. H. (2018). The effects of corpus use on second language vocabulary learning: A multilevel meta-analysis. *Applied Linguistics, 40*(5), 721–753. https://doi.org/10.1093/applin/amy012

Pérez-Paredes, P. (2022). How learners use corpora. In R. R. Jablonkai & E. Csomay (Eds). *The Routledge handbook of corpora and English language teaching and learning* (pp. 390–405). Routledge.

Tyler, A. E., & Ortega, L. (2018). Usage-inspired L2 instruction. Some reflections and a heuristic. In A. E. Tyler, L. Ortega, M. Uno, & H. I. Park (Eds.), *Usage-inspired L2 instruction: Researched pedagogy* (pp. 315–321). John Benjamins. https://doi.org/10.1075/lllt.49.14tyl

Vyatkina, N., & Boulton, A. (2017). Corpora in language learning and teaching. *Language Learning & Technology, 21*(3), 1–8.

Warren, M. (2016). Introduction to data-driven learning. In F. Farr & L. Murray (Eds.), *The Routledge handbook of language learning and technology* (pp. 337–348). Routledge.

Webb, S., & Nation, P. (2017). *How vocabulary is learned.* Oxford University Press.

CHAPTER 11

Using Digital Tools
in the Language Classroom

Contextualization

Digital tools, including apps, social media, online games, podcasts, and many others have become ubiquitous in the English language classroom. While the use of these tools is expected to contribute to the language teaching and learning process, classroom instruction needs to be guided by a set of principles designed to help teachers avoid making random decisions about the use of digital tools in the classroom and, instead, integrate digital tools in such a way that they will contribute to language development and high student and teacher satisfaction. This chapter is designed to help future and novice teachers conceptualize the role that digital tools can play in their classes, identify a set of principles guiding the integration of digital tools in the classroom, and describe a variety of digital tools that can be used to promote language learning.

Case Study: So Many Digital Tools! I Need to Start Using Some in My Classes . . .

A few months ago, a novice English as a foreign language (EFL) teacher was hired to teach full-time for a South American binational center (an institution dedicated to providing American English instruction and promoting mutual understanding between the local community and the United States). Our teacher was assigned to teach a variety of courses, including English for specific purposes (ESP) and general English courses to adult learners and teenage students.

214

In her classes, our teacher noticed the different ways in which her students used digital tools. While her teenage students played online games, posted images and reels on Instagram, and created TikTok videos on their smartphones, her adult learners used their tablets and smartphones to read the news, look up vocabulary in online dictionaries, and play online games. Very early in her classes, our teacher realized her teaching would benefit from integrating digital tools since they would play a motivating role in her students' learning process and, at the same time, provide meaningful language learning opportunities. As our teacher set out to integrate technology in her classes, she decided to take on this new responsibility in the same way she approached the textbook selection process: by applying a principled approach that would allow her to make smart decisions about the selection and integration of digital tools in the English language classroom. This chapter discusses the principled approach to the selection and use of digital tools in their classrooms and describes a variety of emerging tools that can be integrated into the language classroom.

Common Concerns

The questions below are designed to guide novice teachers as they make decisions about the selection and integration of digital tools in the classroom. While the questions address a variety of issues about digital tools, in no way are they meant to be comprehensive, since teachers work in a variety of settings and with many different student populations who have a wide range of language learning goals. Despite these differences, the questions are meant to provide novice teachers with a starting point in their thinking about the integration of digital tools in the language classroom.

- *Q1. What can be understood as "digital tools"? How has technology been used in the classroom?*
- *Q2. What principles should guide the use of digital tools in the classroom?*
- *Q3. What criteria should teachers use to evaluate digital tools to be used in the language classroom?*
- *Q4. What are some examples of reputable, free-of-charge digital tools that teachers can use to plan and deliver instruction?*
- *Q5. What are some exciting examples of emerging technologies that are currently used in language classrooms?*

Implementing Digital Tools in the Language Classroom

- **Q1. What can be understood as "digital tools"? How has technology been used in the classroom?**

In this chapter, the term "digital tools" is understood to include a wide variety of emerging digital technologies like augmented reality (AR), virtual reality (VR), computational thinking, and artificial intelligence (AI) tools such as OpenAI's ChatGPT, Google's Bard, or Microsoft Bing's AI chatbot. Digital tools also include more established software programs, databases, social media sites, and apps. While many of these tools have not been developed for educational purposes, they can still be relevant to the language classroom.

The relatively recent explosion in the use of digital tools in education would give the impression that the use of technology in the language classroom is a thing of the 21st century. However, this is far from the truth. One of the first uses of technology in the teaching of the English language is from the 1950s when the language laboratory (commonly known as the "language lab") was used in support of the audio-lingual method (ALM) and provided language practice in the form of drills. With the growth of the internet, email, listservs, and learning management systems (LMSs) (see Chapter 12 for in-depth information on LMSs), the 1990s brought a new era that promoted student–student interaction, collaboration, and language practice, though instruction was still centered around the desktop. The release of the iPhone in 2007 brought about a new era that was accompanied by the exponential growth of social media tools that promote high connectivity, interaction, and user-generated content. Currently, learner-centered classrooms are promoted by integrating a wide variety of emerging tools. These include, but are not limited to ChatGPT and Bard, for example, which can generate human-like text, and computational thinking—involving "the ability to formulate thoughts and questions in a manner that is communicable to a computer to achieve desired results" (Jacob et al., 2018, p. 12).

The digital tools already available in the market as well as the constantly emerging new technologies can provide language learning benefits—and, as we will explain in this chapter, also present ethical challenges. Therefore, as we will argue in the next section, the selection and integration of digital tools in the language classroom needs to be guided by a set of principles that provide novice teachers with an understanding of why and how digital tools should be used in the language classroom. This is the focus of Question 2.

• Q2. What principles should guide the use of digital tools in the classroom?

By the time novice teachers are assigned to their classes, they have developed—or are in the process of developing—a set of guiding principles that inform their instructional practices. Though these principles will evolve throughout their professional lives, at a minimum, teacher preparation programs have prepared novice teachers to develop an understanding of their values and beliefs about accepted research-based practices in the TESOL/applied linguistics field (Richards, 2017). What is often missing from this set of principles is an understanding of the role that digital tools will play in the teachers' classroom. Considering the significant role digital tools play in society and the increasing demand for teachers to incorporate technology into their classrooms, novice teachers should establish a guiding set of principles that will assist them in deciding how best to utilize digital tools in their teaching. In this way, rather than selecting and using digital tools for random reasons, the integration of digital tools in their classrooms will be meaningful. In this section, we describe five principles that are designed to help teachers conceptualize the role that digital tools will play in their teaching.

Principle 1. The Use of Digital Tools in the Language Classroom Needs to Be Driven by Learner Needs

An important principle in the field of English language teaching (ELT) is that instruction needs to be driven by learner needs (Richards, 2017). To this end, teachers need to understand their learners' target situation (Graves, 2000). They should ask themselves questions like: What are the students' objectives for studying English? What do students want or need to be able to do in English? Do they want to be able to read in English? To write academic papers? To travel? To do business in English? For no particular purpose? The answers to these questions will help teachers identify digital tools that can be used to meet learner needs. For example, if students are enrolled in a writing class, then the teacher could consider using Canva (a free video and graphic design tool) to produce a digital story such as an autobiographical narrative. If students are K-12 English learners (ELs) enrolled in an English language development class in the United States then they would benefit from playing games on iCivics (a nonprofit US website or app that provides motivational educational games and lesson plans promoting civic education).

In summary, in developing their lessons, teachers need to consider how the class goals are designed to meet learners' needs and how the digital tools used will contribute to meeting the classroom goals and learners' needs.

Principle 2. Digital Tools Should Not Be Used as an "Add-On"

Digital tools should be used for meaningful purposes, rather than "just because" they are ubiquitous or are contemporary in the ELT field. To avoid looking at technology as an "add-on" (Koehler & Mishra, 2009, p. 67), teachers need to consider the relationships among their course objectives, their pedagogical practices and beliefs, and their students' technology skills. What this means is that digital tools should be used to meet course objectives. Doing this will ensure that digital tools are a good fit for the course or, to put it another way, are integrated for meaningful purposes (see Koehler & Mishra, 2009 for their work on technological pedagogical content knowledge). In addition, this view of digital tools as having a purposeful role in the classroom will prevent teachers from feeling that digital tools are something that needs to be used on top of or as an extra to the work they do.

Principle 3. Digital Tools Are Motivating; Therefore, They Stimulate the Language Learning Process

Digital tools provide students with exposure to high-quality materials and authentic language input, and allow students to produce output and learn authentic language (Li, 2017). Therefore, when they are used for relevant and meaningful purposes, they enhance the language teaching and learning process. Digital tools are also extremely powerful because they promote a high degree of cognitive and emotional engagement that is sometimes not possible when teachers use traditional classroom tools (Cummins et al., 2007; Grabe & Gabe, 2004).

Principle 4. Digital Tools Can Play Different Roles in the Language Classroom, and These Roles Will Place Different Demands on Teachers and Their Classrooms

English language teachers are busy professionals. Therefore, as they reflect on the role that digital tools will play in their classrooms, they need to take into account the various demands that different technology tools will place on them. A practical framework to help teachers understand such demands is provided by Puentedura's (2013) SAMR (substitution, augmentation, modification, and redefinition) framework. This framework presents two levels of technology integration (*enhancement* at the lower level and *transformation* at the higher level). Within the lower level, *enhancement*, digital tools can be used to *substitute* traditional classroom materials (for example, a textbook reading passage could be replaced with a reading passage from the web) or to *augment* instruction, in which digital tools act as a direct substitute of a traditional tool with some functional improvement (a handwritten biography, for instance, could be replaced by the publication of the same biography in a public blog that would receive readers' comments). Substitution and augmentation do not place great demands on language teachers since they do not require a major redesign of the curriculum.

In contrast to the *enhancement* level is Puentedura's (2013) *transformation* level, which requires teachers to engage in a significant redesign of the curriculum to integrate digital tools. Within this level, there are two steps: *modification* and *redefinition*. An example of modification could involve having students produce the biography mentioned in the previous paragraph in the form of a digital story integrating images, videos, and PowerPoint slides. Redefinition involves the use of technology for the creation of tasks that were previously inconceivable. An example of this could be teaching a lesson using Nearpod, a digital tool that promotes interactive lessons that can be delivered in person or virtually.

Teachers who engage in a process of transforming instruction will need to engage in a substantial redesign of their classes. However, for teachers of ELs, such a drastic overhaul may not be possible, practical, or realistic given several factors. These factors include the teachers' instructional goals, their knowledge and comfort with technology, and the investment—professional, financial, and emotional—needed to completely revamp a course. Given all of these factors, it is important that, as teachers consider how they will use digital tools in the classroom, they make conscious decisions about the amount of work they are willing to do or are capable of doing to integrate such tools into their teaching. To put it in simple terms, teachers of ELs should remind themselves that in integrating technology tools into their teaching, their goal is to teach language. Therefore, their instruction should be driven by language goals and not by digital tools.

Principle 5. The Degree of Access to Technology Devices Should Guide the Teachers' Decision-Making Process Regarding the Integration of Digital Tools in the Classroom

In deciding the roles that digital tools will have in the classroom, teachers need to consider their students' degree of access to technology devices. While some classrooms may be equipped with one computer with an internet connection, in other classrooms, every student may have access to their own smartphone, tablet, or laptop with an unlimited internet connection. In addition, if teachers are considering assigning homework that relies on digital tools, then they need to understand whether their students will be able to complete the tasks since not everyone will have (reliable) access to the internet. In summary, as teachers consider designing tasks that integrate the use of digital tools, they will need to take into account all of the factors described in this section since they can be a plus or a limitation in completing classroom activities.

In summary, in this section, we identified five principles that should guide teachers' integration of digital tools in the classroom. These principles are:

> Principle 1. The use of digital tools in the language classroom needs to be driven by learner needs.
> Principle 2. Digital tools should not be used as an "add-on."
> Principle 3. Digital tools are motivating; therefore, they stimulate the language learning process.
> Principle 4. Digital tools can play different roles in the language classroom and these roles will place different demands on teachers and their classrooms.
> Principle 5. The degree of access to technology devices should guide the teachers' decision-making process regarding the integration of digital tools in the classroom.

The five principles are interconnected because one principle cannot be considered in isolation from the others. In addition, they provide a rationale for how and why digital tools could be used in the language classroom. Finally, the principles are not meant to be comprehensive. Instead, they should be used to help teachers begin to develop their vision for their integration of digital tools in the classroom.

• Q3. What criteria should teachers use to evaluate digital tools to be used in the language classroom?

After identifying the principles that will guide the teachers' use of digital tools in the classroom, novice teachers are now ready to evaluate the tools they are considering adopting in their teaching. According to Tomlinson (2003, as cited in McDonough et al., 2013), materials evaluation involves assessing the value of a book. In our case, rather than looking at textbooks, the evaluation focuses on digital tools, that oftentimes have not been developed for language teaching and learning purposes.

Teachers are often under pressure to select textbooks that have been sanctioned by their schools or programs. In contrast, most of the time, they have the flexibility to select digital tools they deem appropriate to meet their students' language needs. Despite this seeming difference, one point in common between textbook and digital tool evaluation is that the latter should be conducted in two stages, a point made by McDonough et al. 2013 about the textbook evaluation process. In the first stage, called external evaluation, teachers should do a quick assessment of the digital tool under consideration by analyzing its general fit. To this end, teachers could refer to the guiding principles for using digital tools described in Question 2 in this chapter and swiftly evaluate the digital tool under consideration based on those principles. To complete this task, teachers could use a simple checklist like the one provided in Figure 11.1. In the example, the tool being evaluated is Flip, a free-of-charge video discussion tool.

In addition to focusing on the principles that should guide a teacher's integration of digital tools in the classroom, the external evaluation could also include a review of the available literature on the digital tool under consideration. For example, in the case of Flip (formerly known as Flipgrid), a review by Bell (2018) available on Larry Ferlazzo's (n.d.) blog (one of the best-known and trustworthy blogs focusing on ELT topics) supports the initial results of the external evaluation.

Since the results of the first stage of the evaluation are positive, it is time for the teacher to continue to the second stage of the evaluation process: the internal evaluation. At this stage, the teacher would do a detailed assessment of the digital tool under consideration. To this end, the teacher would rely on the questions provided in Figure 11.2, "Digital tool

Tool: Flip	Principles guiding the use of the digital tool	Yes/no
	Its use is driven by learner needs	Yes
	Its use is meaningful	Yes
	It is a motivating tool	Yes
	It places low demands on the curriculum	Yes
	It can be accessed from a wide range of devices	Yes
	Final assessment: Continue with stage 2 evaluation	

Figure 11.1. Checklist: Tools under consideration v. principles guiding their use in the language classroom.

General Questions
1. What is the name of the digital tool being evaluated?
2. Who are the students with whom the digital tool will be used?
   a. What are the students' ages? Are these children, adolescents, or adults?
   b. What is the students' proficiency level?
   c. How motivated are the students?
3. What is the overall goal of the class in which students are enrolled? To learn English for general purposes? To learn English for survival purposes? For academic study in an English-speaking setting? Or are students enrolled in a content class in an English-medium university? Or are they enrolled in an ESP class (and if so, what is the focus of the class)? Or are they enrolled in an EFL class?

Degree of Appropriateness of the Digital Tool
4. To what extent is the digital tool appropriate for the students in terms of: 1) content knowledge; and 2) linguistic demands?
5. To what extent will the digital tool benefit students in their language learning process?
6. For what purposes can the digital tool be used? To provide input? To promote output in a controlled or independent manner? To engage students in meaningful communication?
7. To what extent is there alignment between the technology tool and the teacher's pedagogical practices?

Instructional Modality
8. What will the learning modality be? Will students be expected to work individually? In pairs? In groups?
9. Will the digital tool be used in the face-to-face classroom? Outside the classroom?
10. If the digital tool is used in the face-to-face classroom, will all students have access to it? How?
11. Will the teacher be able to monitor the students' use of the digital tool?
12. Is the digital tool free of charge or will it require a teacher (or class) subscription?

Tool Design Transparency
13. Can students use the digital tool without effort? Specifically, is it user-friendly?
14. Can the teacher learn how to use the digital tool without much effort? Specifically, is the digital tool transparent enough for the teacher to quickly learn how to use it?
15. Is the design of the digital tool appealing to the students?

General Comments

Adopt? Adapt? Reject?

Figure 11.2. Digital tool evaluation form.

evaluation form," which would need to be considered against or adapted to the teachers' instructional context, a point that Richards (2017) makes for textbook evaluation. The form is designed to address key considerations such as whether the digital tools meet learners' needs, align with course objectives, and offer language benefits. In addition, because most digital tools are "foreign" to the language classroom—that is, they have not been developed for language teaching purposes—the evaluation criteria should also focus on their degree of transparency (ease of use) for ELs and teachers. This is an important factor to consider because, as we have discussed in this chapter, the integration of digital tools in the classroom should not be an add-on or burden to the teacher, the students, and the classroom as a whole.

As can be seen in Figure 11.2, the form focuses on four areas: 1) the students and the class in which the digital tool will be used; 2) the degree of appropriateness of the digital tool for the class; 3) the instructional modality of the class in which the digital tool will be used; and 4) the digital tool's degree of transparency.

So how would the second stage of the evaluation process work with a digital tool like Flip, for example? The results of the evaluation, focusing on the questions in Figure 11.2, show that Flip would work well within a variety of courses, including those focusing on English for survival purposes to those focusing on English for academic purposes. In addition, the evaluation would also show that Flip is highly appropriate for all students since it can be used to provide meaningful input or to promote free output. In addition, Flip is a flexible tool since it can be used by groups or individual students, though it seems to work best when students work independently. Flip is also free of charge, which for teachers on a tight budget is a critical issue to consider. Finally, as already explained, Flip's design is transparent. Students and teachers can learn how to use it without effort and its design is appealing to a wide student population.

The in-depth evaluation of digital tools is an essential component of the digital tool adoption process. While this evaluation is expected to be comprehensive, it should not be a labor-intensive activity since teachers could quickly assess the strengths and weaknesses of the digital tools under consideration. However, we should note that even if a digital tool gets a glowing evaluation, teachers should listen to their students' feedback on the tool. Doing this will contribute to validating the students' voice and, as teachers act on their students' input, enhance the instructional process and classroom climate.

- **Q4. What are some examples of reputable, free of charge digital tools that teachers can use to plan and deliver instruction?**

It would be impossible for this chapter to provide a comprehensive description of the many digital tools available in the market. Therefore, this section is designed to describe a selected number of digital tools that can be used for instructional purposes. In selecting the tools, our emphasis was on those that are free of charge and have a high degree of transparency since this makes them easy to use. In addition, we selected tools that are reliable because, in contrast with other digital tools available in the market, they have not gone through major—and often dramatic—changes in their design or subscription structures. Finally, several of the tools identified are not designed for the specific purposes of language teaching and learning. However, these tools have such a high potential for benefiting language learners that they are, at the very least, worth experimenting with.

We fully acknowledge that the digital tools featured in this section may, in the future, be replaced by other emerging tools or require a paid subscription. However, not describing a variety of selected digital tools and their potential uses in the language classroom would shortchange a chapter that focuses on the integration of digital technology in ELT field.

Table 11.1 features a variety of free-of-charge tools that can be used for lesson and activity planning and delivery purposes. Of particular interest for professionals in the ELT field are TED Talks and the Moth Podcast. These two tools provide authentic presentations (TED Talks) and motivating stories (the Moth Podcast) that can be used to develop listening and speaking lessons for students whose level of proficiency is B1 or higher on the Common European Framework of Reference (CEFR). Another digital tool of great relevance to ELs is TED-Ed, a TED Talk extension that allows teachers to use or easily develop video lessons that can be used with low-level proficiency students. The three digital tools described in this paragraph, TED Talks, TED-Ed, and the Moth Podcast, feature a wide variety of topics that will be of interest and relevance to classrooms around the world.

A digital tool that should be highlighted is iCivics (see Table 11.1). While iCivics has been designed for a US K-12 student audience, it can also be used with adult ELs who are preparing to take the US Naturalization Interview and Test. The value of iCivics lies in its game-like and motivating treatment of civic education.

While all the tools in Table 11.1 are easy to use, they differ in the amount of curriculum modification needed to design activities that integrate their use. For instance, JeopardyLabs, one of the tools listed in the table, requires

Table 11.1. Digital Tools for Lesson/Activity Content Planning and Delivery

Digital tool	Instructional purpose	Description	Special features
TED Talks	To develop listening and speaking activities.	Features 18-min max online videos on diverse topics.	The video playback speed can be customized; closed captioning is available. A clickable time-coded script is available.
TED-Ed	To use available video lessons. To design video lessons on TED Talks.	Features short educational videos and lessons in support of the videos. Allows teachers to upload videos and design lessons using available templates.	The target audience is children, though the videos can be used with adults. Appropriate for language learners. The video playback speed can be customized; closed captioning is available. Lessons can be customized for different age and language proficiency groups.
Moth Podcast	To develop listening and speaking activities.	Features authentic and interesting stories told by storytellers to a live audience.	Appropriate for adult language learners at B2 and higher levels.
Nearpod Silver	To develop or deliver interactive lessons.	Allows the development or delivery of lessons that can be offered in three modes: teacher-fronted, student-paced, or live.	Interactive questions can be embedded in teacher-made or available videos. Up to 40 students per lesson.
iCivics	To engage students in meaningful civics learning.	A non-profit US website and app that provides motivating educational games and lesson plans promoting civics education.	Founded by Justice Sandra Day O'Connor (the first female Justice on the US Supreme Court) to encourage children to become active citizens. Contains lessons for English language learners.

(continued)

Table 11.1. (Cont.)

Digital tool	Instructional purpose	Description	Special features
YouGlish for English	To engage in self-directed learning designed to improve oral skills.	Online tool designed to help users improve their pronunciation and intonation.	Features "Inner Circle" varieties of English and other languages.
JeopardyLabs	To create Jeopardy games or use readily available games.	Online Jeopardy game-design tool. Allows the design of bingo and other games.	The free version makes the games designed available to the public.
Kathy Schrock's Guide to Everything	To provide teachers with tools for professional development in the area of technology.	Features a wealth of tools on assessment, information, digital literacy, pedagogy, and more.	This website is regularly updated and it provides teachers with a wealth of information.

minimal curriculum modification. It can replace traditional paper-and-pencil bingo or Jeopardy games with web-based games that can be easily developed, saved, and revised. In contrast, lessons designed using Nearpod Silver will require significant curriculum redesign; therefore, teachers considering its use will need to plan to spend time learning about its features and design options.

In contrast to Table 11.1, featuring digital tools for lesson and activity planning and delivery, Table 11.2 presents digital tools that can be used for project-based teaching and learning purposes. The two free and easy-to-use digital tools in the table allow students and teachers to engage in creative, engaging, motivating, and meaningful projects, like the design of infographics, photo collages, and brochures. In addition, the tools can be used to engage students in the production of multimodal compositions, which allows writers to shift production from print-only text to the production of compositions that include audio, images, video, and text (Maamuujav et al., 2020).

The last table in this section, Table 11.3 features a variety of digital tools designed to promote meaningful student–student and teacher–student communication through the production of video, audio, or written text. One of the tools on the table, ScreenPal, is an online video-making tool

Table 11.2. Digital Tools for Project-Based Learning

Digital tool	Instructional purpose	Description	Features
Adobe Express	To develop video stories, create flyers and infographics.	Robust, free, online and mobile project design tool.	Similar to Canva, though not as sophisticated as Canva.
Canva	To develop video stories, create flyers and infographics.	Robust, free, video and graphic design tool.	Similar to Adobe Express, though more sophisticated. Widely used for infographic design. Provides templates.

Table 11.3. Digital Tools for Meaningful Communication (Video, Audio, Written)

Digital tool	Instructional purpose	Description	Features
Flip (formerly known as Flipgrid).	To watch and respond to student-made videos and teacher-prompts.	Free video discussion tool (also available in Spanish).	Free of charge, it requires an email address connected to a Microsoft, Google, or Apple account.
Anchor	To have students record and edit their podcasts.	Google product to make podcasts that can be uploaded to Google Podcasts or Spotify, for example.	Free of charge, it has many features that will take time to learn how to use.
Blog	To have students produce and publish their blogs, as well as respond to other students' blogs.	Google-owned Weblog publishing tool that allows the sharing of text, images, and videos.	Free of charge.
ScreenPal (formerly known as Screencast-O-Matic).	To have students or teachers record the screen, webcam, or both.	Online video-making and sharing tool.	Free of charge, it does not require registration.

228 Navigating the English Language Classroom

that teachers can use to make short presentations. In contrast, Flip can be used to engage students in interactive video-based activities. Both tools, ScreenPal and Flip, are very easy to use and do not require major curriculum redesign.

The last digital tool worth describing in this section is the HyperDoc, which is becoming more widely used in the ELT field. The HyperDoc, originally designed for the K-12 classroom, is a practical teacher-designed and self-contained digital lesson that allows students to complete the various steps in the lesson by clicking on the hyperlinks available in the HyperDoc (Highfill et al. 2016). HyperDoc lessons work very well with ELs because they provide students with a cognitive map of how to complete self-directed tasks that require little or no teacher intervention. Figure 11.3 presents an example of a HyperDoc content-based English language lesson titled "Food Waste." As can be seen in the figure, the HyperDoc is visually appealing and allows students to access the content easily since all the steps required to complete the lesson are available in one place.

To conclude, while the technology market provides many more tools than those described in this section, the tools we feature are not only free of charge, but also easy to use and do not require that teachers and students invest time to learn how to use them. ELT professionals are not educational technologists; therefore, it is important that, as they integrate digital tools into their classrooms, they do not lose sight of the fact that the tools should be used to support language objectives.

- *Q5. What are some exciting examples of emerging technologies that are currently used in language classrooms?*

Against the backdrop of the digital tools described in response to Question 4 are several emerging technologies that have great potential for second language teaching and learning. One of these advancements is ChatGPT, an AI chatbot that uses natural language processing to generate dialogue that is often indistinguishable from human interaction. ChatGPT exhibits significant promise for materials design although, as we will discuss, also raises ethical challenges. Though the use of ChatGPT is in its infancy, one of the ways in which it is currently being used in the ELT field involves prompt engineering—the crafting of prompts to train ChatGPT for materials development purposes (Fifield, 2023). Prompt engineering is just in the beginning stages of development and exploitation; however, teachers are already resorting to it since it is a tool that can aid in the design of instructional materials (Fifield, 2023).

Using Digital Tools in the Language Classroom   229

Step 1	Food Waste	Step 2
What is your relationship with food? Take a poll!		Read these questions before watching the video on Step 3.
Step 3		Step 4
Let's watch this video ·· Take notes on the questions from Step 2!		Share your ideas with your classmates.
Step 5 Let's create a Twitter post about food waste! When you finish, post it on Canvas under this week's "Discussion: Food Waste" post.		

Figure 11.3. Food waste HyperDoc lesson.
Source: Natasha Guerrero

Learning how to do prompt engineering requires a step-by-step approach to using ChatGPT. This process could start by providing ChatGPT with instructions that may initially seem specific enough to produce the desired results. For example, the teacher could type something like this: *Produce 10 questions* (use action verbs and specify whether you want questions, sentences, and so on) *for beginner-level ESL students* (specify the students' level of proficiency and the context in which they will be used). This search will result in a list of ten questions. However, if the objective is to develop an activity, then the prompt will need to be much more specific. Figure 11.4 presents a screen capture of the prompt.

The prompt in Figure 11.4 will result in ten questions that integrate action verbs. Now, if the objective is to design a dialog drawing on the ten questions, then the search could be followed by another prompt somewhat similar to the following one: *Utilize the questions generated above to write 2 dialogs of at least 15 lines each suitable for beginner ESL students.* If the dialog needs to be turned into a gap-filled exercise, then the previous prompt can be followed by this prompt: *Insert gaps into the sentences above where students can fill in their own information. Change the speakers to "student 1" and "student 2"*) (Fifield, 2023).

We should note that while working with ChatGPT in a chain of prompts, teachers will be tempted to use the CEFR levels of proficiency. However, at this time, searches using the CEFR levels do not produce consistent and reliable results. Until this happens, teachers may need to rely on terms like "beginner," "intermediate," and so on, as well as "ESL" and "EFL." If these terms do not provide sufficient clarification for ChatGPT, teachers can reword or clarify their prompts by writing something like this: *Substitute academic vocabulary for more spoken terms. Regenerate the last response but shorten/lengthen/add/remove . . .* and so on.

Despite the increased popularity of ChatGPT, as well as Google's Bard and Microsoft Bing's AI, chatbots raise several ethical concerns that teachers should consider as they implement generative AI tools. First, the internet is filled with disinformation; therefore, the output produced by the chatbot may be biased or inaccurate. In addition, the output produced by ChatGPT—and the other chatbots—may infringe on copyright law since it is not uncommon for the internet to reproduce materials that are protected by copyright. Finally, the fact that students in general, and ELs in particular,

Generate a list of 10-wh-questions using the auxiliary verb "do" in simple present tense suitable for beginners in ESL. The subject of each question should be "you." Do not provide answers to the questions. Utilize the following words: play board games, bike, hike, run, exercise, watch TV, read, go to the movies, listen to music, play video games.

Figure 11.4. Sample prompt engineered using ChatGPT.
Source: Nathaniel Fifield

may try to pass ChatGPT-generated output as their own is also problematic; this results in plagiarism, which may stem from students' lack of understanding of academic expectations. This is often the case of younger learners who do not understand academic convention expectations. This may also be the case of lower-level ELs, who lack English language proficiency to paraphrase. Given all of these issues, teachers considering implementing AI tools should do it with extreme caution.

Besides chatbots, two additional innovative technologies that are engaging and offer significant opportunities for language learning are augmented reality (AR) and virtual reality (VR). Both of these technologies leverage computer-generated imagery to create different forms of reality in the digital realm. AR superimposes digital elements onto the users' physical world. VR immerses users into a fully digital environment. The most popular real-world example of AR is Pokémon Go, a game that is designed around its users' ability to find and catch Pokémon in their geographical area. Despite its popularity in the real world, Pokémon may not be well known among ELs, or teachers may not be able (or allowed) to take their students out of the classroom to engage in real-life Pokémon catching activities. Therefore, we propose that teachers engage their students in "Pokémon-inspired" activities. These activities could range from the design of a Pokémon avatar using Canva's free avatar maker followed by pair work or group work in which students share and describe their avatars' features.

Other examples of AR, which have been used in the language classroom, come from companies like IKEA and Amazon, as well as TikTok's filters. Using AR, teachers could ask B1 ELs working with the IKEA app, for example, to view and compare how two pieces of furniture will fit in their own space. Then students could be asked to use comparative adjectives and choose the piece of furniture that would fit best in their space (Issagholian, 2022).

VR involves real-time simulation environments created entirely digitally and achieved using computer technology. VR can be classified into three categories: nonimmersive, which is the case of video games experienced through gaming consoles; semi-immersive, also known as mixed-reality environments, where users engage with avatars displayed on a computer screen or through a headset that presents a blend of the real and virtual worlds; and fully immersive, wherein users are entirely involved in a digital world, completely isolated from their physical surroundings, a state which is almost always facilitated by the use of a headset. While VR technology offers great affordances for the language classroom, so far its use has been limited to Google Earth or Second Life, a desktop platform that has worlds language learners can use to engage in communicative activities with the residents of the various worlds. More recently, the use of VR has involved engaging students in 360-degree videos through the use of Google Cardboard VR headsets (Bonner & Reinders, 2018).

Currently, there are several emerging VR apps, though they require paid subscriptions. Of those that do not require a paid subscription (unless users want to get unlimited storage), we can mention vTime XR, a fully immersive, free social VR network where students can participate in virtual meet-ups in a variety of locations. Similar to ChatGPT, the use of VR apps in the language classroom is in its infancy, as issues of cost, accessibility, appropriateness, and teacher preparation currently hinder their widespread application. In addition, much like ChatGPT, the integration of VR technology in the language classroom needs to be done with caution. As explained by Issagholian (2022), the long-term use of VR technology may cause addiction, mental health disorders, and even physical problems like dehydration, exhaustion, and cardiac arrhythmia.

The final example of new technologies in the ELT field comes from work on computational thinking, understood as "an analytic approach to solving problems utilizing concepts essential to computing" (Wing, 2006, as cited in Jacob et al., 2018). The work by Warschauer and his associates (e.g., Jacob et al., 2018; Jacob et al., 2020; Jacob et al., 2022) has led to the implementation of a variety of computational thinking projects designed to integrate Scratch, a block-based program created by MIT, with English learners in K-12 settings in the United States and other countries around the world.

A basic lesson designed to teach students how to use computational thinking (Jacob, 2018) could start by engaging students in a discussion on the notion of algorithms and how these apply to computational thinking. Then, students would be introduced to the different types of blocks (known as "sprites") available on Scratch, as well as the colors associated with them (motion blocks are blue, looks blocks are purple, sound blocks are magenta, and so on)—with a focus on the most basic blocks. Then students would be directed to Scratch (https://scratch.mit.edu/), where they would pick sprites from the Scratch library to create an interactive collage about themselves. To make their projects interactive—or to make the project look like a movie—students would select an event block (yellow). Once students select the event block, they can publish their Scratch product. Figure 11.5 presents a simple Scratch project produced after two hours of instruction.

Using Digital Tools in the Language Classroom   233

Figure 11.5. Scratch project: About me.
Source: Suky Kaur

The research training programs led by Warschauer and his associates (see Jacob et al., 2018; Jacob et al., 2020; Jacob et al., 2022) have shown that computational thinking greatly contributes to the development of ELs' critical thinking skills, computer science learning, and students' identities. However, its implementation in college-level composition courses and intensive English programs is not yet fully realized. It could be the case that time limitations and lack of teacher preparation prevent instructors from integrating computational thinking into their teaching.

Big Picture and Bottom Line

This is an exciting time because the technology field offers a wide menu of options for novice teachers working in a variety of environments and under different conditions. What is crucial is that the integration of digital technology in the language classroom be done for meaningful purposes, driven by curriculum needs, and designed to promote language and motivational benefits. To this end, teachers' instructional practices need to be guided by a principled approach to the selection and integration of digital tools in the classroom. Only in this way will teachers avoid the common pitfall of integrating digital tools just because they are popular among their students.

Food for Thought

1. After reviewing the information in this chapter, select 1) two of the digital tools described in this chapter, and 2) another tool of your choice, and evaluate their appropriateness and relevance to your classes using the "digital tool evaluation criteria" (Figure 11.2).

2. Identify a digital tool you have used or use as a student or teacher. Then read the five principles supporting the integration of digital tools described in this chapter. Finally, decide whether your use of the digital tool is supported by the five guiding principles.

3. Create a ChatGPT account. Using the steps to prompt engineering described in this chapter, design an activity that is appropriate for one of your classes. Do you agree with our assertion about the benefits of using ChatGPT for materials development? Are there other purposes for which ChatGPT could be used?

References

Bell, J. (2018, Jan 22). *Guest post: Getting started with Flipgrid.* Larry Ferlazzo's websites of the day. https://larryferlazzo.edublogs.org/2018/01/22/guest-post-getting-started-with-flipgrid/

Bonner, E., & Reinders, H. (2018). Augmented and virtual reality in the language classroom: Practical ideas. *Teaching English with Technology, 18*(3), 33–53.

Cummins, J., Brown, K., & Sayers, D. (2007). *Literacy, technology, and diversity: Teaching for success in changing times.* Pearson.

Ferlazzo, L. D. (n.d.). Larry Ferlazzo's websites of the day. https://larryferlazzo.edublogs.org/

Fifield, N. (2023, October 26–28). *Crafting ESL materials with AI: A chatGPT prompt workshop* [Conference workshop]. Annual conference of CATESOL (California Teachers of English to Speakers of Other Languages), Alameda, CA, United States.

Grabe, M., & Grabe, C. (2004). *Integrating technology for meaningful learning* (4th ed.). Houghton Mifflin.

Graves, K. (2000). *Designing language courses: A guide for teachers.* Heinle and Heinle.

Highfill, L., Hilton, K., & Landis, S. (2016). *The HyperDoc handbook: Digital lesson design using Google apps*. EdTechTeam Press.

Issagholian, N. (2022, March 22–25). Virtual and augmented reality in language learning: Advantages, considerations, and ethical concerns [Colloquium presentation]. In L D. Kamhi-Stein (Organizer), *Advances in technology for language teacher preparation* [Colloquium], TESOL 2022 International Convention, Pittsburgh, PA, United States.

Jacob, S. (2018, October 10). Computational thinking for ELs [Paper presentation]. TESL 5650: Using computers in the language classroom. California State University, Los Angeles.

Jacob, S., Nguyen, H., Garcia, L., Richardson, D., & Warschauer, M. (2020, March). Teaching computational thinking to multilingual students through inquiry-based learning. In *2020 research on equity and sustained participation in engineering, computing, and technology (RESPECT)*. IEEE. https://doi.org/10.1109/RESPECT49803.2020.9272487

Jacob, S., Nguyen, H., Tofel-Grehl, C., Richardson, D., & Warschauer, M. (2018). Teaching computational thinking to English learners. *NYS TESOL Journal*, *5*(2), 12–24.

Jacob, S. R., Montoya, J., & Warschauer, M. (2022). Exploring the intersectional development of computer science identities in young Latinas. *Teachers College Record*, *124*(5), 166–185.

Koehler, M. J., & Mishra, P. (2009). What is technological pedagogical content knowledge? *Contemporary Issues in Technology and Teacher Education*, *9*(1), 60–70.

Li, L. (2017). *New technologies and language learning*. Palgrave.

Maamuujav, U, Krishnan, J., & Collins, P. (2020). The utility of infographics in L2 writing classes: A practical strategy to scaffold writing development. *TESOL Journal*, *11*(2), Article e484. https://doi.org/10.1002/tesj.484

McDonough, J., Shaw, C., & Masuhara, H. (2013). *Materials and methods in ELT: A teacher's guide* (3rd. ed.). Wiley-Blackwell.

Puentedura, R. R. (2013). SAMR: Moving from enhancement to transformation [Presentation slides]. 2013 AISNSW ICT management and leadership conference, Canberra, Australia. http://www.hippasus.com/rrpweblog/archives/2013/05/29/SAMREnhancementToTransformation.pdf

Richards, J. C. (2017). *Curriculum development in language teaching* (2nd ed.). Cambridge University Press.

CHAPTER 12

Integrating Learning Management Systems

Contextualization

Learning management systems (LMSs) are software programs designed for the administration, documentation, and delivery of educational courses. They currently play a central role in the English language classroom. This chapter describes a framework for selecting an LMS as well as a set of principles informing the design and implementation of a course hosted on an LMS.

Case Study: It's Time to Use a Learning Management System!

A couple of years ago, an MA in TESOL student-teacher, who was a very experienced instructor, decided to enroll in the teaching practicum course offered in his program. His goal from the outset was to integrate an LMS into his classes. At the time of the practicum course, our student-teacher was leading various English for academic purposes (EAP) classes for sixteen contact hours per week in a small, privately-run intensive English program (IEP). His classes ranged from CEFR Level B2 (high intermediate) to TOEFL and International English Language Testing System (IELTS) preparation courses.

Our student-teacher's purpose in integrating an LMS into his teaching was two-fold. First, he was concerned about how complicated it had become to keep track of the course files because he mainly relied on his email and multiple Google Drive folders to retrieve, store, and distribute instructional materials. Therefore, he thought that an LMS would allow him to better manage his work. Second, the administration of the IEP had not adopted

236

an LMS and left all decisions on whether or how to integrate an LMS up to individual instructors. Regardless of the type of program in which teachers work and whether their program is in an English as a second language (ESL) or English as a foreign language (EFL) setting, teachers and students can benefit from the use of an LMS. The goal of this chapter is to provide novice teachers with a system for finding, evaluating, and implementing LMSs into their teaching.

Common Concerns

The questions below are designed to guide the discussion on the integration of LMSs in the English language classroom. In framing the questions, we paid attention to the principles that English language instructors can use to guide their decision-making process. Each of the questions addressed in this chapter is presented below.

- *Q1. What is an LMS and why should teachers use one?*
- *Q2. What criteria should teachers follow in selecting a learning management system (if they have the flexibility to do so)?*
- *Q3. What are the principles that should guide the design of a course available on an LMS?*

Effective Steps for Working with a Learning Management System

• *Q1. What is an LMS and why should teachers use one?*

An LMS is a software program designed for the administration, documentation, and delivery of educational courses. At a very minimum, an LMS can be used as a repository of materials. Doing this would allow instructors to have their materials for a specific class saved and organized in an LMS for easy retrieval. However, currently LMSs are used for far more extensive purposes, like delivering instruction and engaging students in the learning process.

LMSs began to be adopted in the 1990s. Initially, LMSs like WebCT and Blackboard—which eventually merged under the Blackboard name—were used as a way to enhance, and not replace—face-to-face (F2F) instruction. In the 1990s, the most widely used feature of the LMSs was the discussion board, which engaged students in asynchronous communication outside the confines of the F2F classroom (Kamhi-Stein, 2000). Currently, in addition to their use in F2F classrooms, LMSs are used in two different types of courses: blended and online. Blended courses utilize a flipped model of instruction. In this model, students participate in an asynchronous lesson, designed to present new content or language. After this, they take part in a F2F or synchronous online lesson, where they apply the information presented to them in the asynchronous portion. Although descriptions of the blended model of instruction have focused on the percentage of time that should be spent in the F2F and the online classrooms, the reality is that central to this instructional model is that responsibility for learning greatly falls on the students since they must work independently for much of the class. The instructor's responsibility, as we will explain in this chapter, is to create conditions to promote learning (Caufield, 2011).

LMSs are also utilized in online classrooms, which can operate in either a synchronous or asynchronous manner. In synchronous online classes, all instruction is done in real time since all students meet at the same time through videoconferencing platforms like Zoom, Webex, Microsoft Teams, or even Skype—one of the first voice and videoconferencing tools that became popular around the world. In contrast to synchronous online instruction, in asynchronous courses there is very limited, if any, contact with the instructor, who delivers instruction through the LMS. Much like in the case of the blended model, in the asynchronous course responsibility for learning lies with students, though to a much higher degree than in the case of the blended course (for further information on the various models of instruction, see Chapter 13 in this volume).

While there is a large and growing selection of LMSs on the market, the most popular are Canvas, Moodle, Blackboard, and Schoology. All of these LMSs are cloud-based, eliminating the need for software installation, maintenance, or updates, as they are managed and supported by the companies that develop the LMSs. In contrast to Schoology, which has been specifically developed with a US K-12 audience in mind, all of the other LMSs cater to a broad range of contexts. These include community colleges and universities, as well as intensive English programs (IEPs) in "Inner Circle" countries—settings where English is considered the first or dominant language. Furthermore, these LMSs are utilized in both publicly- and privately-funded English as a foreign language (EFL) teaching institutions globally.

Currently, the most widely used LMS in US community colleges, universities, and IEPs is Canvas. It could be argued that the reason for this is that, in contrast to Moodle, for example, Canvas does not require a significant investment in instructional technology (IT) and customization; therefore, it is easy to use by non-IT experts and busy instructors. Canvas also offers a free version, which, although it does not have all the features of the subscription-based Canvas version, is quite robust and, more importantly, is very easy to use. Moodle also offers a free version; however, to create a course on Moodle, teachers need to have extensive technical skills since the burden of customization lies with the course designer. In addition to its free version, Moodle offers a variety of paid plans with different upgrades and capabilities. Although these versions are significantly more user-friendly than the free ones, they are meant to be used by large numbers of users and are quite costly; therefore, they do not necessarily work for individual instructors on a budget.

In contrast to Moodle and Canvas, Blackboard does not offer a free version. Given all these reasons, the free version of Canvas has become a very popular LMS among ESL and EFL instructors. These educators typically work in smaller programs, such as privately-run IEPs in the United States or neighborhood-based EFL programs owned by local instructors. These instructors are similar to the instructor we described in the case study. They do not necessarily work for programs that have adopted LMSs, and the responsibility of selecting one to organize and deliver instruction falls on them.

We should note that Google Classroom is another platform that is widely used around the world. Google Classroom, although not technically an LMS, is a popular platform for English language instructors thanks to Google's global presence. Google Classroom works exceptionally well across devices and Google products, including Google Workspace for Education (including Google Docs, Google Slides, Jamboard, Google Calendar, YouTube, and Google Forms). In addition, Google Classroom provides users with seamless integration of Google Meet, a free videoconferencing tool that has quickly become a competitor to Zoom since it allows for 60-minute meetings at no charge—in contrast to Zoom's 40-minute free-of-charge meetings.

Google Classroom lacks some functionalities found in Canvas and Blackboard. These other platforms allow designers to manage content, assign and grade tasks, and facilitate interaction with peers and teachers through discussion threads. Additionally, they can be set to require that students read their peers' and instructors' posts before responding. Another source of interactivity available in traditional LMSs—not available in Google Classroom—is built-in conferencing tools. These tools allow for whole class or selected group conferences and chats. Another feature that Google Classroom does not have is one that traditional LMSs offer: the ability to embed apps that allow students to complete tasks (on Padlet or Flip, for example) *without* having to click on a link that takes students to external websites. This feature contributes to the ease of use of LMSs for ESL/EFL students since it reduces the number of clicks that second language learners must make to reach their class materials. At the same time, embedding apps rather than providing clickable links provides students with rich visuals that contribute to reducing the cognitive load. Following is an example of a visually appealing Padlet activity that was embedded in a Canvas course (Figure 12.1). Figure 12.1 shows that, to complete the task assigned by the instructor, all students needed to do was to click on the + sign (not visible) at the bottom of the page and start typing.

In summary, as we explained in this section, ESL/EFL teachers who work for small IEPs or neighborhood institutes do not have access to a paid LMS subscription. Neither do they have access to IT support. Therefore, it is not uncommon for these teachers to face the burden of selecting and designing a course on a free-of-charge LMS. The current LMS market offers these

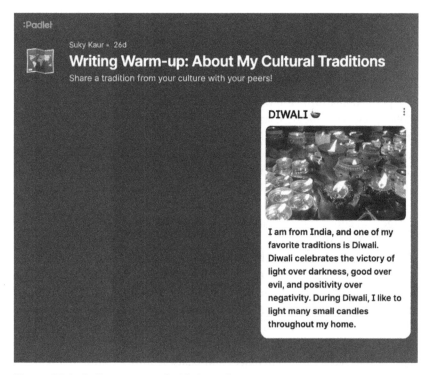

Figure 12.1. Padlet activity embedded in a Canvas course.
Source: Suky Kaur

teachers, who regardless of the setting in which they teach are on a very tight budget, a variety of options from which to choose. After identifying the basic features of the various LMSs available for instruction, novice teachers are ready to implement in-depth criteria for the evaluation and adoption of an LMS that suits their needs.

- **Q2. What criteria should teachers follow in selecting a learning management system (if they have the flexibility to do so)?**

English language instructors are well aware of the importance of developing their courses by drawing on information obtained through a needs analysis (Richards, 2017). Needs analyses provide instructors with much-needed information about their students' needs and wants, the content to be taught, the students' beliefs about the teaching and learning process, as well as issues of assessment. In addition to the central role that needs analyses play in the course design process, equally important are course materials and, more specifically, textbooks since they provide coherence and cohesion to the course at hand.

In this section, we propose the notion that in selecting an LMS, teachers evaluate a variety of LMSs in the same way they would evaluate a textbook for adoption. To find an LMS that best meets instructors' and students' needs, we recommend considering the following criteria:

1. **Identify the purposes for which the LMS will be used.**
   This is an important issue to consider since an LMS can be used for specific and limited purposes, as would be the case of instructors who teach F2F classes and use the LMS as a repository of course materials that students can access before, during, and after class. A more extensive use of an LMS would be in the case of instructors who teach blended/hybrid courses. In this model, the F2F setting (or synchronous online setting) engages students in hands-on, meaningful activities that stem from the work done asynchronously in the LMS. This system is utilized for direct instruction, which can involve teaching language, content, or both, often through media like videos and PowerPoint presentations. In the case of the blended/hybrid course, the LMS will most probably also be used to engage students in asynchronous discussions in which they can participate in a variety of formats, including text, audio, and video. Students would also complete quizzes and polls, submit assignments, and receive feedback in different

formats (text, audio, video). The third and most extensive use of an LMS occurs in asynchronous online classes, in which students and instructors use the LMS for all teaching and learning purposes. As instructors get ready to embark on their course design process, it is important to review the various LMS features and make a conscious decision about which LMS features will be used, why they will be used, and how they will be used.

2. **Decide whether students will be required to interact with content, content and peers, and/or content and instructor.**

   While LMSs like Canvas and Blackboard provide students with features that allow student–student interaction, Google Classroom is limited in this respect. Therefore, in selecting an LMS, it is important to consider who or what students will be expected to interact with.

3. **Decide whether access to the LMS will be equitable.**

   Regardless of whether students and teachers are teaching digital natives (people born in the digital age) or digital immigrants (those who adopted technology during their adult life), it is important to provide equitable access to the LMS course. Therefore, as instructors select the LMS to use in their course, they need to make sure that the LMS can be accessed through a desktop, a laptop, a tablet, or a smartphone. In fact, regardless of the tool used to access the LMS, the LMS needs to be accessible to *all* students. This means that the LMS course is free of barriers and promotes equitable access to the course materials. The framework known as Universal Design for Learning (UDL) is designed to enhance learning by providing equitable access to all students by drawing on research focusing on effective learning. Initially, UDL was meant to be implemented with students with disabilities; however, more recently, the education field has embraced UDL as a framework to support all learners. In the case of language learners, there are several features in the UDL framework that are designed to provide equitable access to an LMS course. These include, but are not limited to, the use of:

   a. consistent and preset text styles and sizes throughout the LMS course;

   b. color combinations that provide contrast between foreground and background;

   c. images and figures that are supported by alternative text;

   d. clearly labeled tables;

e. preset layouts and bullet-pointed and numbered lists;

f. captioned instructional videos.

All of these features, designed to provide accessibility to LMS users, should be exploited since they will result in equitable access to diverse students (CAST, 2018). Well-known LMSs like Canvas and Blackboard are designed to provide features that are consistent with UDL. In fact, they provide diverse learners, like language students, organizational advantages that Google Classroom does not necessarily offer. Therefore, instructors who choose to use Google Classroom will have to pay special attention to how they structure their courses to make them accessible to all students.

4. **Decide which of the LMSs under consideration provides you the most benefits at no charge.**

The student-teacher in our study adopted the Free-for-Teacher version of Canvas. This choice was driven by the platform's high functionality and cost-effectiveness, which is a critical consideration for instructors lacking institutional or IT support. In addition, the free version of Canvas offers strong functionality, is easy to use, and provides equitable access features. On the other hand, MoodleCloud offers a free 45-day trial for a maximum number of 200 users, and Blackboard allows a 30-day free trial. Therefore, unless the teacher's school or institution acquires a subscription, these platforms may be out of the question due to their high subscription costs.

In summary, not all LMSs are created equal. Evaluating an LMS as one would evaluate a textbook will help teachers gain a clear understanding of the strengths and weaknesses of the LMS. Once teachers have made their selection, they are ready to design their LMS courses. In the next section, we identify the principles that should guide the LMS course design process.

• Q3. What are the principles that should guide the design of an LMS course?

Regardless of whether teaching is done F2F, in a blended classroom—in which instruction is done in part synchronously and in part asynchronously—or in a completely asynchronous format, we see good teaching on an LMS as relying on four interrelated principles. These are: 1) backward design; 2) scaffolding; 3) transparency; and 4) instructor and student presence for cognitive and social engagement.

244   Navigating the English Language Classroom

The first LMS design principle, backward design, is central to the field of ESL/EFL curriculum development (Richards, 2017). However, backward design plays an even more central role when instructors have to develop an LMS course because there is an extra layer of complexity added to the course design and instructional process. In practical terms, backward design involves aligning student learning outcomes with the various modules or weekly content. This should then be reinforced by the activities contained within each module or week. To ensure that this happens, before the beginning of the term, instructors could start by filling out a worksheet like the one shown in Figure 12.2 as the first step in the course design process.

As instructors fill out the worksheet, they should pay attention to the extent to which student learning outcomes are supported by the objectives in the weekly modules. The weekly activities, instructional materials, and assignments should be designed to support the objectives set for each week or module. These, in turn, should align with and work towards the overall objectives that students are expected to achieve by the end of the course.

After completing the worksheet, instructors are now ready to move on to the syllabus design process. However, in working on the syllabus, instructors will go through a process of backward *and* forward design (Richards, 2017). This involves engaging in an iterative process in which instructors draw on the information contained in the worksheet to develop the course syllabus.

Course Title: **Student Learning Outcomes:** **By the end of the course, students will be able to:**			
Module/ Week	**Objectives**	**Activities and Instructional Materials**	**Assignments**
Module/ Week 1			
Module/ Week 2			
Module/ Week 3			
Module/ Week 4			

Figure 12.2. Aligning student learning outcomes with weekly activities and assignments.

As they work on it, they make revisions to the worksheet, which may subsequently result in syllabus modifications. Traditionally, in the language classroom, students receive a copy of the course syllabus. However, for greater transparency purposes, students will benefit from receiving a copy of the finalized worksheet too, since it will contribute to greater student awareness about the course expectations and the ways in which the course expectations will be met.

The second principle, scaffolding, is widely implemented in the ESL/EFL classroom. Scaffolding involves providing students with the support they need to complete course tasks (Wood et al., 1976). In the context of the F2F classroom, it is the instructor or more knowledgeable peers who, through scaffolds, help language learners achieve the independent functioning level. In the context of an LMS, scaffolds can be provided in two ways. First, they can be provided by sequencing weekly modules in such a way that activities move from guided to independent practice, a principle implemented in lesson planning for language learning (Purgason, 2014). Scaffolding will also be achieved by breaking down complex tasks into manageable ones. When doing this, the emphasis should be placed on making sure that students understand how each task contributes to the completion of the final one. To achieve this objective, the instructor could write or record (through video or audio) a simple statement explaining how each individual task will help students achieve a course objective. In doing this, it is important to use clear and simple instructions, provide models of expected products (sample papers, for example, just as we would in the language classroom), and identify challenges faced or questions asked by previous classes or provide a list of dos and don'ts about the task at hand. Central to these ideas is that in the LMS course, instructors will not be able to answer questions as they would in the F2F classroom. Therefore, in designing the LMS course, instructors need to predict potential challenges and questions faced by students and preempt them as they design the course.

In addition to the above scaffolds, other scaffolds are directly relevant to LMSs. These involve releasing content strategically and gradually—what is known as "conditional release" (Fisher et al., 2015)—as a means to prevent students from: 1) feeling overwhelmed and instead keep them focused on the content already released; and 2) skipping tasks that may be critical to the construction of knowledge. Conditional release needs to be supported by tasks designed to make students accountable for learning. For example, a video presentation designed to provide input on the use of the simple present needs to be followed by an exercise or a quiz that allows students to check how much they understood from the presentation. Having students complete a task that is based on content that has been released strategically ensures that students avoid engaging in a process of clicking on pages without any particular focus, and instead they work with and through the content presented as much as they would after a teacher presentation in the F2F classroom.

The third principle that should guide the design of an LMS is centered around the notion of transparency. It is a known fact that in the F2F classroom, instructors can provide immediate clarification of ideas, backtrack when they realize that there is a need for further clarification, explain the rationale of what they expect students to do, or provide as many examples or models as needed before having students engage in an activity. In designing an LMS course, it is important to keep in mind that none of the above modifications are possible. Therefore, it is critical to provide clear information on *what* students are expected to do as well as on *how* and *why* they are expected to complete a task. The latter two features are part of the Transparency in Learning and Teaching (TILT) framework (Winkelmes, 2016), which is concerned with providing equitable access to higher education. Despite an apparent lack of focus on language learners, we view the TILT framework as central to language teaching. Providing students with an understanding of the *what, how,* and *why* of a module (or lesson) would contribute to helping students become mindful of why they are doing what they are doing. This, in turn, could result in higher student motivation and investment.

Transparency in a Canvas course involves preparing students for the forthcoming module (or lesson). This is achieved by giving them an overview of the topic covered in the forthcoming module or lesson and providing step-by-step instructions on what the readings (for example, chapters in assigned books or journals) and tasks to complete during the week (for example, participating in an online discussion or view a video) are, as well as on how to complete the tasks. In addition, transparency would involve explaining why the module (or lesson) is relevant to the class in which students are enrolled. Following is an example of what transparency looks like in an educational sociolinguistics course offered in an MA in teaching English to speakers of other languages (TESOL) program.

This week, our focus will be on the topics of code-switching and translanguaging in the language classroom. Code-switching and translanguaging are important topics because they have direct implications for your current and future teaching. In preparation for our F2F class, you will: 1) review the reading guide on this page; 2) read the

(Cont.)

> relevant materials; and 3) participate in a Canvas discussion designed to help you reflect on where you stand on the ideas presented by the authors.
>
> As you engage in the discussion, remember to respond to your peers' questions and comments. Agree or disagree with them by providing a rationale for your ideas. Remember to call your peers by their first names and use a professional tone. Enjoy the readings and the discussion!

Although the above example is from an MA in TESOL course, transparency is critical for *all* students, regardless of their level of English language proficiency and the course they are taking. Providing students with a clear understanding of the *what*, *how*, and *why* of a lesson will promote better learning since it will give students a cognitive map or a rationale for what they are doing in the classroom.

The fourth critical component in the design of an LMS course is instructor and student presence for cognitive and social engagement (Darby, 2019). In our years of teaching, we have found that, regardless of whether we teach in a F2F, blended/hybrid, or asynchronous environment, instructor presence results in higher student motivation and involvement (a point made by Darby, 2019). Higher instructor presence can be achieved by posting instructional videos, making announcements, providing feedback to students, and engaging students in threaded discussions and chats. Instructor presence can also be achieved by giving feedback to students, making themselves available for instructor–student meetings, and offering instructor webinars—prerecorded or live—focusing, for example, on a topic of difficulty for students. To achieve high student presence in the form of student engagement, instructors can engage students in extensive opportunities for student–student interactions through group activities, group projects, and asynchronous and synchronous discussions. Student engagement can also be achieved through scaffolded activities and conditionally released lessons.

Instructor and student presence are also necessary to create a classroom community. To achieve this goal, instructors and students should introduce themselves through video, voice, or text (or a combination of the three) at the beginning of the term. These introductions should be personalized and accompanied by pictures so that students can see the humanity behind their instructor. Doing this would contribute to breaking the wall between students and instructors. Other strategies contributing to creating a classroom community include encouraging students to communicate with their peers by calling them by their first names, engaging students in peer feedback by teaching them how to give meaningful feedback, and designing activities that require that students collaborate. At the most basic level, instructor presence can be achieved when instructors contact individual students asking them how they are doing or why they were absent or did not participate much in a previous class. While this may seem overly personal, we have found it to be critical in promoting a sense of instructor caring and student belonging in the course.

While all of the above principles are central to the design of a course available on an LMS, two caveats are in order. First, an LMS course should be seen as a living tool. This means that in designing a course, it is important to provide structure and at the same time be flexible. For example, the course instructor could consider negotiating LMS deadlines with students to make class assignments more manageable for students *and* the course instructor, encourage students to lead LMS activities, and invite students to lead discussions focusing on topics of their interest.

The second caveat that needs to be considered when creating an LMS course is that instructors need to implement the principle that "what is said in the course stays in the course." Student privacy is central to creating an atmosphere of instructor–student and student–student respect. We learned this a few years ago when, surfing online, we found a US university practicum course in which sensitive discussion postings were available to anyone. The lesson for us was to always make sure we check the privacy features of our LMS courses.

Big Picture and Bottom Line

Using an LMS will enhance the teaching and learning process and, at the same time, make novice English language instructors' professional lives more manageable. We recommend that as teachers embark on the LMS selection and design process they "start small" and focus on one course until the designer feels the model implemented is ready to be replicated in other courses. Even when instructors are satisfied with the LMS course they have designed, it's important to remain open-minded and flexible. Instructors should not hesitate to make adjustments to the LMS course while the term is in progress. Students often appreciate such changes since they understand they are intended to better meet their needs.

Food for Thought

1. After reviewing the information in this chapter, find two colleagues who have been using two of the LMSs described in this chapter and interview them to understand:
   a. The principles they follow in making their courses available on an LMS.
   b. The challenges they face in designing their LMS courses.
   c. The benefits of using the LMSs selected.
2. Drawing on the information in this chapter, identify two changes that you would make to your teaching in relation to the use of LMSs.
3. If you have used an LMS as a student or as a novice teacher, identify two or three modifications you would make that draw on the ideas presented in this chapter.

References

CAST. (2018). *The UDL guidelines version 2.2.* https://udlguidelines.cast.org

Caufield, J. (2011). *How to design and teach a hybrid course: Achieving student-centered learning through blended classroom, online, and experiential activities.* Stylus.

Darby, D. (with Lang, J. M.) (2019). *Small teaching online: Applying learning science in online classes.* Jossey-Bass.

Fisher, L., Brinthaupt, T. M., Gardner, J., & Raffo, D. (2015). The effects of conditional release of course materials on student performance. *Journal of Student Success and Retention, 2*(1). https://www.jossr.org/wp-content/uploads/2015/11/CR-Research-FisherFinal-Sept23-15.pdf

Kamhi-Stein, L. D. (2000). Looking to the future of TESOL teacher education: Web-based bulletin board discussions in a methods course. *TESOL Quarterly, 34*(3), 423–455.

Purgason, K. B. (2014). Lesson planning in second/foreign language teaching. In M. Celce-Murcia, D. M. Brinton, & M. A. Snow (Eds.), *Teaching English as a second or foreign language* (4th ed., pp. 362–379). Heinle Cengage Learning.

Richards, J. C. (2017). *Curriculum development in language teaching* (2nd. ed.). Cambridge University Press.

Winkelmes, M-A. (2016). *Transparency in learning and teaching project.* TILT Higher Ed. https://tilthighered.com/transparency

Wood, D., Bruner, J. S., & Ross, G. (1976). The role of tutoring in problem solving. *Journal of Child Psychology and Child Psychiatry, 17*(2), 89–100. https://doi.org/10.1111/j.1469-7610.1976.tb00381.x

CHAPTER 13

Teaching beyond
the Face-to-Face Classroom

Contextualization

Chapter 11 in this volume focuses on the integration of digital tools in the language classroom. Chapter 12 deals with learning management systems (LMSs). This chapter is complementary to Chapters 11 and 12 in that it focuses on virtual classrooms; that is, classrooms in which teaching and learning occur beyond the face-to-face (F2F) environment. The chapter describes the various models of instruction that go beyond F2F classrooms. Then it describes the affordances and challenges provided by online synchronous environments and identifies a variety of strategies teachers can implement to actively engage students in learning. The chapter concludes with a list of teacher-implemented strategies designed to create an equitable environment that contributes to an inclusive learning community.

Case Study: This Synchronous Online Class Is Way Different from My F2F classes!

Liza, the novice instructor in this case study, was assigned to teach a synchronous online course in a community-based English as a second language (ESL) program. As Liza opened her class, she quickly observed her students were not comfortable participating through Zoom, the videoconferencing platform she was required to use to deliver instruction. In fact, after asking her students a couple of questions about their prior use of videoconferencing platforms, she noticed that for most of her students, this was the first time taking a synchronous online class. Most of Liza's students were working full-time and had families to support. Therefore, despite their lack of familiarity with synchronous online instruction, they decided to take the plunge and enroll in the class because it was more convenient than attending F2F classes. Our novice teacher initially panicked. Although she had received training in how to teach online, she wondered how she could lead the ESL class and, at the same time, teach her students how to be comfortable using Zoom to participate in a synchronous online course. In the end, Liza's students met the course objectives and developed a sense of comfort in the Zoom environment. In fact, on the last day of class, Liza's class organized a digital potluck, something that Liza would not have predicted when the term started.

Liza's initial concerns about the virtual classroom are not uncommon for novice teachers. Although they are well prepared to teach in F2F environments, the reality of the English language teaching (ELT) job market around the world now requires that teachers also be able to deliver instruction in online settings. For this reason, this chapter focuses on the strengths and weaknesses of virtual classrooms and identifies a variety of strategies teachers can implement to help students develop a sense of belonging and maximize student engagement.

Common Concerns

The questions below are designed to guide novice teachers as they make decisions about their instructional practices in virtual classrooms. The questions are meant to provide novice teachers with a starting point in their thinking about factors that contribute to and challenge the successful delivery of instruction in a variety of online settings, with a special focus on synchronous online environments.

- *Q1. What are the various models of instruction beyond the F2F classroom?*
- *Q2. What are the limitations of videoconferencing platforms, and how can teachers address such limitations to promote ESL/EFL student engagement in their synchronous online classes?*
- *Q3. How can teachers create an equitable community of learners in synchronous online environments?*

Effective Practices for Teaching beyond the F2F Classroom

- *Q1. What are the various models of instruction beyond the F2F classroom?*

The ELT field has changed significantly over the last few years. Instruction is no longer limited to the confines of the F2F classroom. In fact, besides this traditional model, several other instructional models have grown in popularity. One of these, *blended learning*, is a flexible model that looks different depending on institutional requirements and expectations (Eaton, 2020). Blended instruction can be viewed on a spectrum. At one end of the spectrum is the traditional blended model of instruction, in which students participate in F2F classes and synchronous online instruction. A variation of the blended model is the *blended/hybrid model* which offers a combination of F2F and asynchronous online instruction. At the other end of the spectrum is bichronous online learning, which integrates features of asynchronous and synchronous online instruction. Regardless of the format the blended model takes, the assumption is that instruction is flipped. What this means is that the F2F or synchronous online portion of the lesson is dedicated to helping students apply the information they are presented with during the asynchronous portion of the lesson.

A more recent model that grew out of the blended model is known as *hyflex* (hybrid/flexible). In this model, students are given the option of attending classes either F2F or synchronously online through a videoconferencing tool. All students participate as part of the same class and the course objectives are the same for all students (Martin et al., 2020).

In contrast to blended learning, online instruction can be synchronous or asynchronous. Synchronous online courses are those in which all instruction is done in real time, since all students are expected to attend the class at the same time, though this can be done from any geographical location. Asynchronous online courses are those in which all the content is delivered online through an LMS (for information on LMSs, see Chapter 12). Although no F2F instruction is done in this model, there may be individual student–teacher meetings scheduled to address student concerns about the course. Massive open online courses (MOOCs) are the last online instruction model. By definition, MOOCs are online courses that are massive and open to an unlimited number of participants who are not enrolled in any particular institution (Sokolik, 2022).

The models of instruction that include videoconferencing tools, and more specifically Zoom, have been in use for several years. In fact, in the 2010s Zoom was a niche tool used by tech companies, and it was not until

2020, with the COVID-19 pandemic, that Zoom became a nearly indispensable tool around the world (Bailenson, 2021; Molla, 2020). Although there are other videoconferencing platforms (such as Google Meet, Microsoft Teams, Webex, Skype, among others), Zoom has become the default platform in academia (Bailenson, 2021). Some of its strengths include its easy access and consistent look, its audio and video qualities, its flexible screen view and voice detection capabilities, its live chat box, and its host controls (MVS Audio Visual, 2023). Despite its many strengths, Zoom also presents some weaknesses that create challenges for synchronous online instruction. The next section identifies some of its weaknesses, especially concerning ESL and English as a foreign language (EFL) students.

- • *Q2. What are the limitations of videoconferencing platforms, and how can teachers address such limitations to promote ESL/EFL student engagement in their synchronous online classes?*

F2F interactions have traditionally played an important role in the language classroom (Brown, 2014). Teachers are well prepared to engage students in interactive activities in F2F settings. However, the nature of Zoom—and other videoconferencing platforms, which have not been specifically designed for instructional purposes, present a variety of limitations. If these limitations are not addressed, they may curtail the students' ability to interact in synchronous online classes (Cheung, 2021, Kohnke & Moorhouse, 2022; Moorhouse et al., 2023).

The educational psychology and ELT fields have specifically identified at least six technical and pedagogical limitations of Zoom—though the limitations are also characteristic of other videoconferencing platforms. The first limitation is the reduced interpersonal distance between participants—what Bailenson (2021) calls "the eye gaze at a close distance" (p. 2). This short distance makes communication awkward since the close and direct view of one another's eyes is typical of intimate relationships. The Zoom environment also affects participants owing to the constant self-evaluation prompted by Zoom's self-view. As explained by Bailenson (2021), this issue can be easily solved by changing the settings to "hide self-view." However, in our experience observing synchronous online ESL/EFL classes offered through Zoom, the hide-self-view setting is hardly ever used. The third limitation of the Zoom environment is that it promotes reduced participant mobility since students stay near their devices (Bailenson, 2021).

A further limitation associated with the videoconferencing tool is the cognitive load on the students, who must manage the video and audio demands of the platform (Bailenson, 2021). It could be argued that in the case of

ESL/EFL learners, the cognitive load is even higher due to their more limited English language proficiency; therefore, teachers will need to pay great attention to this issue. The fifth limitation observed in the Zoom environment is its lag—or delay—in connectivity (Boland et al., 2022; Moorhouse et al., 2023), which in at least one study was found to prevent non-ESL/EFL interlocutors from initiating their turns without effort, leading them to produce longer but fewer turns (Boland et al., 2022). The final limitation in the Zoom environment observed in the ELT field is what has been called the "empty room" (Moorhouse et al., 2023, p. 125). The "empty room" or "the black square effect"—as many teachers in the ELT field call it—involves students avoiding turning on their webcams. It is not uncommon to hear teachers attribute this problem to institutional policies that prevent them from requiring that students turn on their webcams due to equity concerns that include privacy issues, students' lack of private space, and an unreliable internet connection. Teachers have also attributed the "black square effect" to their students' competing obligations, which result in multitasking (Moses, 2020).

Taken together, the limitations contribute to what is known as "Zoom fatigue," a term that has been made popular by Bailenson, (2021, p. 1). However, the limitations should not prevent or discourage teachers from using Zoom—or other videoconferencing platforms—as there are many strategies that they can implement to address Zoom's challenges and, at the same time, engage students in active learning. To this end, in this section, we provide eight suggestions designed to promote synchronous online student interaction and engagement. The suggestions are grounded in recommendations, practices, and research from the fields of general education, ELT, and educational psychology (Apigo, 2021; Bailenson, 2021; Boland et al., 2022; Cheung, 2021; Eaton, 2020; Kohnke & Moorhouse, 2022; Moorhouse et al., 2023; Pawan et al., 2022; Rehn et al., 2018).

1. Chunk the lesson into small segments so that the lesson includes several brief cycles of direct instruction—or input—followed by interactive activities. For example, in a one-hour lesson Apigo (2021) suggests that teachers integrate two 15-minute cycles of direct instruction—or lectures—followed by two cycles of activities. It remains unclear what the pedagogical basis is for the 10–15-minute direct instruction period. What is important, though, is that the cognitive and linguistic loads be kept low so that students are not overwhelmed managing the various demands of the video and audio features of Zoom. In addition, given that a variety of

guides focusing on synchronous online instruction (e.g., Apigo, 2021; Office of Teaching and Learning, University of Guelph [n.d.]; SMC Academic Senate Distance Education Committee, 2021) do not refer to ESL/EFL learners, teachers working with these student populations should pay extra attention to the length and level of complexity of their input. In this way, they can prevent student disengagement in the lesson.

2. Encourage—though do not require—students to turn on their webcams. When students are in their "black squares," ensure that they are following the lesson by implementing a variety of nomination strategies designed to engage students in class. These could include using one of the many free randomizers available on the web (such as wheelofnames.com and wheelgenerator.com). However, using one would add complexity to the lesson delivery since online randomizers require the sharing of the screen, which often results in the lesson losing its flow. Therefore, a more practical idea involves using less sophisticated tools such as name sticks (popsicle sticks with the students' names), the students-nominating-students technique, and the random selection of students to answer questions or comprehension checks.

3. Engage students in a variety of activities that will go beyond those that require oral-aural communication. For example, design activities that require the use of the chat box, Google Docs and slides, YouTube, the Zoom whiteboard, as well as Jamboard (a Google digital interactive whiteboard that can be used for online collaboration) or Padlet (a whiteboard that has limited free-of-charge features), as well as other digital tools. This will allow students to better connect with and process the materials presented. Use the course LMS to save or link any documents produced.

4. Elicit student participation through the chat box. Specifically:
   a. Use the chat box as a communication tool that your students can resort to throughout the lesson. Keep an eye on the chat box as your students use it to ask questions and raise concerns, or ask students to answer their peers' questions in the chat box during the lesson. In this way, they will be more engaged and contribute to their own and their peers' learning. Save and make the chat history and the lesson recording available to your students for review purposes.
   b. Implement the "waterfall technique" (J. Litten, personal communication, February 2019). This technique involves getting

students to post responses or summaries and so on in the chat box, without releasing their posting until you direct students to do so. This form of wait time serves two purposes. First, it reduces the students' cognitive load since they will have time to think through their answers without pressure for an immediate response. In addition, the waterfall technique promotes participation from all students, something that would not be the case if only a couple of students were called on or had the opportunity to respond.

5. Move away from the webcam to capture your arms and your lower body. In this way, you will be able to use nonverbal cues, which ESL/EFL teachers are extremely adept at using to make language comprehensible. Even if you are teaching in a small space, do not hesitate to use your body language to teach, just as you would in the F2F classroom. By using and demonstrating nonverbal cues in your teaching, you can enhance the clarity of instruction, potentially reducing the students' cognitive load.

6. Get students to move away from their devices, stand up, and physically engage in the lesson. For example, you could get students to take breaks and participate in "yoga" breaks in which students use their bodies to stretch, while at the same time, they are receiving comprehensible input in English.

7. Engage students in a warm-up activity that draws on the work they have done in the previous lesson. This warm-up could be undertaken individually, but ideally students should work in small groups. In this way, the expectations for student interactivity will be established from the beginning of the lesson.

8. As the lesson comes to an end, engage students in a closing activity, just as you do in the F2F environment. This activity should be brief and result in a product students will have access to after the day's class.

In summary, the strategies listed above are meant to help novice teachers engage their online synchronous students actively in learning. Although the strategies will not solve all the problems associated with Zoom (and other videoconferencing platforms), they will contribute to maximizing student participation and engagement. However, as teachers implement these strategies, it is indispensable to reflect on the extent to which they influence teachers' expected outcomes. Only by doing this will teachers be able to adapt their instruction and exploit Zoom (and other videoconferencing platforms) so that, despite its limitations, it contributes to ESL/EFL learning.

Teaching beyond the Face-to-Face Classroom 257

• *Q3. How can teachers create an equitable community of learners in synchronous online environments?*

To explain teaching and learning in online environments, researchers have relied on the "community of inquiry" framework (Garrison et al., 1999). This framework is characterized by three elements: *social presence*, involving the learners' ability to feel part of a community in which they feel a sense of belonging and acceptance; *cognitive presence*, involving the extent to which the learners can construct knowledge through their participation in the class; and *teaching presence*, involving the teachers' design and facilitation of instruction. While the interaction of the three elements contributes to the creation of learning communities in synchronous and asynchronous online environments, missing from the framework is the notion of *equity* (Reinholz et al., 2020). In this chapter, equity is understood to mean the removal of barriers that prevent student participation in online environments. Doing this will ultimately contribute to the students' ability to function effectively, without barriers, in the class.

In Chapter 1 of this volume, we described various strategies that ESL/EFL teachers can implement in F2F settings to help students develop a sense of community. However, the nature of the synchronous online environment necessitates an expansion of the instructional strategies ESL/EFL teachers have in their repertoire. They must implement a range of equity-based strategies. This will facilitate the management of the virtual classroom and concurrently cultivate the students' sense of belonging in an inclusive, equity-based environment.

Following is a list of principled pedagogical practices that have been implemented to train students to successfully participate in synchronous online environments so that they can develop a sense of membership and belonging in an equitable learning community (for example, Arasaratnam-Smith & Northcote, 2017; Cheung, 2021; Darby, 2019; Koh & Kim, 2003/2004; Kohnke & Moorhouse, 2022; Moorhouse et al., 2023; Reinholz et al., 2020; Sokolik, 2018; Tobin & Behling, 2018). The practices are meant to provide novice teachers with initial ideas on how to work in a virtual environment.

1. Before the first day of class, share some information about yourself that reflects your personality. Sharing information about your life and interests will humanize you (Darby, 2019; Nguyen, 2023). In class, have students ask follow-up questions on the information you shared. Throughout the term, get students to reveal information that reflects their personalities. Have students answer follow-up questions from their peers.

2. Train students in the use of Zoom controls. Specifically:

   a. Teach students how to use the "Thumbs up" and "Raise your hand" controls. To do this, engage students in a motivating Total Physical Response (TPR) (Asher, 1969) activity, just as you would in the F2F classroom. When students feel comfortable, get them to lead the activity and give the commands. An alternative to this activity could involve having students create yes/no color-coded signs. These signs would show agreement or disagreement, serving as a visual aid during the TPR activity. Having students create and use the signs may seem more cumbersome than using the Zoom controls. However, this practice contributes to students' physical engagement in the lesson, which, in turn, can lead to increased cognitive engagement and higher comfort with Zoom.

   b. Teach students how to use the "Mute/Unmute" and the "Share Screen" Zoom controls. After students feel comfortable with the controls, use self-made color-coded "Mute/Unmute" signs and engage students in a TPR activity similar to the one in (a) above. Throughout the term, alternate between the use of the Zoom controls or the self-made sign to maintain student cognitive and physical engagement.

3. On Day 1, give a virtual tour of the setting from which you are teaching. If there is time, have students participate in a game-like recall activity that requires you, the teacher, to turn off your webcam and ask yes/no questions about your space. To answer the questions, have students use their self-made yes/no signs. As a follow-up, assign students to give tours of their settings early in the term. Warn students about the activity ahead of time so that they can decide where they will be located on the day of the virtual tour (Nguyen, 2023). If students choose not to have their webcams on, they can still do their virtual tours as their peers take notes on the presentations.

4. Encourage—but do not require—students to turn on their webcams. Instead, require that students who do not turn on their webcams use an image of or create a hand-drawing that reflects their personalities or preferences. Have them post the image or the hand-drawing in their "black square" (as their Zoom profile picture) and have them explain how the picture or the drawing reflects their personalities or preferences. If needed, before engaging students in the activity, create a tutorial, with

Teaching beyond the Face-to-Face Classroom   259

images and simple text, explaining how to post the image in their "black squares."

5. Be aware of Zoom's communication lag and delays in muting, which often result in students talking over their peers. Alert your students to these issues so that they do not feel embarrassed when their speech overlaps with their peers'.

6. Explain the important role the chat box will play in your class. At the beginning of the term, implement activities that will require students to ask or answer questions as a way to train them how to use the chat box. Continue using the chat box throughout the term.

7. Explain how your synchronous online lessons will be structured. For example, you could say: "Our class will always begin with a short warm-up activity. After that, we will continue with a brief teacher presentation, followed by a small group activity. In this activity, you will use online tools (for example, Google Docs, Jamboard, and so on) so that you can access them after our lesson is over. Another short teacher presentation and another small group activity will follow. We will end the lesson with a brief takeaway activity. I will always record the lesson and the chat box, making them available in our LMS for review purposes." While the language used to explain will need to be modified to address the students' level of English language proficiency, central to the explanation is the idea that students need to understand how their synchronous online lessons will be organized.

8. Show enthusiasm for the class and keep an upbeat tone throughout the term since this will contribute to your students' sense of enjoyment.

9. Engage students in mindfulness activities to help them develop a sense of well-being and improve their attention in the online environment.

10. Be sensitive to accessibility factors that may prevent some of your students from accessing class materials. Specifically, to address this, use alt-text descriptions for images, and create video captions and transcripts for audio and video content. (For further information on this issue, visit the Described and Captioned Media Program website at https://dcmp.org/learn/captioningkey.)

11. Educate yourself on accessibility issues. Consult resources such as the CAST (2020) website, which describes Universal Design

for Learning (UDL), a framework aimed at improving teaching and learning for everyone (for further information on UDL, see Chapter 12 in this volume). Consult the various Microsoft guides available on the web to learn how to design accessible PowerPoint slides.

In summary, as we have shown in this section, an equity-based learning community is one in which teachers implement strategies designed to dismantle the access barriers inherent to Zoom and other videoconferencing platforms. To achieve active participation and language learning, teachers need to be intentional and reflect on how they will help their students feel safe in an online environment. Although the strategies listed in this section are by no means exhaustive, they will provide teachers with some initial ideas on how they can promote equitable access to synchronous online classrooms. Only by doing this will students feel they are participating in truly inclusive and authentic learning communities.

Big Picture and Bottom Line

Online ESL/EFL instruction requires that teachers develop a repertoire of instructional strategies that go beyond those implemented in their F2F classrooms. To do this, teachers need to consider the factors that contribute to and hinder "participatory equity" (a term coined by Reinholz et al., 2020) in online teaching and learning environments. While learning and implementing new strategies may initially be time-consuming, teacher and student satisfaction will increase as a result of higher student participation in an inclusive learning environment.

Food for Thought

1. After reviewing the information in this chapter, interview two language learners who have participated in synchronous online classes. Ask them about the challenges they faced in their classes. Then ask them about the strategies their teachers implemented to foster student participation. Are the challenges and strategies different from those identified in this chapter? If they are, add them to the ideas presented in this chapter.

2. Which of the ideas presented in this chapter are you most interested in exploring for your classroom? What, if any, adjustments would you make to meet your classroom needs?

3. In this chapter, we identified the structure of a one-hour class designed to promote active learning. Strategize how you would structure your own ESL/EFL synchronous online classroom to engage students in the learning process.

References

Apigo, M. (2021, March 29). *Beyond lectures: Synchronous student-student interaction.* California Virtual Campus: Online Network of Educators. Retrieved May 20, 2023, from https://onlinenetworkofeducators.org/2021/05/07/beyond-lectures-synchronous-student-to-student-interaction/

Arasaratnam-Smith, L. A., & Northcote, M. (2017). Community in online higher education: Challenges and opportunities. *The Electronic Journal of e-Learning, 15*(2), 188–198.

Asher, J. J. (1969). The Total Physical Response approach to second language learning. *The Modern Language Journal, 53*(1), 3–17. https://doi.org/10.1111/j.1540-4781.1969.tb04552.x

Bailenson, J. N. (2021). Nonverbal overload: A theoretical argument for the causes of Zoom fatigue. *Technology, Mind, and Behavior, 2*(1). https://doi.org/10.1037/tmb0000030

Boland, J. E., Fonseca, P., Mermelstein, I., & Williamson, M. (2022). Zoom disrupts the rhythm of conversation. *Journal of Experimental Psychology: General, 151*(6), 1272–1282. https://doi.org/10.1037/xge0001150

Brown, H. D. (2014). *Principles of language learning and teaching* (6th. ed.). Pearson.

CAST. (2020). *About Universal Design for Learning.* https://www.cast.org/impact/universal-design-for-learning-udl

Cheung, A. (2021). Synchronous online teaching, a blessing or a curse? Insights from EFL primary students' interaction during online English lessons. *System, 100,* Article 102566. https://doi.org/10.1016/j.system.2021.102566

Darby, F. (with Lang, J. M.) (2019). *Small teaching online: Applying learning science in online classes.* Jossey-Bass.

Eaton, M. (2020). *The perfect blend: A practical guide to designing student-centered learning experiences.* International Society for Technology in Education.

Garrison, D. R., Anderson, T., & Archer, W. (1999). Critical inquiry in a text-based environment: Computer conferencing in higher education. *The Internet and Higher Education, 2*(2–3), 87–105. https://doi.org/10.1016/S1096-7516(00)00016-6

Koh, J., & Kim, Y-G. (2003/2004). Sense of virtual community: A conceptual framework and empirical validation. *International Journal of Electronic Commerce, 8*(2), 75–93. https://www.jstor.org/stable/27751097

Kohnke, L., & Moorhouse, B. L. (2022). Facilitating synchronous online language learning through Zoom. *RELC Journal, 53*(1), 296–301. https://doi.org/10.1177/0033688220937235

Martin, F., Polly, D., Ritzhaupt, A. (2020, September 8). *Bichronous online learning: Blending asynchronous and synchronous online learning.* Educause Review. Retrieved May 20, 2023 from https://er.educause.edu/articles/2020/9/bichronous-online-learning-blending-asynchronous-and-synchronous-online-learning

Molla, R. (2020, December 4). *The pandemic was great for Zoom. What happens when there's a vaccine?* Vox. Retrieved May 20, 2023 from https://www.vox.com/recode/21726260/zoom-microsoft-teams-video-conferencing-post-pandemic-coronavirus

Moorhouse, B. L., Li, Y., & Walsh, S. (2023). E-classroom interactional competencies: Mediating and assisting language learning during synchronous online lessons. *RELC Journal, 54*(1), 114–128. https://doi.org/10.1177/0033688220985274

Moses, T. (2020, August 17). *5 reasons to let students keep their cameras off during Zoom classes.* The Conversation. Retrieved May 20, 2023 from https://theconversation.com/5-reasons-to-let-students-keep-their-cameras-off-during-zoom-classes-144111

MVS Audio Visual. (2023). *What are Zoom cloud meetings and why are they so popular?* MVS Audio Visual. Retrieved May 20, 2023 from https://mvsav.co.uk/2023-update-of-features-and-benefits-of-zoom-cloud-meetings/

Nguyen, T. (2023, March 21–24). Ten engaging online activities and micro-lessons [Colloquium presentation]. In H. M. Khamis (Moderator), *A simple approach to designing digital interactive materials* [Colloquium]. TESOL 2023 International Convention and English Language Expo, Portland, OR, United States.

Office of Teaching and Learning, University of Guelph. (n.d.). *Adapting your teaching and learning activities for the remote environment: Instructor planning guide.* University of Guelph. Retrieved May 20, 2023 from https://otl.uoguelph.ca/crdi#Activities

Pawan, F., Daley, S., Kou, X., & Bonk, C. J. (2022). *Engaging online language learners: A practical guide.* TESOL Press.

Rehn, N., Maor, D., & McConney, A. (2018). The specific skills required of teachers who deliver K-12 distance education courses by synchronous videoconference: Implications for training and professional development. *Technology, Pedagogy and Education, 27*(4), 417–429. https://doi.org/10.1080/1475939X.2018.1483265

Reinholz, D. L., Stone-Johnstone, A., White, I., Sianez, L. M., Shah, N., & Schussler, E. (2020). A pandemic crash course: Learning to teach equitably in synchronous online classes. *CBE: Life Sciences Education, 19*(4), https://doi.org/10.1187/cbe.20-06-0126

SMC Academic Senate Distance Education Committee. (2021). *Principles and practices for effective, equitable synchronous online classes.* Retrieved from https://www.smc.edu/administration/governance/academic-senate/committees/documents/distance-education/2021-2022/Principles-and-Practices-for-Effective-Synchronous-Online-Teaching-Fall-2021.pdf

Sokolik, M. (2018). The nexus of accessibility and pedagogy: What every online instructional designer should know. *TESL-EJ, 21*(4). Retrieved May 20, 2023 from http://tesl-ej.org/wordpress/issues/volume21/ej84/ej84int/

Sokolik, M. (2022). Teaching online: Design for engagement. In E. Hinkel (Ed.), *Handbook of practical second language teaching and learning* (pp. 195–208). Routledge.

Tobin, T. J., & Behling, K. T. (2018). *Reach everyone, teach everyone: Universal design for learning in higher education*. West Virginia University Press.

SECTION V

The Professionalization Process

CHAPTER 14

Building a Professional Identity

Contextualization

This chapter addresses the need for new instructors to establish a living and evolving sense of professional presence. Because of the typically high cost of living in large metropolitan areas, it is very common for novice teachers to work multiple jobs as they seek full-time positions, which are very competitive because they pay higher salaries, include benefits, and provide better job security. To improve their ability to find and attain such positions, it is recommended that novice teachers create a personal library with documentation of their professional work and skill sets. Considering the challenges posed by the competitiveness of the current job market, this chapter aims at providing useful strategies for deciding on the ideal career path, and for writing (and maintaining) curriculum vitae, resumes, cover letters, teaching philosophy statements, digital teaching portfolios, and other important documents that might be required during a job search process. This chapter offers helpful tips for interviews, job talks, teaching demonstrations, and video demonstrations, and provides a review of best practices for the larger application process and follow-up correspondence needs.

Case Study: Opportunity Does Not Knock until You Build a Door.

It can be hard for novice teachers to land the teaching position they want right after completing a teacher-training program because of their lack of experience as they enter the job market. But in order to get the experience that most jobs require, someone needs to decide to offer them a chance to prove their worth. There are certain tell-tale signs that employers can look for that might indicate that an applicant can become a great teacher even though they have little or no teaching experience to show for. For example, a recent masters in TESOL graduate asked one of the authors of this book for a letter of recommendation, and she also asked for help building up her teaching portfolio and curriculum vitae (CV) because she had little teaching experience. The things she was able to include in her CV were her TESOL certificate, her tutoring of international students on campus, her one-semester appointment at the Graduate Writing Center on campus, the practicum she took at a local community college, which included the responsibilities she had as a training teacher there, and all the professional conferences she had attended and presented at (such as the CATESOL regional and annual conferences, and the Graduate Student Forum at the TESOL annual convention). In this particular case, this student had pursued enough professional development opportunities to show a potential employer that she could become a great teacher if given the chance. In fact, she was hired by a language school in Los Angeles right after she graduated.

This particular example illustrates the need for teachers-in-training and novice teachers to seize opportunities to develop skills that may be useful in the future. Showing evidence of being a proactive go-getter and an opportunity seeker, as well as having the required educational background—and even some desirable personality traits (which can transpire during a job interview)—are tell-tale signs that a candidate has good potential. Then when asked about their experience with lesson planning, assessment, and trouble-shooting classroom challenges, novice job candidates will be able to refer to their experience with tutoring, volunteering at community centers, working at writing centers, or as a teaching assistant.

Common Concerns

The following are common questions that we are often asked related to improving one's chance to find an ideal job and develop a professional identity.

- *Q1. What are the career options for language teaching professionals?*
- *Q2. There are so many different teaching settings, so what training does a teacher need for each, and what should they consider before choosing a career path?*
- *Q3. The market is highly competitive, but what can teachers do as they prepare to apply for a job in order to ensure that they are a strong candidate and that they have a fighting chance?*

- *Q4. When a novice teacher is entering the job market, what should they do in terms of promoting themselves?*
- *Q5. Once a novice teacher has found a job, how do they keep it?*

Effective Practices for Building a Professional Identity

- *Q1. What are the career options for language teaching professionals?*

First of all, options can vary based on the geographical location where a teacher would like to work. If they would like to work in a country where English is the primary language, like the United States, there are a number of educational institutions where they can teach English as a second language (ESL) to speakers of other languages. If a teacher doesn't live in an English-speaking country, then the most widely available teaching pathway will be that of an English as a foreign language (EFL) instructor. Certain locations might have more opportunities than others, and oftentimes local or international teaching organizations will list job openings. For example, TESOL's Career Center has an ongoing job board that is free to search, and it contains filters to help users narrow down the listings to positions that might be more relevant to them (see https://careers.tesol.org/jobs/).

If a person lives in an English-speaking country such as the United Kingdom, Australia, the United States, and Canada, one pathway to consider is working with English language learners (ELLs) at primary and secondary schools as an ESL teacher. Although the duties of primary and secondary grade ESL teachers will vary depending on students' age, grade, and grade level, a typical job description may include the following responsibilities: to plan, organize, and provide instruction in English that meet state or national standards; to provide instruction that is consistent and coordinated with the district's or school's instructional program; to address all aspects of communication through appropriate instruction that develops each student's ability to read, write, speak, and listen in the appropriate content area; to administer academic and language assessments for the purpose of evaluating student progress for meeting academic learning targets and progress in language acquisition; and to maintain complete and accurate records of student progress and evidence of growth and progress.

Another language teaching career path to consider if the person lives in an English-speaking country is that of ESL instructor at a community college or at an intensive English program (IEP) at a four-year university.

The former involves teaching students from non-English speaking countries who are on a path to transfer to a four-year university, and the latter involves teaching students from non-English speaking countries already enrolled in a university. The most common duties required of community college and intensive English program ESL teachers include: teaching the material in weekly or biweekly classroom sessions; developing and managing the course syllabus; ensuring that the syllabus meets department and college standards and student learning outcomes; advising students on how to be successful in class; planning and creating lectures; facilitating in-class discussions and activities; grading assigned papers, quizzes, and exams; reporting on students' progress and achievement of learning outcomes; collaborating with colleagues on course curriculum and rubrics on an annual or biannual basis; and attending faculty meetings.

A much more widely available English language teaching career pathway that is available in both English-speaking and non-English speaking countries is that of an ESL or EFL instructor, or tutor at an English language school or program. The primary duties of an instructor will include: teaching language or test preparation courses; lesson planning; creating and grading assignments; reporting on students' progress and achievement; and attending faculty meetings and professional development meetings. Some schools have a dedicated program coordinator who is typically charged with creating and updating tests, curricula, syllabi, and rubrics, alleviating some of the responsibilities assigned to instructors. Tutors, on the other hand, will work one-on-one with students, and if they work at an educational institution, they may be required to report what they covered during the tutoring session. But if they work privately, their arrangement with their client, who is typically the student they will work with one-on-one, can vary based on their needs and demands.

- **Q2. *There are so many different teaching settings, so what training does a teacher need for each, and what should they consider before choosing a career path?***

Besides considering the geographical location and the duties and responsibilities of various teaching career paths, novice teachers also need to consider what types of training, certificates, and degrees are required for each career path (Johnston, 1997; Watt et al., 2012).[1] More specifically, a

---

1. For more tips on getting your career going, see: https://www.weareteachers.com/how-to-become-a-teacher/

person pursuing a career in teaching English to speakers of other languages (TESOL) must make sure they have the hard and soft skills typically needed for each type of career. Hard skills consist of the specific knowledge gained during any professional teacher training (that is, professional training from a TESOL certificate, in- or pre-service teacher training, a degree in TESOL or applied linguistics, and so on), while soft skills comprise a novice teacher's *people* skills, which are not necessarily taught in professional development programs and yet are very much needed for professional and personal advancement (Noah & Aziz, 2020, p. 4611). Both skill sets complement each other and are equally important in order to obtain and retain a job (see TESOL International Association, n.d.)

The types of professional qualification needed for each career path will vary depending on the job and setting (England, 2020; Leung, 2022; Plonsky, 2020). For example, if a person wants to work with ELLs in public primary and secondary school settings in the United States, this person needs to obtain a teaching credential from a program approved by their state's department of education. Different programs are designed to meet the state requirements for either an initial license or an add-on ESL endorsement. Qualifications to become an ESL teacher in the United States vary from one state to the next, as state boards of education are responsible for setting minimum standards for ESL licensure and additional ESL endorsements. Although many teachers seeking an ESL add-on endorsement at the secondary level are licensed in English or language arts, it is common for teachers of other subjects to seek ESL certification so as to best serve their multilingual classrooms. ESL educators in the United States may pursue one of two ESL certificate programs: graduate certificates and independent certificates. Both types of ESL certificate program require candidates to possess a bachelors degree. Teachers who want to apply their ESL credits toward the completion of a masters degree usually seek graduate-level certificates. Independent certificates, on the other hand, are designed to focus on practical training and the different methods for teaching English to ELLs.

Preparation to become a community college teacher or an instructor at a university's IEP requires a masters degree in TESOL, applied linguistics, English, education, second language, linguistics, or other related field, and a minimum one year experience of teaching ESL, preferably on a college or university campus. Foreign language coursework, living abroad, and multicultural experience are typically treated as preferred qualifications.

Teaching positions at ESL/EFL language schools can vary widely in their professional and educational background requirements. These can range from simply being an English native speaker to having TESOL training and certificates or an advanced degree in the field (Craig & Haworth, 2016). Sazdovska and Soproni (2020) distinguish TESOL teacher *training* from TESOL teacher *education*, and according to them, certain training certificates like CELTA (Certificate in Teaching English to Speakers of Other Languages) only give teacher-candidates the essential basic knowledge and skills to help them gain confidence in teaching and become qualified to teach globally.[2] In contrast, longer programs like graduate degrees in TESOL provide more teacher education and knowledge, as several classes cover pedagogical theory, with hands-on practice being limited to class assignments and the practicum course, when students are placed in a real classroom in order to complete the fieldwork requirement.

In a nutshell, while TESOL certificates and masters and doctoral degrees can open interstate and international teaching opportunities, teaching credentials are typically state/country-specific and are only accepted by the issuing state or country. Doctoral degrees should only be considered when a teacher knows that they want to apply for higher education positions and if they are interested in publishing and conducting research. Therefore, it is crucial to reflect on what they consider to be their ideal job, and if they will find personal happiness and professional fulfillment in doing it. According to Erten (2014), reasons for selecting teaching as a profession may include motivational factors such as ability, intrinsic career value, personal utility value (job security; time for family; job transferability), social utility value (shaping the future of children and adolescents; enhancing social equity; making a social contribution), and prior teaching and learning experience. Other equally important personal considerations to reflect on before making career decisions are:

- Do I want to stay in the city, state, or country of my education? Do I have family restrictions that prevent me from moving? Am I able to go wherever the job market takes me?
- What is the cost of living, and do the jobs in that location pay well enough for me to afford living expenses (and possibly student loans) there?
- If I am looking internationally, will potential employers help with a work visa and residency? How proficient am I in the local language? Can I live far away from friends and family?

---

2. See here an explanation of the differences between teaching certificates that are typically useful for those interested in teaching abroad: https://www.internationaltefl academy.com/blog/tefl-tesol-tesl-celta-delta-differences

- Is it a job that appeals to me and that I can see myself doing day in and day out? Do I agree with the larger curriculum of that educational setting?

The bottom line when deciding on a career path in education is a person should envision their future self, five years down the road, and critically ask themselves how professionally satisfied that future self will be. Ultimately, it is a person's background, experiences, self-perception, career opportunities, and goals that will affect their career choices and outcomes (Lent & Brown, 2019; Moodie & Greenier, 2023).

- **Q3. The market is highly competitive, but what can teachers do as they prepare to apply for a job in order to ensure that they are a strong candidate and that they have a fighting chance?**

There are a few things anyone planning to apply or preparing to apply for teaching positions should do. First, they should strive to get as much experience as they can, in any way that they can, and to never pass on the odd job or pro bono volunteering opportunity. The skill sets that these experiences can bring to a novice applicant's profile should not be underestimated as it is impossible to predict what will turn out to be a useful experience or skill in a future job application. In addition, besides doing their best to learn the ropes teachers-in-training should also try to make a good impression on their master teachers and supervisors when undergoing a practicum class, supervised teaching, or fieldwork. A positive relationship with them can afford a stronger letter of recommendation in the future and even job referrals.

There are other ways to increase relevant professional experience. For example, teachers-in-training and novice teachers should (i) seek opportunities to tutor or work as a teaching assistant (TA) in their academic programs, (ii) look for community teaching and coaching opportunities that might be open to the public, (iii) become a member of and actively participate in ELT professional organizations such as the TESOL International Association, CATESOL, ACTFL, AAAL, CARLA, among others, as this is a good way to network with people in the field, and (iv) volunteer for conferences, which can help them not only build professional experience but also lower the cost of registration and membership dues (Rimmer & Floyd, 2020). They can also join Facebook and Twitter (now called X) groups that relate to language teaching as those groups are generally very active and often share resources and announcements in their areas and fields. Some professional

274   Navigating the English Language Classroom

organizations like the TESOL International Association provide resources for novice teachers to plan their professional careers (see https://www.tesol.org/careers/career-tools/).

Teachers-in-training and novice teachers should also explore any professional services that their school or training center might offer. If their school has a career center, they should make an appointment and get their teaching portfolio, CV, and resume checked.[3] Career centers can evaluate these documents from a larger, wider, and most importantly, a current perspective. A career center can also help with mock interviews and offer job application advice. If the novice teacher does not have access to a career center, they should consult with peers who have recently been hired for teaching positions and have therefore been recently on the job market and may be able to offer useful advice and insight based on their experiences.

Next is learning when and where a novice teacher should start searching for a position. It is important to start searching sooner rather than later, as many jobs have early applications for subsequent years. Novice teachers should start familiarizing themselves with the job search sites that might be helpful, such as Linguist List, HigherEdJobs, the Chronicle of Higher Education, Indeed, and so on. Some of these might go out of fashion, but they will inevitably be replaced by others if they do, so it is the principle that is important here: online job search engines can help novice teachers navigate what is out there and how to contact people. However, note that many jobs are not widely advertised, so they might have to search individual systems in localities to find the jobs that are open (for example, community colleges post jobs on their own websites). If they have their own application system, prospective teachers can apply via their system, but they might still want to reach out to the program chair or director to show interest and to put themselves on their radar.

Finally, novice teachers should not underestimate the occasional odd job here and there. When offered a one-off position, they should consider taking it to get their foot in the door, or to increase (or widen) their teaching experience. This is a common way in which new teachers begin to make themselves valuable to a group of potential hirers. They should not wait for the dream job to present itself; instead, they should be proactive. Moreover, novice teachers should consider many positions (such as substitute teacher, fill-in, part-time, one semester, tutoring gigs, and so on) to expand their opportunities and the likelihood that they will get a response from potential

---

3. Find sample CVs: https://grad.illinois.edu/sites/default/files/pdfs/cvsamples.pdf

Building a Professional Identity 275

hirers. A broader scope increases their chances, especially if the return rate is low (which it may be for new and less experienced teachers). Novice teachers should remember that they need to be ready with all the relevant qualifications and required experience for when their dream job does present itself.

- **Q4. When a novice teacher is entering the job market, what should they do in terms of promoting themselves?**

First of all, the biggest mistake a teacher can make when looking for a job is to send the exact same resume to multiple job posts. No two job posts will be identical, so why should resumes? What's more, this practice conveys the impression that an applicant didn't put in the effort to apply for that job, which can be perceived by the employer as a negative sign. Therefore, it is advisable that applicants have different kinds of base CVs and resumes that cater to different types of jobs, educational settings, ESL levels, locations, and so forth. Then, before applying for a job, they should make the revisions necessary to all application documents to only include relevant experience and training that were listed on the job post. Employers do not want to read an extensive (multiple-page) resume looking for what they think is relevant experience. The job applicant is the one who needs to highlight those and bring their main qualities to the employer's attention. Another suggestion is to make sure their resume looks current and strong, and one way to do that is to collect CVs and resumes from successful professionals in their field to look at how they are promoting themselves and how they position themselves as professionals in their academic areas.

Along with CVs and resumes, cover letters should also match the job novice teachers are applying for, so they should not use a simple generic letter that fails to fully demonstrate their qualifications for a specific position and educational setting.[4] Instead, they should explain exactly how they match the job description's requirements and preferred qualifications, and why they think they are a strong candidate. Then they should make sure to tailor all application documents to target keywords and phrases that are emphasized on the job post—a strategy that should be used on all the application materials. Another piece of advice is for job applicants to mind the tone of the cover letter. It should not be overly friendly, and it should try to convey a more formal tone, and whenever possible it should address the exact person in charge of the hiring decision.

---

4. See some tips and sample cover letters here: https://www.weareteachers.com/teac her-cover-letter-examples/

Teachers seeking work opportunities should also have ready their diversity statement. Diversity statements have become an integral part of the materials submitted as part of an application for employment. They are just as important as the resume, cover letter, and writing sample. A diversity statement is a personal essay that is a depiction of your past experiences and explains how these experiences have contributed to your personal and professional growth. It allows the applicant the opportunity to explain to a hiring person or committee the distinct qualities and commitment they can bring to the table.

Other documents can prove very useful to have handy during job interviews, so novice teachers should consider creating a digital teaching portfolio (see Figure 14.1).[5] As most applications are now digital, they can get ahead of the competition by uploading current samples of videos (such as teaching demos), materials and handouts (showing actual work that they created), student evaluations, syllabi, course calendars, screenshots of course management systems they put together, a sample of their feedback to students, letters of recommendation, accolades, teaching philosophy, publications, research agenda for the future or a research dossier, presentation material, collaborations, and more. This portfolio would show employers who they actually are in the classroom, and they can be highly helpful to set them apart from other candidates, or when they do not have a lot of extensive experience but shine at development, creativity, and ideas. This is how they can demonstrate their skills, and if they have actual teaching experience, they can further strengthen their demonstration of ability.

A lot of employers use LinkedIn, Interfolio, Academia, ResearchGate, and social media (Twitter [now X], Instagram, Facebook, and so on) to learn more about job applicants. It is essential in today's digital world that a novice teacher have an online presence, as this is often a consideration in hiring processes (see Figure 14.2). For example, interviewers might want to look up novice teachers and see how they are promoting themselves outside of the interview process. New teachers in search of career opportunities must keep these locations up to date and respectful, as controversy may be a disqualifier. Another thing for novice teachers to consider is that social media is a great way to extend the documents that they submit; for example, having a link to a LinkedIn profile on their CV or resume will give interviewers an option to look at more if they desire, and this can offset applications that

---

5. See some advice and sample teaching portfolios here: https://www.weareteachers.com/teaching-portfolio-examples/

Create teaching blogs	Participate in discussions on teacher professional websites, such as myTESOL	Create teaching videos and post them on YouTube
Create your own logo and use it on all your materials	Create a professional website and a digital portfolio	Create professional (i.e., not personal) profiles on social media to interact with your students
Present at professional conferences and PDs and share your logo and the links to your blogs and website	When sharing your self-marketing materials online, tag professional organizations and other relevant keywords to reach more followers	Use high-quality (and copyright-free) images on your promotional materials

Figure 14.1. Suggestions of strategies for online self-promotion.

To get the word out about your services in a competitive professional environment	To showcase your teaching abilities and build confidence in your services	To increase your income by attracting more students
To keep connected to the online educational environment	To reach a wider audience for your materials	To energize your students and get them more involved
To bridge communication gaps between you and your students and/or their parents	To be searchable by an employer during a job interview	

Figure 14.2. Reasons to market oneself online and/or create an online presence.

restrict what can be submitted. Employers might not limit their search to only professional media outlets, and they might go through personal social media profiles. When maintaining their social media accounts, novice teachers should remember to keep it clean and respectful. They may think that their posts are private, but there may be settings that open it to the general public through friends' comments, reposts, and likes. Posting compromising images or messages that might stir intense disagreement and lead to possible uncomfortableness should be avoided.

When preparing for job talks and interviews, novice teachers should confirm all the information that they will need about dates, times, location, parking, documents to bring, graphic needs, audio needs, PowerPoint projection, and they should consider bringing snacks (like protein bars they can eat in the bathroom in case they get hungry). When a job applicant is invited for a campus visit for a college or university position, they typically spend all day there as they will be interviewed by several different people (search committee, program chair, division/department chair, and dean, followed by a job talk or teaching demonstration). During the application and interview process, interactions should be kept formal. Formal titles (that is, Mr, Mrs, Ms, Miss, Professor, or Doctor before the person's last name) should be used before and after they meet people. First names should not be used unless after an invitation from the person to do so or after seeing an email sign off that indicates a first name basis). Lastly, during a job talk, the job candidate should interact with the audience in a manner in which they are made to feel valued and heard.

Novice teachers should keep in mind that getting hired is not always a straightforward and transparent process. A person can be a highly qualified candidate and not get the job if the search committee has specific needs in addition to the posted required minimum qualifications, such as to improve their faculty diversity of gender, race, or ethnicity, or a need for a specialization or a skill set that is lacking in their program. Especially at the college and university level, where jobs are scarce and candidates are abundant, search committees might have to choose among several highly qualified applicants, and the final decision can be based on something that was not listed on the original job post. One example of an internal and not always publicized need that might sway a search committee to choose one among equally competent candidates is when they need to hire someone who speaks a specific foreign language, even when it was not in the job description, only because many of their students are native speakers of that language, so being able to speak their language is then seen as a valuable skill. Although this practice is likely to happen for higher education jobs, it is less likely to happen in the K-12 system, where there is a higher demand for teachers and the qualifications are more standardized. In some cases, when there are multiple candidates that are equally qualified for a job, the hiring decision can at times come down to a candidate's personality and self-presentation during the interview and selection process. After all, employers are making a long-haul commitment, so hiring someone they can get along with is just as important as hiring someone who can do the job.

Finally, it is a good idea to send a thank-you note after an interview, and if enough time has passed and they have not been notified, it is OK to send an email inquiring about the employer's hiring decision. When they do so, they should make sure to keep their tone highly formal and professional.

• Q5. Once a novice teacher has found a job, how do they keep it?

It is an amazing accomplishment to find a good job, but that's just half the battle! Once a teacher has the job, it is only the beginning of their professionalization path. New teachers need to stay current with the pedagogical literature and be prepared to enter into pedagogical conversations with peers. Showing currency in the field will come into play when merit reviews come up and they have to show continued progress. For example, they should make sure they know the current trends in antiracist and inclusive pedagogy and are able to apply such principles to their own teaching (Maamuujav & Hardacre, 2022). Such practices can increase student satisfaction and can be reflected in course and instructor evaluations. Even if teachers think their school does not conduct merit reviews that would take into account students' satisfaction with their classes and instructors, employers do make merit-based decisions when considering, for example, who to rehire for the following semester or year, and a teacher whose students are often displeased might not get rehired.

Another suggestion we can offer is attending faculty meetings and school events. Teachers who attend these regularly are typically favored over those who don't—for good reason: these are ways to show investment and professionalism. So, when a school tells part-time teachers they are not required to attend faculty meetings and campus events, keep in mind that although this might be the policy on paper, and that part-timers may really not be paid for those hours spent on extracurricular school events, that participating in them nevertheless might be the best way to show employers that they are a valuable asset to the program and school. Attending faculty meetings, volunteering when they can, and chipping in if possible are proactive actions that will show their employers that they are a team player who is invested in

280   Navigating the English Language Classroom

the students, program, institution, and field, and that they should be kept around (as in rehired every semester). Over time, once they feel out the ethos of the department and the true expectations, they might be able to reassess some of these points, but until that time comes, it is best to demonstrate investment to all stakeholders involved.

Once a novice teacher starts on their new teaching job, they must speak to their peers and their coordinator or supervisor, as they have been around longer and know the ropes. That doesn't mean they are necessarily more qualified, but it does mean that they have been exposed to more scenarios and situations at that school site, and the information they can potentially share with the new teacher could help to inform their pedagogy and ease the burden of the new job. Besides befriending faculty, they should also develop a friendly relationship with staff. Teachers need both faculty and staff on their side to be successful at a new job because they usually have different perspectives that can help to inform their work on the job. For example, department staff can help them work through student issues such as enrollment, attendance, grades, forms, technical issues, and more.

Professional development opportunities need to be factored in, such as attending symposia, colloquia, conferences, and other events. Also, from time to time actually presenting or participating on panels with peers at professional conferences would showcase to their employers their continued involvement in their professional field as well as their professional growth. According to Crandall and Miller (2014), there are a number of professional development opportunities that teachers should consider getting involved in, among which are the following groups of activities: (i) workshops, podcasts, webinars, conferences; (ii) summer institutes, academies, and graduate courses; (iii) grant and award applications; (iv) publishers, clearing houses, resource centers; (v) observing, mentoring, coaching, team teaching; (vi) joining professional organizations; (vii) participating in online discussions, blogs, wikis, and Twitter (now X); (viii) reading professional books, journals, and web resources (p. 633). Professional teacher organizations such as the TESOL International Association are an excellent place to start a search for professional development opportunities (see https://www.tesol.org/professional-development/).

Big Picture and Bottom Line

If a novice teacher is still at the beginning of their teaching career, this is the ideal moment to reflect on where they envision themselves professionally in five, ten, and fifteen years. It is really important to consider all the factors in this decision, taking into account not just their vocation, but also the job's location, cost of living, and repercussions to their personal life. Different teaching paths require different types of degrees and preparation, and options vary on time commitment and financial investment. While obtaining the required qualifications, they should also be actively pursuing relevant experiences that could bolster their resume. Getting that initial experience under their belt is crucial to moving up through the chain and attaining the positions they ultimately want. Apply to each job opportunity as if it were their dream job, putting thought and attention into the application documents. And once they get the job, they should keep working hard not only to be the best teacher that they can be for their students, but also to ensure job security.

Food for Thought

1. Look at the three types of language teaching jobs below, and discuss with a partner how they differ in terms of expectations from the teacher and pedagogical approaches required to cater for these students. Then, create teaching philosophy statements for these language teaching positions, making sure they are slightly tailored to fit these contexts:

    a. ESL instructor for adult learners who have recently immigrated to the United States and have been placed at a multiskill elementary level class (CEFR A2). The setting will be an adult school with classes that meet in the evening, once a week for three hours.

    b. ESL adjunct instructor for young adults who are students at a community college in an English-speaking country and have been placed in a reading/writing lower intermediate (CEFR B1) level course. This class meets in the morning once a week for three hours.

    c. English language learner (ELL) teacher for fourth-graders at a public elementary school. This is a multilevel setting with students placed in levels 1 through 3 (namely, 1: Entering; 2: Beginning; 3: Developing; see TESOL Pre-K-12 English Language Proficiency Standards Framework).

2. Question 2: Perform an online search to try to find the CVs of three well-known people in your field. They may be posted on their personal homepages or on their professional social media

accounts (for example, Academia, LinkedIn, or ResearchGate). If you can't find some of them, use the CVs of three people you are connected with through one of your online professional accounts. Work with a partner to compare and contrast these CVs, looking for features that you think worked well and highlighting features that didn't work so well. Select the characteristics you would like to adopt in your own CV and build or revise your CV to match those characteristics.

References

Craig, C., & Haworth, P. (2016). Reflecting on the changing nature of English language teaching internationally, the status of the profession, and future visions for teacher education. In P. Haworth & C. Craig (Eds.), *The career trajectories of English language teachers* (pp. 237–247). Symposium Books.

Crandall, J., & Miller, S. F. (2014). Effective professional development for language teachers. In M. Celce-Murcia, D. M. Brinton, & M. A. Snow (Eds.), *Teaching English as a second or foreign language* (4th ed., pp. 630–648). Heinle Cengage Learning.

England, L. (2020). *TESOL career path development: Creating professional success.* Routledge.

Erten, I. H. (2014). Understanding the reasons behind choosing to teach English as a foreign language. *Novitas-Royal: Research on Youth and Language, 8*(1), 30–44.

Johnston, B. (1997). Do EFL teachers have careers? *TESOL Quarterly, 31*(4), 681–712. https://doi.org/10.2307/3587756

Lent, R. W., & Brown, S. D. (2019). Social cognitive career theory at 25: Empirical status of the interest, choice, and performance models. *Journal of Vocational Behavior, 115*, Article 103316. https://doi.org/10.1016/j.jvb.2019.06.004

Leung, C. (2022). English as an additional language: A close-to-practice view of teacher professional knowledge and professionalism. *Language and Education, 36*(2), 170–187. https://doi.org/10.1080/09500782.2021.1980003

Maamuujav, U., & Hardacre, B. (2022). The politics and praxis of academic English: Toward antiracist language pedagogy. *TESOL Journal, 13*, Article e668. https://doi.org/10.1002/tesj.668

Moodie, I., & Greenier, V. (2023). "I promised growing up I would not become a teacher": Exploring the career trajectory of a language teacher through social cognitive career theory. *TESOL Journal.* https://doi.org/10.1002/tesq.3235

Noah, J. B., & Aziz, A. B. A. (2020). A case study on the development of soft skills among TESL graduates in a university. *Universal Journal of Educational Research, 8*(10), 4610–4617. https://doi.org/10.13189/ujer.2020.081029

Plonsky, L. (2020). *Professional development in applied linguistics: A guide to success for graduate students and early career faculty.* John Benjamins. https://doi.org/10.1075/z.229

Rimmer, W., & Floyd, A. (2020). Teaching associations and professionalism. *ELT Journal*, *74*(2), 126–135. https://doi.org/10.1093/elt/ccaa003

Sazdovska, J., & Soproni, Z. (2020). ELT teachers' perceptions of professional requirements. In A. Fekete, M. Lehmann, & K. Simon (Eds.), *UPRT 2019: Empirical studies in English applied linguistics in honour of József Horváth*, 261–281.

TESOL International Association. (n.d.). *Beginning your career*. Retrieved June 25, 2021, from https://www.tesol.org/careers/career-tools/beginning-your-career/

Watt, H. M. G., Richardson, P. W., Klusmann, U., Kunter, M., Beyer, B., Trautwein, U., & Baumert, J. (2012). Motivations for choosing teaching as a career: An international comparison using the FIT-Choice scale. *Teaching and Teacher Education*, *28*(6), 791–805. https://doi.org/10.1016/j.tate.2012.03.003

CHAPTER 15

Balancing Responsibilities with Life

Contextualization

This chapter explores the hard-to-navigate yet essential-to-tackle concept of work–life balance. When new instructors enter the language classroom for the first time, it can be difficult to determine and establish personal and professional boundaries that are fair for the many students who demand professional expertise and guidance, while also remaining fair to teachers who have complex lives that must be balanced with student needs. Because it is an area of the profession that depends highly on individual circumstances juxtaposed against a backdrop of institutional requirement, teachers are often left feeling as if the only good decision in their career is one in which the professional is prioritized over the personal. Imbalances such as these can, however, often lead to resentment, such as when work obligations negatively impose themselves on personal time (Da Silva & Fischer, 2020). To use a term coined by psychologist Freudenberger (1974, p.160), "burnout," which stems from feelings of general "exhaustion and fatigue" (p. 160), becomes a major consideration. Because imbalances affect teacher retention over time, work–life equilibrium presents as a prime concern. Given the gravity of this issue, this chapter explores a range of questions and potential solutions that can be considered and possibly adopted by teachers who are struggling to balance their home and work lives.

Case Study: A Tale of Two Teachers

In two separate yet related accounts, one involving a primary school teacher and one a new university-level teaching assistant, one common work–life concern that stood out was the role of email. The primary school teacher

284

explained that she often checks her email and responds to messages from students and school administrators right away, regardless of when they are sent. In this way, she replies to work emails during and after work, into the night, and often over the entire weekend. It is no surprise then that this teacher also expressed that she feels that emails are slowly taking over her life given the fact that they tether her to her computer and to her class' many stakeholders. Conversely, the university teaching assistant explained that she is very good at not responding to emails after 5pm. Instead of constantly looking at her inbox, she merely replies after 8am the next business day; if anyone, including students, emails her on Friday afternoon, she lets them know in advance that their email will most likely not receive a reply until Monday morning. In this scenario, the teacher has regained some sense of control in terms of balancing her lifeworld with her professional world, though she also expressed apprehension in some scenarios as she was unsure as to whether she was doing a disservice to her students.

Though these two examples represent notably different scenes, what these teachers have in common is that they are both trying to find ways to bring the professional into harmony with the personal. Even experienced teachers will admit that this is a struggle from time to time, but for novice teachers, it can be debilitatingly discouraging, often leading to imbalances that drive teachers into different professions due to untenable burdens. In this way, finding a home life/work life balance, just to illustrate one concern, presents itself as a problem area that must be addressed if new teachers are to establish and maintain a healthy teaching career over time.

Common Concerns

The questions below address a wide swathe of subissues that orbit the notion of home life/work life balance. There is certainly more to this topic than can be covered in a simple chapter, and this is—at least in part—because the lives of teachers are idiosyncratically rich and kaleidoscopically complex. Despite the variation educators encounter when examining their lives, there is often common ground that can be found and exploited to improve the home life/work life balance across vastly different scenarios or contexts. The following questions elucidate some of the central concerns that might help teachers navigate this tricky area of their profession.

- *Q1. How should novice teachers approach balancing their personal life and their professional goals?*

286   Navigating the English Language Classroom

- *Q2. Good teachers set boundaries for themselves. But what many new teachers don't understand is how they can set those boundaries and then adhere to them. Any advice?*
- *Q3. Teaching is a passion, but the amount of additional work beyond the classroom is often unbearable. How do new teachers optimize this extra work so that it becomes more manageable?*
- *Q4. Teachers are in this profession for the long haul, but they have to find ways to work smarter, not harder. What strategies can help with this?*
- *Q5. As new teachers, the workload can sometimes feel overwhelming and discouraging with regard to new responsibilities. What advice is there for new teachers to help alleviate this anxiety?*

Effective Practices for Achieving Balance

- *Q1. How should novice teachers approach balancing their personal life and their professional goals?*

Teaching, unlike many other professions, is a job that requires interaction with others for success. These interactions, however, often flow well beyond the boundaries of the actual classroom and its many teaching experiences. For primary and secondary school teachers, the day often starts early in the morning at around 8 a.m. and goes until roughly 3 to 4 p.m. depending on the system. For these settings, teachers are consistently busy with little downtime, often leaving planning and grading for the evenings and weekends. In a similar yet distinct vein, although community colleges, colleges, and universities are somewhat different in their general teaching structure, where teachers typically teach on specific days and during specific windows of time, they are no less difficult to master in terms of planning and grading. In addition, community college instructors typically teach a heavier annual load than university instructors, depending on the institution or system. Higher education instructors are also frequently required to perform additional administrative duties or are knee-deep in research projects, and this is on top of their normal preparation, teaching, and grading. As can be deduced from both groups, the demands of the job are alarming for the larger profession given that overwhelming workloads have indeed been shown to correlate with teacher burnout (El Helou et al., 2016), which can in turn result in teacher attrition (Madigan & Kim, 2021).

What these scenarios indicate is that teaching is not a nine-to-five job, where instructors can simply turn it off after they walk out of the classroom.

Balancing Responsibilities with Life 287

The bottom line is that teachers have to get the job done, and this often means forging a pathway that works for them and is sustainable over time. This often translates into doing extra work during off-time, but most teachers would quickly acknowledge that it is not "extra;" rather, it is just a part of the job. To put it bluntly, educators cannot treat their job as if they are tellers at a bank with clearly defined hours and the ability to call it a day once the closing bell tolls.

Culturally speaking, teaching is revered in some cultures and underappreciated in others. When it is underappreciated, as it often is with language teachers, it can lead to lower salary and, in turn, a need to take on additional work through additional classes, extracurricular activity supervision, or secondary workplaces (National Center for Education Statistics, 2021). In addition, some instructors have multiple preparations (teaching a writing class while also teaching a pronunciation class, for example) as well as multiple geographical considerations that add nonproductive time to one's schedule (for example, working at multiple educational institutions; private tutoring in residential areas; remote or freelance work). In this way, the value a society places on teaching may result in more or less tenable outcomes for teaching professionals, and this will ultimately impact one's home life/work life balance.

Despite the hurdles that many teachers face in terms of work location and course load, there are many areas that can be targeted to improve their quality of life. For instance, educators understand that teaching is not limited to just teaching. This is because teachers also have to prepare by conceptualizing and creating lesson plans (see Chapter 4), to provide feedback on graded assignments and exams (see Chapter 9), to assist students with learning objectives in the moment and as they arise through teaching actions (see Chapters 3 and 5), to meet with students outside of class to provide additional support (see Chapter 9), and to ensure that the classwork aligns with university expectations such as adequately setting up websites, posting materials, and creating digital interactions, among others (see Chapter 2). Following this logic, achieving an effective balance will require time management skills such as a well-organized and up-to-date calendar or schedule as well as some flexibility in that calendar or schedule as things come up. Balance will also require forethought in terms of class design and execution, as this will create space in which instructors can budget their time without a last-minute rush. Teachers can also potentially work with their administration, in some cases, to seek out the most opportune schedule possible, especially when working across geographical locations separated by extreme distance. In short, a healthy way to approach balance is to see balance as a

288   Navigating the English Language Classroom

game of give and take, where the weight of the personal may outweigh the professional on one day, and the reverse is just as likely the next.

To truly address the notion of achieving balance, teachers first have to pose a few additional questions: How much personal life are teachers willing to sacrifice? Do teachers have a family, a partner, kids, or elderly parents who require extra attention, for whatever reason? Is their family supportive of the extra time they need to put into work after business hours? Will teachers choose to watch that movie with their partner, or will they sit and do the grading that needs to be done? The answers to these questions are uncertain from a collective perspective, as they essentially depend on what each individual educator's professional goals are and how motivated they are to achieve them. One person's yes is another person's maybe or no, so the bottom line is each person has to come to terms with how much time they are willing to invest. Setting boundaries may mean that a person is seconded to the go-getter (and it is often the go-getter who gets the promotion), but if the goal of those boundaries is to ensure home-life harmony, then it may indeed be worth it to take a step back. As Shakespeare (1623/2012) once poignantly wrote in *Hamlet,* "to thine own self be true" (1.3.84), and in no other profession do these words ring truer.

- **Q2. Good teachers set boundaries for themselves. But what many new teachers don't understand is how they can set those boundaries and then adhere to them. Any advice?**

Understanding the need for limits and setting those limits and adhering to them are two different things (see Chapter 9 for how this can be seen through feedback, for example). It is simple to say that instructors will not respond to emails after business hours; however, the real world is oftentimes antithetical to rigid approaches to thresholds. The limits educators set are often easily swept aside for the sake of their students, for keeping up with their own work, or even for addressing a project that a superior might be inquiring about.

One common conundrum in terms of respecting one's boundaries that is complex for newer teachers to navigate is how to weather their position as a new addition to a larger team. In other words, being the newest member may lead to feelings of anxiety that stem from a need to please superiors and colleagues or to be successful as an educator who may not have as much experience. If a person is an overachiever, for example, then that person may have trouble saying no when asked to stay late, direct an extracurricular activity, take on another class, develop a new class or new curriculum, or work on a service-oriented committee they don't really have time for. In this way, teacher status asymmetries can impact the labor balance in ways that are covertly skewed in favor of those with more time and job protection. By knowing the ins and outs of their position, including, for example, its official duties and expectations, novice teachers can better advocate for their own work–life health by basing their decisions on a more realistic understanding of commitment. In other words, saying no can be a healthy aspect of professional boundary development and adherence as long as the no aligns with the parameters of the job.

But balance is not just achieved among fellow faculty and job details; in fact, novice teachers can also explore boundary adherence and its relation to balance by clarifying expectations for their students through clear and reasonable policies and protocols. Take, for example, the syllabus, which is often seen as a labor contract between instructors and their pupils (Chanie, 2013). When writing syllabi, instructors certainly need to consider the time commitment for students in terms of readings, assignments, projects, attendance, and so forth, but they also have to consider the time commitment for themselves, including planning, designing, teaching, grading, counseling, and overall management of the classroom setting. New teachers can sometimes aim for the stars in terms of what they believe they can accomplish, but seasoned teachers know that practicality and realism will always win out in the long run. For instance, providing feedback on a five-page essay draft for twenty students can be burdensome, so teachers need to build enough time into their calendar to allow them to review student work in a thoughtful manner that still leaves enough time for the students to then receive the feedback, potentially counsel with the instructor, and then perform revisionary writing before the next task is due. To save time, teachers might want to build in more in-class workshopping in preliminary stages, more peer review sessions before drafts are due to teachers, and more focused feedback practices so that teachers do not feel the need to treat all concerns at all times, instead allowing them to focus on core concerns in performance that will be impactful for the students' overall growth and development without overloading them (see Chapter 9 for more insight on the grading/feedback process).

It is important when reflecting on boundary enforcement to remember that ultimately it is educators who will always have their own best interest in mind. This means that when working with colleagues as a part of a team, asserting agency may be the only way to achieve personal and professional happiness; likewise, asserting agency over classroom design practices in ways that positively impact the labor of both teachers and students may also aid in nurturing professional boundaries over time.

- *Q3. Teaching is a passion, but the amount of additional work beyond the classroom is often unbearable. How do new teachers optimize this extra work so that it becomes more manageable?*

When new teachers are starting out, it is understandable that they might follow preset curricula and lessons if they can; these can reduce the learning curve and workload significantly. However, not all programs will have this type of material at the ready; in these cases, new teachers will be generating more than they might expect. When instructors have to generate materials, they will quickly see that they have to do a lot of trial and error to get to a point where they feel comfortable and confident. New teachers shouldn't deprive themselves of this experience because it is normal: all teachers go through trial and error, and all teachers have to feel out the burden of running a course, for better and sometimes for worse (see Chapter 4 for more on how lessons are sometimes spaces for trial and error experimentation).

One area that new teachers often undervalue is the recycling of materials, as well as how this can positively impact planning labor—as well as improve student interest and motivation (Mukundan et al., 2016). Indeed, many new teachers share thoughts that indicate they are not doing their job well if their classes are not jam-packed with new materials and activities on a daily basis. Though this can be true, it is equally important to remember that every new material brings with it an additional cognitive load for the students. What this means is that by changing materials frequently, teachers essentially hit the reset button with each switch. One way to lessen this cognitive burden is by reusing readings from one day to the next, or even one unit to the next—only in noticeably different ways. For example, if a reading is used one day to look at compound-complex sentence structure and usage, then depending on what the reading presents, it might also be viable a second day to talk about passive versus active structures. In this way, the teacher double-dips, so to speak, into the reading, hitting it from two instructional angles while requiring students to grapple with only one set of content and ideas.

As indicated in the previous question, feedback on student performance is another way in which educators can optimize their work beyond the classroom. New teachers shouldn't let the need for student feedback take over their lives. It is easy to spend excessive amounts of time commenting on student performance, but teachers have to set boundaries for themselves; otherwise, they might end up tethered to their computer and to the grading process itself. This is not productive for the teacher or the student, as excessive feedback leads to instructional burnout while also depriving the student of critical thinking moments in which they themselves can drive performance revision and improvement. By setting feedback limits, new teachers in turn establish space for their students to take on more agency, thereby alleviating some of the weight placed on the instructor's shoulders (see Chapter 9 for more on managing feedback).

One additional way in which educators can optimize work beyond the classroom is by reenvisioning the idea of the lesson plan. To elaborate, for some teachers a lesson plan is a document that is typed up in full and held at the ready in the classroom while teaching. For others, it is a checklist of items that are to be ticked off as a given lesson unfolds. One more recent way of looking at lesson planning is to see it as the creation of a digital narrative. For instance, many newer teachers develop lessons within presentation software such as PowerPoint, Keynote, Google Slides, or Prezi, to name a few. In terms of their role in lesson planning and building, if teachers can use presentation software to flesh out the overall narrative of a lesson, they essentially transform visual support into a type of active lesson guide, reducing their dependence on a separate document and facilitating student engagement through visual interaction with the lesson itself. If the developed digital lesson is intuitive, it can, therefore, guide the teacher through the day. One caveat is that students do not want a lesson plan in digital form, as this can easily lead to boredom, so if a teacher makes use of this approach, it is essential that it be highly interactive and student driven (see Chapters 4 and 5 for more on planning and delivering lessons).

- **Q4. Teachers are in this profession for the long haul, but they have to find ways to work smarter, not harder. What strategies can help with this?**

One easy-to-employ tactic that new teachers can make use of to work smarter, as opposed to harder, is to see all of their ideas, actions, developments, explorations, successes, and failures as productive components in the development and application of their teacher identity. What is meant by this is that all instructional experiences help to generate a larger sense of professional context, for better or worse, and within that context is a wealth of *dos and don'ts* as well as *go-to items* that can be drawn on in order to improve the instructional context and its demands (see Chapter 14 for more on building a professional identity).

In terms of dos and don'ts, it is only through experience that educators come to understand what constitutes effective or ineffective practice within the classroom. Over time, teachers new to the field begin to see, intuitively, actions that lead to nonproductive pathways. Through a series of trials and errors, new teachers learn to feel out what works and what doesn't work, and this in and of itself can be exceptionally impactful in long-term work–life management. For instance, one *do* that all teachers—new or veteran—can apply to make their job less burdensome over time is to make thoughtful notes the moment things come up or actions are attempted. By reflecting on classroom actions in real time, teachers ensure that they have to rely less on memory, and less reliance on memory means a lessened process of relearning classroom materials with each successive encounter. Teachers should set up good practices of annotating lessons, slides, or materials as they are used, so if there is no time for actual revision, the notes can guide them through in future attempts (see Chapter 5 for more tips on delivering lessons).

With regard to go-to items, one habit that novice teachers can never over-nourish is creating and using materials repositories. In addition to online materials sharing sites (Fincher et al., 2010, August), many teachers develop digital or manual filing systems that are intuitive and easily accessible at a moment's notice. To illustrate, teachers might develop a filing system in which they collate articles or readings that emphasize the use of the present perfect tense or a certain web of imagery present within the vocabulary used. When new instructors encounter a potentially useful document online or in their program, they should make a copy of it and add it to their developing handout collection, either to use or adapt, depending on permissions. This can reduce time spent on original creation by rechanneling creative energies into processes of adaptation, which are less time-consuming.

When browsing online for resources, teachers should also download videos that make for great resources, as long as they are downloadable. Teachers can start a video collection that can supplement explanations or take the place of detailed handouts that would need to be designed and distributed. If videos cannot be downloaded owing to copyright, one strategy would be to keep a running log of the videos, along with their titles and their respective links. The title is important because if a source link becomes obsolete through one carrier, it may be possible to locate the video through another provider through its identifying characteristics. These actions may seem like overkill in the time of easily searchable terms, but the long-term payout is worth more than the short-term effort if it makes for more effective classroom planning over time.

Teachers can also start setting up lesson plan repositories as well as digital slide set collections as early as possible. Even if they are not used regularly, they can become a resource database where teachers can go to work through ideas in new ways that are grounded in previous experience. Teachers can also position these repositories as omni-accessible by shifting them into cloud-based systems that provide multiple access points, in turn rendering the planning process more fully accessible no matter the geographical constraints.

Lastly, new teachers can work smarter in the pursuit of work–life balance by positioning themselves as an active giver and taker within their professional community. What this means is that they can offer ideas to and learn from interchanges with immediate colleagues: they can join online teacher chat forums to exchange with an extended community; they can continue to read up on new research or even provide their own as they find innovative pathways; or they can participate in the active sharing of information through professional symposia, colloquia, and conferences. Some of these strategies can be costly, such as attending a conference, but many if not most are fully accessible through simple access to colleagues or to the internet.

- ● *Q5. As new teachers, the workload can sometimes feel overwhelming and discouraging with regard to new responsibilities. What advice is there for new teachers to help alleviate this anxiety?*

As a new educator, it is sometimes helpful to embrace one's status as new in order to become the master of the emotions that accompany this newness. Any time new instructors are starting out at something, they will inevitably be anxious about what they have to do and how they will do it. Indeed, for English as a foreign language (EFL) instructors, Sammephet and Wanphet (2013) posit that anxiety is often a combination of teacher personality, teaching context, and supervisory context. But English as a second language (ESL) teacher anxiety is not any different from, for example, a nurse who works at a hospital for ten years and then goes to another hospital: they will still have to learn the way things are done at the new hospital, and their success will likely also be tied to questions of personality, context, and supervision. Yes, their medical training will be the same, but there will be different policies, practices, and expectations that create a learning curve for them. The same is true for any teacher who is starting out. Novice teachers have the training, and they have to find some sense of confidence in this fact, but they also have to learn to navigate the job they are moving into, with all of its many twists and turns. The same was true for the teachers who came before them, as it will be true for those who follow.

One simple action to combat stress and anxiety is to practice self-care. Physical and mental health are very important, and new instructors must find the time to pause and relax, as this allows for energy recharge and space for reflection. They should work to build in personal time and activities that facilitate a healthy outlook on life. For instance, novice educators should allocate specific windows of time for exercise, meditation, sleep, personal interactions, hobbies, travel, and so on. They should avoid leaving their diet to chance by planning meals in advance, shopping with purpose, and preparing foods that will keep them feeling healthy and nourished through those stressful moments. They should listen to their body and adapt their approach as needed when it is telling them something is wrong, such as when tension or stress leads to lower backaches, migraines, or stomach problems. If depression enters the fray, they shouldn't underestimate the power of a good therapist—most teachers the authors know have had experience with therapy, and most report that it was exactly the thing they needed to manage their anxiety and stress levels.

Another important aspect of managing stress and anxiety as an educator is not to be afraid of mishaps. Mishaps are where educators learn, and they can lead to beautifully productive outcomes that can enhance abilities and improve the learning experience for the students. All teachers have to start somewhere, and that starting point is just that, a starting point. Once new teachers find their preliminary footing, they can then start taking baby steps in various directions that add new or unfamiliar pathways to their educational dossier. Some of these steps will be well received, and others will fall flat on their face. If a teacher is a perfectionist, they might want to rethink what perfection means in a language classroom. It is not about getting it right the first time; it is about finding productive pathways that work for very diverse personalities and learning styles, which are ever-changing. In other words, anxiety and stress can be alleviated by rethinking the role of the teacher as a participant on a journey that is dynamic while also being contextually bound. Instructors are not expected to be walking encyclopedias, so they shouldn't set that standard for themselves. Likewise, they are not machines, so their lessons and approach should not be seen as static and inflexible but alive and adaptive (see Chapters 4 and 5 on building and delivering lessons).

Lastly, teacher anxiety is not just about teaching; it is also about how professional anxiety impacts their personal lifeworld. When considering how work anxiety bleeds into personal life, new teachers should try talking to family members in advance about bursts of time that they will need for work, especially when they know they will be extra busy and less available to them. Chances are that loved ones can help with house chores, family obligations, or errands on an as-needed basis. By openly discussing professional obligations with family and friends, teachers can let them know that there are windows in which they simply need time to themselves to get things done. They also soften the blow of behavior that might be seen as erratic and unpredictable to others by ensuring that those other people understand the workload. At the same time, teachers actually have to make devoted time for others as well so that their idea of balance is not skewed in a one-sided direction their loved ones cannot relate to. Small requests for flexibility are usually met with productive responses, but if every day means sacrificing for work, it can lead to resentment from family and friends, which increases stress and anxiety. In other words, be sure to nurture both the professional and the personal in a balanced way so that stress and anxiety are lessened through open and productive communication. Table 15.1 recaps some of the more productive tips to keep in mind when seeking balance.

Big Picture and Bottom Line

There are a lot of factors that will impact how new educators manage their job and personal life. At the end of the day, however, each individual instructor is ultimately the only person who can weigh their options, consider the repercussions, and make the decisions that must be made. Knowing this will help new teachers preserve their mental health as they work to establish a professional identity among peers; it will also help them preserve their personal lifeworld as they meld it with their professional goals and objectives. In short, new teachers must attend to their professional responsibilities in ways that are conducive with their long-term career and personal goals, and this is no easy feat; but with a little practice, and trial and error, it is something that can be achieved.

Food for Thought

1. Examine a major assignment for a language class that you have taught, are teaching, or will teach in the future. Rethink the assignment in terms of making it less burdensome with regard to your assessment practices. For instance, how might you reformulate your approach to feedback so that it is more time-efficient for you? What can you do to reduce time spent outside of class assessing the assignment without sacrificing its educational integrity? Be ready to share two potential strategies with peers.
2. Reflect on your own lesson preparation practices. What are some strategies not mentioned in this chapter that might help you work

smarter rather than harder when it comes to planning, generating materials, creating classroom activities, and fostering productive student–student or student–teacher interactions? Be creative and innovative in your line of reasoning, and be prepared to share your thoughts with peers or in whole-class discussion.

Table 15.1. Tips for Relieving New Teacher Anxiety

Tips for relieving new teacher anxiety
New teachers should trust in their pedagogical training and remain open to the pedagogy of others, as there are always things to learn that were not covered in their own training coursework.
New teachers should keep in mind that learning is ongoing, especially for educators, so continued learning should be embraced as a necessary part of their profession.
New teachers should welcome insights from more experienced others who have already dealt with the issues they are experiencing; they should trust in these insights as a source of knowledge to give them pathways towards success.
New teachers should remember that mistakes or misjudgments happen, but that they are also windows for continued learning; they should recognize their role as necessary steps in moving toward greater understanding.
New teachers should rethink perfectionism in favor of exploration and experimentation; they should envision teaching as a journey of discovery that will unveil new pathways for success as the pathways are traveled.
New teachers should consider flexibility and adaptability as prized qualities that will enhance their overall experiences in the classroom and with their students.
New teachers should prioritize physical self-care practices (e.g., striving for a proper diet to fuel their actions; attending to aches and pains before they get out of control).
New teachers should prioritize good mental health practices (e.g., creating designated times for friends, family, and fun; making time for a good night's sleep so the mind can recharge).
New teachers should keep family and friends informed about what their profession entails so that they understand the nature of the work and the pressures new teachers are under.
New teachers should talk to the people they live with about sharing the domestic workload, especially when things at work are creating pressure (e.g., grading exams or essays; teaching a new course for the first time; carrying out extracurricular duties or service-oriented duties associated with the job).
New teachers should keep in mind that they should not be sacrificing happiness for work; the two can coexist, but they can sometimes be extremely difficult to balance.

References

Chanie, B. S. (2013). Conceptions about language syllabus and textbook based instructions: TEFL graduate students in focus. *Online Journal of Education Research, 2*(4), 66–71.

Da Silva, J. P., & Fischer, F. M. (2020). Understudied school teachers' work/life balance and everyday life typologies. *Chronobiology International, 37*(9–10), 1513–1515. https://doi.org/10.1080/07420528.2020.1808010

El Helou, M., Nabhani, M., & Bahous, R. (2016). Teachers' views on causes leading to their burnout. *School Leadership & Management, 36*(5). https://doi.org/10.1080/13632434.2016.1247051

Fincher, S., Kölling, M., Utting, I., Brown, N., & Stevens, P. (2010, August). Repositories of teaching material and communities of use: Nifty assignments and the greenroom. In *ICER '10: Proceedings of the sixth international workshop on computing education research* (pp. 107–114). Association for Computing Machinery. https://doi.org/10.1145/1839594.1839613

Freudenberger H. J. (1974). Staff burn-out. *Journal of Social Issues, 30*(1), 159–165. https://doi.org/10.1111/j.1540-4560.1974.tb00706.x

Madigan, D. J., & Kim, L. E. (2021). Towards an understanding of teacher attrition: A meta-analysis of burnout, job satisfaction, and teachers' intentions to quit. *Teaching and Teacher Education, 105*, Article 103425. https://doi.org/10.1016/j.tate.2021.103425

Mukundan, J., Zarifi, A., & Kalajahi, S. A. R. (2016). Developing reading materials for ESL learners. In M. Azarnoosh, M. Zeraatpishe, A. Faravani, & H. R. Kargozari (Eds.), *Issues in materials development*, pp. 65–73. Sense. https://doi.org/10.1007/978-94-6300-432-9_6

National Center for Education Statistics (2021, March 17). Outside jobs among U.S. public school teachers. National Center for Education Statistics. Retrieved June 15, 2023, from https://nces.ed.gov/pubs2021/2021007/

Sammephet, B., & Wanphet, P. (2013). Pre-service teachers' anxiety and anxiety management during the first encounter with students in EFL classrooms. *Journal of Education and Practice, 4*(2), 78–87.

Shakespeare, W. (2012). *Hamlet.* (B. A. Mowat & P. Werstine, Eds.). Folger Shakespeare Library. https://www.folger.edu/explore/shakespeares-works/hamlet/read/1/3/#line-1.3.84 (Original work published 1623)

CHAPTER 16

Additional Resources for Professionalization and Teaching

Contextualization

Teacher socialization, involving teacher participation in professional communities like language teacher associations (LTAs) and informal support networks, plays an important role in teachers' professional lives. It is through their engagement in professional communities that future and novice teachers partake in professional development activities and receive mentorship from more experienced professionals. With the advent of the web and social media, professional development opportunities are no longer limited to LTAs. This chapter describes several leading LTAs in the field of teaching English to speakers of other languages (TESOL) and discusses the value of joining one while concurrently enrolled in a teacher preparation program. Additionally, the chapter highlights the significance of mentoring and proposes a variety of strategies that future and novice teachers can employ to find and collaborate with a mentor in the TESOL field. The chapter concludes with a description of a variety of organizations and informal teacher support networks available on the web that offer free-of-charge professional development activities and classroom resources.

Case Study: How Do I Keep Growing and Learning as a TESOL Professional?

When I moved to California, I had just graduated from my MA in teaching English to speakers of other languages (TESOL). I knew that the TESOL International Association had a strong state affiliate, California TESOL (CATESOL); therefore, I decided to attend the annual CATESOL conference and become a CATESOL member. The association changed my life! It became my professional home, a home where I found mentors that gave me opportunities to grow as a professional, learn from others, and, at the same time, help other professionals grow!

—Teacher 1

It is hard for me to attend and participate in LTAs. I prefer to go on the web and seek professional development opportunities in a setting that is less bureaucratic than an LTA.

—Teacher 2

These two stories summarize two different realities that can be commonly observed in the TESOL field. While LTAs have traditionally played a critical role in teachers' professional development, the growth of the web and social media sites currently provides future and novice teachers with a variety of opportunities for continuous professional development. In this chapter, we describe leading LTAs and identify informal support networks that future and novice teachers can draw on to learn from others, network, and advance professionally (see Appendix 16.1 at the end of this chapter for a list of the organizations and websites cited).

Common Concerns

The questions below are designed to guide our discussion on the leading LTAs and informal support networks that are available to teachers in the English language teaching (ELT) field. Rather than being exhaustive, the discussion below is meant to guide novice and future teachers as they make decisions about their potential membership in LTAs and informal networks.

- *Q1. What are some of the leading LTAs in the ELT field? When and why should future teachers join an LTA or find a professional community in which to participate?*
- *Q2. What role should mentoring play in the professional development of future and novice teachers?*
- *Q3. What are some of the web and social media sources that provide English language teachers with opportunities for professional development at no charge?*

Effective Practices for Professionalization

- *Q1. What are some of the leading LTAs in the ELT field? When and why should future teachers join an LTA or find a professional community in which to participate?*

As we explained above, teacher socialization involves the process of becoming a participant in a professional community. For future teachers, this process starts when they are enrolled in their teacher preparation programs as they interact with their peers, professors, and field experience mentor teachers (Ashcraft, 2018). In addition, it is not uncommon for future teachers to be encouraged to participate in LTAs since these provide their members with the structures, tools, and opportunities for professional development and personal advancement (Kormpas & Coombe, 2023; Selvi et al., 2018).

There are numerous LTAs in the field of ELT. Therefore, as future and novice teachers begin to consider membership in LTAs, they need to understand the various foci of the leading professional associations in the ELT field to decide which one will benefit them the most. The two largest LTAs are Teachers of English to Speakers of Other Languages (TESOL) International Association (commonly known as TESOL or TESOL International) and the International Association of Teachers of English as a Foreign Language (known as IATEFL). Both associations have an international focus and offer a variety of benefits that include but are not limited to access to online publications, virtual seminars, lower registration fees to annual international conventions than nonmembers, participation in advocacy activities, and more (Kamhi-Stein, 2016; Paran, 2016).

Both TESOL and IATEFL have a large network of affiliates (TESOL) or associates (IATEFL). These are independent regional, state/provincial, or country-wide associations that provide professional support to English language professionals in their localities; therefore, they are sensitive to the professional development needs of local members. In many ways, local associations mirror the offerings of their international counterparts, though they do so at a smaller level since their reach is more locally focused than that of their international counterparts. However, we should note that the extent to which affiliates and associates function greatly depends on their local leadership; therefore, there may be some associations that work effectively, while others may face challenges and struggle to achieve their goals.

Another LTA is the National Association for Bilingual Education (NABE), a US-based organization that is popular among future and novice teachers working in bilingual and dual immersion programs in K-12 settings

(National Association for Bilingual Education, 2020). Much like TESOL, NABE has state and regional affiliates and, more recently, has expanded its presence internationally. Unlike the associations mentioned earlier that primarily focus on teachers and teaching, the International Association of Applied Linguistics (AILA) has a different emphasis. This organization targets applied linguistics, an interdisciplinary field that addresses various language and communication issues. Like the other associations described in this section, AILA has a variety of national affiliates ranging from those in Australia to the United States (American Association for Applied Linguistics, AAAL).

In our capacity as teacher educators, we are often asked the following question: When and why should I become a member of an LTA? Although there is nothing wrong with teachers joining a professional association once they graduate from their teacher preparation programs, we usually encourage our students to join a professional association *while* they are enrolled in their programs. From a practical standpoint, membership in an LTA helps future teachers build their resumes. Since membership dues for future teachers are lower than other membership fee categories, the return on investment can potentially be significant. In fact, in the highly competitive job environment in which teachers currently function, it is not uncommon for program administrators to favor hiring novice teachers who demonstrate some initial commitment to professional involvement (Van Houten et al., 2022).

Becoming a member of an LTA is the first step down the path of professional development. In addition to that, volunteering in an LTA is a good way to become involved *beyond* being a simple member. One of the benefits of volunteering is the opportunity to network with more established professionals outside the classroom setting. Volunteering opportunities can range from working at an annual conference for a couple of hours to serving on an LTA's board of directors (BoD). In fact, several state and regional TESOL affiliates have BoD slots specifically designated for future teachers. In doing this, the LTAs give voice to the needs and interests of future teachers and, at the same time, contribute to the development of the associations' future leaders (Ashcraft, 2018).

Future and novice teachers may question the value of volunteering at a time in their lives when they have to juggle balancing their work and personal lives. However, there are real-life examples that point to the fact that volunteering in a limited role such as serving on a conference committee alone can lead to an invitation to apply for admission to a doctoral program or interview for a teaching position. This was the case of a student of ours who, after striking up a conversation with a program administrator during a conference committee meeting, was invited to interview for a teaching position. A couple of weeks after the interview, our student was teaching ESL to adult immigrant students. While future and novice teachers should not expect a "direct return" from volunteering within an LTA, it is important to be prepared for the professional advancement opportunities that may arise from volunteering. Specifically, when attending professional events, future and novice teachers should be prepared with electronic or hard copies of their resumes since they need to be ready to seize any potential opportunities to apply for a position or be recruited by a school or program.

When novice professionals assess the potential of various LTAs, it's important to think strategically about the promotion of volunteering opportunities, as these not only offer significant pathways for their professional growth but also provide critical contributions to the LTAs themselves. In general, state and regional organizations welcome volunteers because they bring innovative ideas that help the associations remain current and relevant to their whole member population. It is often the case that new members, who are just being initiated into the profession are eager to implement fresh ideas when they see there is a need to fill a gap in their association. Doing this kind of work benefits both the association *and* the volunteer members. An example in point is the case of a group of MA in TESOL students who established a new interest group (IG) in the CATESOL Association (CATESOL's LGBTQ+ IG) (D. Collings Ralph, personal communication, February 21, 2022). The CATESOL members who established the IG made a significant contribution to their LTA. In addition, as they continue to be involved in the IG, they obtain valuable hands-on leadership development experience and gain a sense of professional identity and worth.

We should note that while LTAs are always seeking members who can contribute to the association, future and novice teachers may find it more accessible to engage with their local affiliates or associates than with their international counterparts. Local affiliates tend to be more flexible and less bureaucratic than their international counterparts; therefore, future and novice teachers may gain more benefits from their participation in their local affiliates than in their international LTAs.

The final point that future teachers should consider as they evaluate LTAs is whether their conferences provide presentation slots to students enrolled in teacher preparation programs. Even though presenting at a conference as a student enrolled in a teacher preparation program can seem daunting, most future teachers have the opportunity to receive guidance from their professors. It is often the case that professors guide students through the conference proposal submission process, teaching them to: 1) review sample presentation proposals available on the conference website; 2) assess the conference organizers' expectations reflected in the proposal evaluation rubric (also available on the conference site); 3) write and revise their conference proposal; and if accepted, 4) prepare their presentation. In our role as teacher educators, we encourage our students to take advantage of the support they can obtain from us, their professors, so that the burden experienced as a first-time presenter can be shared and reduced.

In summary, while it is never too late to join an LTA, becoming an LTA member early in one's professional path has some advantages. However, in deciding which LTA to join, consideration should be given to a variety of factors, including the potential LTA members' budgetary concerns, as well as their level of comfort functioning in different association types (larger versus smaller, local versus national or international). Other important points to consider are the networking, leadership, and professional development opportunities provided by LTAs to new members. At the same time, potential LTA members should consider the degree of involvement they expect to have in the association. Thinking strategically about all these factors before joining an LTA will prevent future and novice teachers from selecting an association that does not meet their professional or personal expectations.

• Q2. What role should mentoring play in the professional development of future and novice teachers?

Mentoring support is critical as teachers go through their professional lives in many ways. It provides future and novice teachers with opportunities for professional development, contributes to higher teacher satisfaction, and supports and guides future and novice teachers as they become initiated into the teaching profession (England, 2020). As future and novice teachers become initiated into the TESOL profession, they should investigate the mentoring opportunities provided by professional associations and informal support networks. In addition, rather than looking at mentoring as a one-directional endeavor—with the mentor imparting knowledge and the mentee gaining knowledge—mentoring should be seen as a "dyadic—two-way—relationship" (Kamhi-Stein & de Oliveira, 2008, p. 40). In this relationship, both the mentee *and* the mentor benefit from the relationship since they collaboratively create learning opportunities for each other.

Mentoring can take one of two forms: formal or informal. Formal mentoring includes those opportunities provided within an LTA's organizational structure. Although these mentoring opportunities are designed to promote benefits to the mentee, ultimately they are meant to strengthen the future leadership of the professional association. This is the case of the TESOL Association's "Leadership Mentoring Program" (LMP), which pairs selected LMP recipients (with preference given to TESOL members from underrepresented groups) with TESOL leaders who mentor the LMP recipients for a year. While the LMP is valuable in that it provides benefits to the mentee, it is also problematic since the mentor and mentee may not know each other prior to the LMP. Sometimes, this approach to pairing results in a lack of mentor–mentee compatibility. Therefore, we suggest that those considering applying for participation in the LMP or another mentoring program offered by professional associations 1) identify a mentor in advance of their application, and 2) collaborate with the potential mentor on the application.

In contrast to formal mentoring, in which the mentor–mentee relationship is established by the LTA, informal mentoring refers to a mentoring relationship that develops and evolves naturally and, at the same time, can occur within or outside an LTA. While seasoned professionals can make excellent mentors, future and novice teachers need to look beyond just professional credentials when selecting a mentor. The success of the mentoring relationship also hinges on a certain degree of personal and professional rapport between the mentor and the mentee (Kamhi-Stein & de Oliveira, 2008).

Finding a mentor with whom one would like to work takes initiative on the part of the potential mentee. Table 16.1 identifies a list of strategies future and novice teachers can implement to identify a potential mentor.

We should note that, as future teachers look for a mentor they should have realistic expectations about the mentoring experience. The mentoring relationship will evolve with time; therefore, the mentor and mentee should start their relationship by working on small, focused projects. As the relationship grows, so will the scale of collaborative projects (Kamhi-Stein & de Oliveira, 2008).

In addition, as we explained in this section, we propose a dyadic approach to mentoring. As future or novice teachers contact potential mentors, they need to think about ways in which they can support or contribute to their mentors' scholarship as much as they expect to be supported by their mentors. Because of the power differential between mentors and mentees, the latter may initially feel nervous about proposing a research or teaching idea. However, experienced professionals often welcome the idea of working with novice teachers because of their fresh perspectives and enthusiasm.

To conclude, whether it is formal or informal mentoring, future and novice teachers should seek the opportunity to work with experienced professionals. Ultimately, this work will contribute to the development of all involved in the mentoring relationship.

Additional Resources for Professionalization and Teaching 305

Table 16.1. Strategies Designed to Identify a Mentor

Strategies designed to identify a mentor
1. Do some initial research on potential mentors and find some commonalities with them, either professional (areas of interest; work setting, etc.) or personal (cultural and linguistic background, etc.).
2. Attend a presentation given by a potential mentor and try to strike up a conversation during or after the session with them; OR
3. Email a potential mentor and introduce yourself and your work to them (avoid contacting more than one individual at a time). Explain why you are seeking that person's mentorship. Make sure your conversation (in 2) or email reflects your knowledge of your potential mentor's work.
4. If you get a positive response, try to schedule a meeting (F2F or virtual) to help you establish some rapport with your potential mentor. At that meeting, describe your future career goals and help your mentor understand how they can help you reach that goal. In turn, explain how your mentor can benefit from the relationship. Remember that for a mentoring relationship to work, both the mentor and the mentee need to obtain benefits.
5. Make sure that:
a. all email communication follows accepted protocols (include a subject heading, check your grammar and punctuation, and communicate positively and professionally);
b. you feel comfortable communicating with your potential mentor; and
c. you do not feel discouraged if the potential mentor declines your invitation.

- *Q3. What are some of the web and social media sources that provide English language teachers with opportunities for professional development at no charge?*

Even as LTAs continue to play an important role in the professional advancement of future and novice teachers, the rise of social media has significantly broadened access to a multitude of resources for professional growth, all available at no cost. In this section, we identify four established organizations that provide teachers with classroom resources and professional development opportunities free of charge.

The first two organizations that are worth highlighting are the British Council—the United Kingdom's international organization for cultural relations and educational opportunities—and the United States Department of State, which provides resources for teaching and learning about US English and culture. The British Council Teaching English website (https://www.teachingenglish.org.uk) is a comprehensive site that offers resources for teacher and teacher educator professional development; teaching resources for different grade levels; recorded webinars and conference sessions; and information on free-of-charge training courses. The second organization, the United States Department of State, offers a website (https://americanengl ish.state.gov), which provides access to a variety of social media resources, including Facebook pages for English language learners (ELLs) and educators. The website also offers access to an American English YouTube channel, which features teacher webinars, teaching methodology videos, and short animated videos for ELLs. In addition, the website provides access to an extensive array of materials teachers can use in their classes. The website also provides information for US educators who may be interested in participating in programs sponsored by the US State Department (for example, Fulbright English Teaching Assistant Program, among others). The final focus of the website is *English Teaching Forum*, a free-to-download quarterly journal for English language teachers around the world. This is an excellent journal whose articles are authored by English language teachers who work in diverse settings. The articles in the journal are not only practical but also based on current research and thinking. Taken together, both the British Council and the United States Department of State offer a wealth of resources that teachers can access at no cost. Given the fact that ELT professionals' salaries around the world are low, access to the high-quality free-of-charge resources provided by the two organizations is a welcome opportunity for teacher professional development and growth.

In addition to the mentioned resources, the web offers access to two other US-based organizations. These organizations are highly respected and provide numerous opportunities for teacher learning and professional development. One of these is the Center for Applied Linguistics (CAL, https:// www.cal.org), a leading nonprofit organization that is the source for language research, resources, and policy analysis. Novice teachers will benefit from CAL's Commentary page (https://www.cal.org/resource-center/cal-commentary), which provides readers with current thinking on a variety of topics (fairness in assessment, culture, and language in the age of diversity, for example). In addition to these, CAL offers interesting free-of-charge webinars that teachers can access live or through the videos available on the CAL website.

The second nonprofit association that provides opportunities for professional development is the International Research Foundation for English Language Education (TIRF) (https://www.tirfonline.org). Of interest to novice and future teachers is the organization's generous funding for a variety of competitive awards, including dissertation and masters thesis awards. Moreover, the TIRF website provides access to comprehensive reference lists covering a wide range of topics that are relevant to the ELT field. The depth

Additional Resources for Professionalization and Teaching   307

and breadth of TIRF's reference lists make them a must-visit resource for any TESOL or applied linguistics professional interested in conducting initial research on a topic of interest to them.

Table 16.2 presents a summary of the information provided in the previous paragraphs.

In addition to the organizations described in this section, social media offers many informal networks that provide teacher support and a community of peers. A popular network available on Facebook is "Teacher

Table 16.2. Web and Social Media Professional Development Sources

	Web and social media sources for professional development			
	British Council Teaching English https://www.teachingenglish.org.uk/	*United States Department of State American English* https://americanenglish.state.gov/	*Center for Applied Linguistics* https://www.cal.org/	*The International Research Foundation for English Language Education* https://www.tirfonline.org/
Content	• Resources for teacher & teacher educator professional development • Publications, including resource books & research reports • Teaching resources for different grade levels • Recorded webinars • Information on free-of-charge training courses	• A YouTube channel with teacher webinars, teaching methodology videos, & short animated videos for ELLs • Instructional materials focusing on the four skills, comics, US culture, music, & games • Free-to-download *English Teaching Forum* journal For US educators: • Information on the Fulbright English Teaching Assistant Program & the English Language Specialist Program	• CAL's Commentaries on a variety of topics of interest • Information on free-of-charge webinars that can be accessed live or through CAL's website	• Information on funding for competitive awards for MA theses, doctoral dissertations • Comprehensive lists of references

Voices: Professional Development," administered and maintained by Dr. Willy Renandya, a professor at the National Institute of Education, Nanyang Technological University. The target audience of this group is teachers, graduate students, textbook writers, curriculum specialists, and researchers in ELT around the world. This network provides information on free webinars and conferences and gives access to discussion forums where teachers engage in conversations relevant to their work. The network also provides access to a wealth of downloadable, well-researched, and informative instructional materials on skill areas (reading, writing, grammar), curriculum development, technology use, and more.

Another resource, designed to provide future and novice teachers with a myriad of practical instructional ideas, is Larry Ferlazzo (@Larryferlazzo on X, formerly Twitter), a highly respected high school ESL teacher. Ferlazzo publishes a valuable blog (https://larryferlazzo.edublogs.org) that features a wealth of classroom resources. His blog includes a dedicated section titled "Around the Web in ESL/EFL/ELL," focusing specifically on all issues related to ELLs. Teachers visiting Ferlazzo's blog need to be ready to spend quite some time there since it provides a wealth of practical information that is anchored in TESOL, applied linguistics, and educational research.

Finally, we should note that the popularity of instant messaging tools like WhatsApp or video communication platforms like Zoom, for example, has facilitated the exchange of ideas among ELT professionals working across the world. In fact, it is not uncommon for novice or experienced teachers working on different continents to establish study groups that meet on Zoom with a specific objective in mind (for example, analyze how artificial intelligence can be used in their classes, or read and discuss an article that is relevant to the teachers' lives). These meetings promote both teacher professional growth and a sense of teacher autonomy since their focus is driven by the teachers' interests and self-perceived professional needs.

In short, the ELT field offers future and novice teachers a variety of resources that can contribute to their professional development. These resources, which range from traditional LTAs to free-of-charge nonprofit associations, social media sites, and study groups, will provide future and novice teachers with some initial ideas about the various sources of professional development. While all the resources described in this section are excellent examples of highly reputable and reliable resources that reflect current thinking in the ELT field, it will be up to individual future and novice teachers to decide which ones match their professional interests and budgets.

Big Picture and Bottom Line

As we explained in this chapter, the role that teacher socialization, understood as teacher participation in professional communities and informal support networks, can't be underestimated. It is through socialization that teachers become stronger professionals, develop their leadership skills, are mentored by more experienced peers, and, eventually, mentor novice professionals. Because teaching can be a lonely profession, teachers must find a professional community that can provide them with the professional and social support necessary to thrive in the ELT field.

Food for Thought

1. After reviewing the information in this chapter, interview two teachers who currently participate in professional associations to understand:
   a. the perceived professional benefits from participating in the associations;
   b. the perceived social benefits of participating in the associations;
   c. any perceived drawbacks from participating in the associations.
2. Drawing on the information in this chapter, search online for two potential associations, one international or national and the other one at the regional, provincial, or state level. Make a list of the potential benefits and drawbacks arising from participating in both. Then, decide which association meets your current professional needs and budget.
3. Consider finding and working with a mentor. To this end, develop a strategic plan designed to identify a teaching or research idea on which you would like to work. Then reflect on who would be a potential mentor with whom you would feel comfortable working. Write an email introducing yourself and describing your ideas. Before pushing the Send key, share your email with a colleague and get feedback. Are you ready to send your email?

References

Ashcraft, N. (2018). Engaging future professionals: How language teacher associations facilitate the involvement of student members. In A. Elsheikh, C. Coombe, & O. Effiong (Eds.), *The role of language teacher associations in professional development* (pp. 53–68). Springer. https://doi.org/10.1007/978-3-030-00967-0_5

England, L. (2020). *TESOL career path development: Creating professional success.* Routledge.

Kamhi-Stein, L. D. (2016). The non-native English speaker teachers in TESOL movement. *ELT Journal, 70*(2), 180–189. https://doi.org/10.1093/elt/ccv076

Kamhi-Stein, L. D., & de Oliveira, L. C. (2008). Mentoring as a pathway to leadership: A focus on nonnative English-speaking professionals. In C. Coombe, M. L. McCloskey, L. Stephenson, & N. J. Anderson (Eds.), *Leadership in English language teaching and learning* (pp. 38–49). University of Michigan Press.

Kormpas, G., & Coombe, C. (2023). English language teacher education and development through language teacher associations: Opportunities and challenges. In L. England, L. D. Kamhi-Stein, & G. Kormpas (Eds.), *English language teacher education in changing times: Perspectives, strategies, and new ways of teaching and learning* (pp. 66–76). Routledge. https://doi.org/10.4324/9781003295723-8

National Association for Bilingual Education. (2020). *About NABE.* https://nabe.org/about-nabe/

Paran, A. (2016). Language teacher associations: Key themes and future directions. *ELT Journal, 70*(2), 127–136. https://doi.org/10.1093/elt/ccw012

Selvi, A. F., de Oliveira, L. C., & Kamhi-Stein, L. D. (2018). Leadership, mentoring and transformation in language teacher associations: A tripartite dialogue. In A. Elsheikh, C. Coombe, & O. Effiong (Eds.), *The role of language teacher associations in professional development* (pp. 215–228). Springer. https://doi.org/10.1007/978-3-030-00967-0_16

Van Houten, K., Ernst, M., Issagholian, N., Lee, E., & Kamhi-Stein, L. D. (2022, September 30–October 1). The changing face of ESL instruction in California [Conference session]. 2022 California TESOL Conference, Pasadena, CA, United States.

Appendix 16.1

Professional Associations, Websites, and Social Media Sites

- California TESOL (CATESOL) https://www.catesol.org
- Center for Applied Linguistics (CAL) https://www.cal.org
- International Association of Teachers of English as a Foreign Language (IATEFL) https://www.iatefl.org
- Larry Ferlazzo's Twitter (now X) handle @Larryferlazzo
- Larry Ferlazzo's blog https://larryferlazzo.edublogs.org
- National Association for Bilingual Education (NABE) https://nabe.org
- "Teacher Voices: Professional Development" Facebook group https://www.facebook.com/groups/teachervoices
- Teachers of English to Speakers of Other Languages International Association https://www.tesol.org

- The British Council Teaching English website https://www.teachingenglish.org.uk
- The United States Department of State American English website https://americanenglish.state.gov
- The International Research Foundation for English Language Education (TIRF) https://www.tirfonline.org
- The International Research Foundation for English Language Education (TIRF) reference lists https://www.tirfonline.org/reference-lists

Epilogue: End as Beginning

Dear readers,

The book is in your hands now. Our journey is complete. When we set out to write this volume, our goal was to produce a book that would be informed not only by the literature in the TESOL field but also by the experiences of the hundreds of ESL/EFL learners and teachers we have worked with over the years. We are convinced that the value of our book lies in its balance between the sound pedagogical principles and practices described in its chapters and the real-life classroom stories and examples that come from novice and experienced teachers.

As we explained in this volume, the transition from teacher-in-preparation programs to the real classroom is complex. As you go through this transition, or as you are assigned to read the volume in your teacher preparation program, we hope you become inspired by the many ideas presented in the chapters. More than anything, we hope that the volume will help you explore the value of experimenting with and reflecting on the pedagogical practices described in the book.

We thank you for joining us on our journey. Now it is time to write your own story.

Lía D. Kamhi-Stein, California State University, Los Angeles
Bahiyyih Hardacre, California State University, Los Angeles
Jeremy Kelley, University of California, Los Angeles

Index

Abeywickrama, P., 144
Access to technology, 219–20
Ahangari, S., 181
Al-Maamari, F., 78
Al-Mahrooqi, R., 78
Al-Seghayer, K., 78
Al-Siyabi, J., 78
Alber, R., 92
Alignment of objectives and
    expectations, 109
Allaw, E., 88
Alrabai, F., 180
Álvarez, J. A., 88
American Educational Research
    Association, 132
American Psychological Association, 132
Anderson, T., 257
Annual conferences, 268, 301
Apigo, M., 254
Arasaratnam-Smith, L. A., 257
Archer, W., 257
Artificial intelligence (AI):
    Google's Bard, 230; Microsoft Bing's
    AI chatbot, 230; Open
    AI's ChatGPT, 216, 228–32,
    234; prompt engineering, 228–30, 234.
    See also emerging digital
    tools
Ashcraft, N., 300, 301
Asher, J. J., 258
Assessment design, 130

Assessment planning, 130, 144–45;
    frequency, 145; location, 145; purpose,
    144–45; task type, 145; timing, 144–45
Atkinson, D., 189
Authentic language, 210, 218
Authenticity in assessment, 130–31, 134
Awareness of current literature, 279, 312
Aziz, A. B. A., 251

Baecher, L., 107
Bahous, R., 286
Bahrami, M., 138
Bailenson, J. N., 253–54
Ball, S. J., 32
Baralt, M., 88
Baumert, J., 270
Bax, S., 192
Behling, K. T., 257
Bell, J., 221
Bennett, C., 95
Bérešová, J., 57, 135
Beyer, B., 270
Beyond-the-classroom evaluations, 127
Bitchener, J., 165
Bohlander, R. W., 30
Boland, J. E., 254
Bonk, C. J., 254
Bonner, E., 232
Borg, S., 60
Boruah, P. B., 54–55
Bouckaert, M., 59

Boulton, A., 191
Bowen, N. E. J. A., 55
Bowles, A. R., 189
Brake, A., 14–17
Braun, A., 32
Braun, S., 191
Breton, G., 57, 135
Bright, A., 135
Brindley, G., 153
Brinthaupt, T. M., 245
Brinton, D. M., 164
British Council, 305–7
Brown, H. D., 131–32, 144, 254
Brown, K., 218
Brown, N., 292
Brown, S. D., 292
Bruner, J. S., 245
Burt, M., 164
Byrd, P., 52
Byrnes, H., 189

Callies, M., 192
Career centers, 269, 274
CAST, 243, 259
Castro, T. B., 110
Caufield, J., 238
Celce-Murcia, M., 164
Center for Applied Linguistics, 306–7
Chaluvarayaswamy, R., 47
Chambers, A., 192
Chandler, J., 172
Chang, J. S., 189
Chang, J.-Y., 192
Chanie, B. S., 289
Chen, H., 75
Chen, M.-H., 189
Chen, X., 111
Cheung, A., 254–55, 257
Chomsky, N., 152
Christison, M. A., 19
Cirocki, A., 107
Clarifying expectations, 289
Classroom, 8–17; action zone, 9;
    agreement, 12–13, 17; atmosphere, 8,
    17; cohesiveness, 10–12; community,
    10, 24; desk location, 9; floor plan,

9; layout, 9; participation, 12–14,
    18; physical and emotional distance,
    9–10; positive classroom climate, 11;
    rules, 12
Classroom documents, 34, 36; course
    calendar, 34, 145, 276; syllabus, 34–43
Classroom participation, 103–4; group
    work, 104–6, 108, 111; pair work,
    104–6, 110–11, 117; solo work, 111;
    student identity, 112–14; student
    investment, 114–18; student
    engagement, 104–8, 113, 117–18;
    student motivation, 103–10, 116, 119
Classroom participation management,
    12–4, 104–11; clear instructions,
    106–7; clear syllabus and policy,
    106–7; comprehension checks, 106;
    cultural expectations, 108, 111–15;
    designing activities to match
    students' learning styles, 109–10;
    engaging all students, 109–10, 116–18;
    mindful teacher positioning, 107–8;
    monitoring, 107–8; use of technology
    and tools, 107–8; varied student
    interactions, 106–8, 116–18
Classroom Policy, 29–30, 33, 36, 38;
    class specific learning outcomes, 30,
    32, 40, 48, 50, 74, 108, 148, 244, 270;
    cold calling, 40; teacher agency, 32,
    37, 76, 289; teacher flexibility, 41, 46,
    76, 295–96; teaching philosophy, 40,
    50–52; unofficial policies, 40
Closing of a lesson, 83, 85, 90–91;
    exit ticket, 91, 128, 137; formative
    assessment, 90–91, 128, 136–39, 174;
    homework assignment, 90
Cobb, T., 191
Collective investment, 118
Collins, P., 226
Collocations, 189, 205–7, 211
Common employers, 269–70;
    community colleges, 267–71, 281,
    286; intensive English programs
    (IEPs), 236, 269, 271; primary and
    secondary schools, 271, 286; tutoring,
    270, 273

Common lesson problems, 94; backup activities, 94–95; overly complex activities, 94; planning too much, 94; student questions, 95; technology problems, 95

Common European Framework of Reference for Languages (CEFR), 12, 17, 48, 57–58, 60–62, 94–95, 98, 135, 139–40, 224, 230, 236, 281

Community of Inquiry Framework, 257; cognitive presence, 257; social presence, 257; teaching presence, 257

Competency, 166–69

Concordance, 196

Conventions, 205, 231; register, 112, 175, 189, 205, 211; style, 205; writing, 205

Cook, C. R., 10

Cook, L. S., 108

Coombe, C., 300

Corpora, 51, 61, 189–97; American National Corpus (ANC), 195; Bank of English (BoE), 194; British Academic Written English Corpus (BAWE), 195–96; British National Corpus (BNC), 194, 196; Collins Birmingham University International Language Database (COBUILD), 193–94; Corpus of American Soap Operas (SOAP), 194; Corpus of Contemporary American English (COCA), 193, 196, 198; Corpus of English Wikipedia, 193; Corpus of Historical American English (COHA), 194; Global Web-based English (GloWbE), 193; Google Ngram Viewer, 194, 196; Intelligent Web Corpus (iWeb), 196–97, 199, 205, 211; Michigan Corpus of Academic Spoken English (MICASE), 195–96; Michigan Corpus of Upper-Level Student Papers (MICUSP), 195–96; Movie Corpus, 194; News on the Web Corpus (OEC), 193; Santa Barbara Corpus of Spoken American English (SBCSAE), 195, 196; TED Corpus Search Engine (TCSE), 195;

The Strathy Corpus of Canadian English, 194, 196; Time Magazine Corpus (TIME), 194; TV Corpus, 194

Corpus adoption, 192, 204

Corpus in materials creation, 204; assessment materials, 204; authentic classroom materials, 204, 207; classroom activities, 204; textbook materials, 204

Corpus in the classroom, 208

Corpus interface, 197–203

Corpus linguistics, 189, 192; English text corpora, 204, 206–7; text corpus, 189–92, 197, 204, 210–11

Corpus size, 193

Costa, R. D., 110

Council of Europe, 12, 48

Course types, 238, 252; blended, 238, 252; online, 238, 252

Cover letter, 275–76

Craig, C., 272

Crandall, J., 280

Crookes, G., 86

Crossley, S., 191

Csomay, E., 205

Cui, Y., 59

Cummins, J., 218

Curriculum, 47; academic content, 47, 51; assessments, 47, 51, 52, 57, 59; pedagogical guidelines, 47, 52, 59; student learning outcomes, 50–51

Curriculum Vitae, 267–68, 274–76, 281–82

Da Silva, J. P., 284

Daikos, C., 10

Daley, S., 254

Dallimore, E. J., 40

Dang, T. N. Y., 205

Danielewicz, J., 149

Darby, D., 247

Darby, F., 257

Davidson, J., 59

De Costa, P. I.

de Oliveira, L. C., 135, 303–4

Deng, Z., 31–33

Denman, C., 78
Dewaele, J. M., 111
Diagnostic tests, 57, 129, 152
Digital teaching portfolio, 267, 276
Digital tools, 215; access, 219–22, 228, 232; applications, 232; as an "add-on", 218, 220, 223; computer software, 216; databases, 216; evaluation, 220–23; evaluation form, 222; implementing digital tools, 216; integration, 215–24; learner needs, 216–23; meaningful purposes, 217–19; principles, 217–21; roles in the language classroom, 217–20; social media, 216
Digital tools for lesson/activity content planning and delivery, 225–26; iCivics, 217, 224–25; JeopardyLabs, 224, 226; Kathy Schrock's Guide to Everything, 226; Nearpod Silver, 219, 225–26; TED-Ed, 224–25; TED Talks, 224–25; The Moth Podcast, 224–25; YouGlish for English, 226
Digital tools for meaningful communication, 227; Anchor, 227; Blog, 227; Flip, 221, 223, 227–28, 238–39; ScreenPal, 226–28
Digital tools for project-based learning: Adobe Express, 227; Canva, 59, 217, 227, 231
Direct marking, 176
Diversity statement, 276
Doran, M., 189
Dörnyei, Z., 9–12, 102, 105
Doughty, C., 181
Doyle, W., 29
Duff, P., 189

Eaton, M., 252, 254
Education technology tools and Apps: Canva, 59, 217, 227, 231; ClassDojo, 59; Google Docs, 59, 239, 255, 259; Google Slides, 53, 59, 239, 291; Kahoot, 59, 87, 128; Keynote, 53, 71, 291; Padlet, 59, 239–40, 255; Pinterest, 59; PowerPoint, 10, 53, 71, 98, 219–20, 241, 260, 278, 291; Prezi, 53, 59; Schoology, 59, 238

Effort, 165–69
El Helou, M., 286
Elbow, P., 149
Ellis, N. C., 189
Ellis, R., 147
Emerging digital tools, 215–16, 224, 228, 232; artificial intelligence (AI), 216, 228, 230–31; augmented reality (AR), 216, 231; computational thinking, 216, 232–33; Scratch, 232; virtual reality (VR), 216, 231–32
Engagement, 10, 41, 49, 80, 82, 87, 103–8, 113, 117–18, 174, 179, 218, 243, 247, 251, 253–58, 291, 298
England, L., 271, 303
English Language Teaching (ELT), 13, 85, 133, 189, 192, 217, 251, 270, 299
Equity, 254, 257, 260
Ernst, M., 301
Erten, I. H., 272
Evaluating digital tools, 220; external evaluation, 221; internal evaluation, 221
Excessive feedback, 164–65, 170, 175, 290; feedback fatigue, 290; overcorrecting, 180
Experiences, 273–74, 276, 281, 286, 291, 296, 312
Extending, 78

Face-to-face (F2F), 175, 222, 237, 238, 241, 243, 245–47, 250–60; classroom, 238, 245–46, 250–52, 256, 258, 260; instruction, 252
Fairness, 40, 55
Farrell, T. S. C., 85
Feedback style, 171–76; face-to-face conferences, 175; variation, 180; peer-review, 176, 181
Feedback translation, 178–79; grading schemes, 179; programmatic alignment, 179
Feldon, D. F., 90
Ferlazzo, L. D., 221
Ferris, D. R., 147, 176
Fiat, A., 10
Field, J., 89

Fifield, N., 228
Fincher, S., 292
First day of class, 8; class rules and expectations, 12; get to know you activities (ice breakers), 11, 18; student gender pronouns, 18; student names, 18; student profiles, 18–19
Fischer, F. M., 284
Fisher, L., 245
Fleming, N. D., 110
Flowerdew, L., 189
Floyd, A., 273
Fonseca, P., 254
Formative assessment, 136–38; exit tickets, 91, 128, 137; teacher's feedback, 137; teacher's questions, 137; peer-assessments, 137; self-assessments, 137
Formative feedback, 58, 129, 136, 144–45
Foster, P., 181
Fostering motivation and participation, 102–19
Frank, T., 149
Frank, V. M., 189
Fraser, D. W., 79
Free digital tools, 50, 53, 59, 72, 221–24, 226–28, 231–32, 239–43, 255
Frequency, 206–7, 209
Freudenberger H. J., 284
Freynik, S., 189
Fry, P. G., 108

Gan, Z., 137
Ganske, K., 90
Gao, Y., 59
Garcia, L., 232
García, O., 13
Gardner, H., 19–20, 115
Gardner, J., 245
Garrison, D. R., 257
Gay, G., 15–16
Genre, 85, 192–95, 204–5, 211
Genre analysis, 205
Gilabert, R., 88
Gilquin, G., 204
Global errors, 164, 169
Goh, C. C. M., 89

Goldsmith, J., 88
Gollin, J., 68
Golonka, E. M., 189
Google classroom, 239, 242–43
Gornitzka, Å., 30
Grabe, C., 218
Grabe, M., 218
Grabe, W., 89–90
Grade review and negotiation, 149–51; grade inflation, 150; instructor feedback, 149
Grades versus feedback, 173; process-oriented, 174; product-oriented, 174
Grading expectations, 148; contract grading, 148–49; models and samples, 146, 148, 151–53; outcomes, 148–49, 153; performance standards, 149–53; processes, 149; product, 149; results, 149
Grant, R., 54
Graves, K., 217
Gray, J., 54
Greenier, V., 273
Güvendir, E., 112, 128, 136, 147

Hall, J. K., 189
Hammer, A. L., 100
Hammerly, H., 68
Han, Z., 149
Hansen-Thomas, H., 135
Hard skills, 271
Hardacre, B., 112, 128, 136, 147, 192, 279
Harmer, J., 84–85, 92
Harris, S., 15
Haworth, P., 272
Hertenstein, J. H., 40
Hewagodage, V., 136
Highfill, L., 228
Hilton, K., 228
Holistic feedback, 176, 178
Holland, E. A., 10
Hooks, S. D., 79
Hopper, D., 55
Horwitz, E. K., 112
Huang, J., 37
Huang, L.-S., 196

Huang, S.-T., 189
Hubbard, P., 135, 192
Hunter, R., 85
Hyland, F., 150
HyperDoc(s), 228–29

In-the-moment feedback, 170–71, 176, 180–81
International Association of Teachers of English as a Foreign Language (IATEFL), 300
Individual feedback sessions, 170; cultural biases, 172; teacher-student investment, 171
Informal support networks, 298–99, 303, 309
Inoue, A. B., 149
Instant messaging teacher groups, 308
International standards, 135–36
Internet access, 190, 208
Institutional Policy, 28–31; accreditation standards, 30–32; discipline, 30–32; plagiarism, 28, 30–35; workload, 30
Investment, 104–8, 112–18
Issagholian, N., 231–32, 301

Jacob, S., 216, 232–33
Jacob, S. R., 232–33
Job boards, 269
Job interviews, 268, 276–77
Job preferred qualifications, 271, 275
Job required qualifications, 271, 275, 278–79, 281
Johnson, E. J., 34
Johnson, K. E., 79, 189
Johnston, B., 270

Kalajahi, S. A. R., 290
Kalir, J. H., 36
Kamhi-Stein, L. D., 205, 238, 300–1, 303
Kang, E., 149
Kanno, Y., 2
Kennedy, K. D., 19
Kilgarriff, A., 196
Kim, L. E., 286
Kim, Y-G., 257

King, J., 13
Kiparsky, C., 164
Klusmann, U., 270
Knoch, U., 165
Koehler, M. J., 218
Koh, J., 257
Kohnke, L., 253–54, 257
Kolb, D. A., 110
Kölling, M., 292
Konopak, B., 108
Kormpas, G., 300
Kou, X., 254
Krishnan, J., 226
Kunnan, A. J., 133
Kunter, M., 270

Lamb, C., 13
Lambert, C., 72
Landis, S., 228
Lang, J. M., 247
Language characteristics, 196; English language varieties, 193, 196, 226; spoken language, 172, 194–96; written language, 196
Language lesson, 83–94; closing, 83, 85, 90–91; dimensions, 83–86; goals and objectives, 30, 35–40, 45–51, 56–60, 65–67, 75–76, 83–86, 91–94, 98–99, 108–9, 126–27, 131, 133, 136, 142, 180, 207, 217, 228, 244; opening, 76, 83–91, 96; pacing, 83, 92–97; pre-reading, while-reading, post-reading, 88–89; sequencing, 83–88, 96
Language standards, 30–40, 56–57, 67, 69, 76, 125–27, 135–37, 148–49, 160, 169, 269–71, 281
Language teacher associations (LTAs), 298–309
Lantolf, J. P., 189
Larsen–Freeman, D., 189
Larson, M., 10
Lau, A. M. S., 174
Le Foll, E., 192
Learner motivation, 103–6, 108–10
Learner needs, 217, 220–21

Learning agreements, 12, 13

Learning management systems (LMS), 33, 39, 53, 108, 216, 236–53, 255, 259; Canvas, 53, 59, 238–39, 242–43, 247; Blackboard, 53, 237–39, 242–43; Moodle, 53, 238–39, 243; Schoology, 59, 238; WebCT, 237

Learning responsibility, 104, 118

Learning style, 20, 109–11, 116, 164, 294; auditory learning, 110–11; kinesthetic learning, 110–11; visual learning, 110–11

Lee, E., 301

Lee, H., 205

Lee, J. H., 205

Lent, R. W., 273

Lesson plan fit, 75; cohesion, 89–91; double-dipping, 75; expansion opportunities, 49

Lesson plan models, 84–85; engage, study, activate (ESA), 84–85; guided to independent, 84–85, 88, 245; Hunter model, 85; present, practice, produce (PPP), 84–85, 99–101

Lesson planning, 66–81; checklists, 20; deductive lessons, 68–69; digital narratives, 217, 291; inductive lessons, 68–69; outcome-defined, 67; presentation software, 71, 291; reverse engineering, 72–73; schedule-defined, 67

Lesson planning adjustments, 77–79; reframing, 78; pivoting, 78, 80; replacing, 78; referencing, 78; omitting, 78; extending, 78

Leung, C., 137

Lexicon, 205

Li, L., 218

Li, M., 115, 146

Li, S., 149

Li, Y., 253–54, 257

Limitations of videoconferencing, 251, 253; cognitive load, 253–54, 256; interpersonal distance, 253; participant mobility, 253; self-evaluation, 253

Liou, H.-C., 189

Little, D., 181

Littlewood, W., 181

Liu, N.-F., 181

LMS course design, 243–49; asynchronous and synchronous discussions, 241, 247; backwards design, 243–44; conditional release, 245, 247; instructor and student presence for cognitive and social engagement, 243, 247; scaffolding, 243, 245, 247; sequencing, 245; transparency, 243, 245–47; weekly modules, 244–45

Local errors, 164, 169

Lockhart, C., 9, 14

Lynch, T., 75

Maamuujav, U., 226, 279

Maclean, J., 75

Madigan, D. J., 286

Madyarov, I., 107

Maftoon, P., 115

Maguire, M., 32

Mahshanian, A., 138

Maor, D., 254

Martin, F., 252

Martínez Marín, J. D., 127

Martínez-Alba, G., 12

Master, P., 78

Masuhara, H., 220–21

Material recycling, 75, 290

Material repositories, 71, 237, 241, 292

McCaulley, M. H., 110

McConney, A., 254

McCreary, J., 181

McDonough, J., 88, 220–21

McGriff, S. J., 174

McLaughlin, C., 10

McMartin-Miller, C., 182

McNamara, D., 191

Mejía Vélez, M. C., 127

Membership in professional organizations, 273, 299–301

Mentoring support, 303; formal, 303–5; informal, 303–5

Mermelstein, I., 254

Messick, S., 132
Micro-adjustments, 77
Miller, S. F., 280
Mills, C., 110
Mishaps, 294
Mishra, P., 218
Models of online instruction, 252–53; blended, 238, 241, 243, 247, 252; blended/hybrid, 241, 247, 252; hybrid, 31–31, 241, 247, 252; hyflex, 252; massive open online course (MOOC), 252
Molla, R., 253
Momentum, 91–95; activity timing, 92; activity variety, 89, 92; adequate preparation, 93; clear instructions, 92–93; effective presentation, 93; grouping variation, 92
Montoya, J., 232–33
Moodie, I., 273
Moore, C., 108
Moorhouse, B. L., 253–54, 257
Morphological features, 206
Moses, T., 254
Moskowitz, G., 11–12, 20
Motivation, 104–6
Mukundan, J., 290
Multiple Intelligences, 19, 115; bodily-kinesthetic, 22, 115; existential, 20, 23, 115; interpersonal, 20, 23, 115; intrapersonal, 20, 23, 115; logical -mathematical, 22, 115; musical, 20–22, 115; naturalistic, 20, 23, 115; verbal-linguistic, 22, 115; spatial-visual, 22, 115
MVS Audio Visual, 253
Myers, I. B., 110

Nabhani, M., 286
Nagro, S. A., 79
Nation, P., 60, 206
National Association for Bilingual Education, 301
National Council on Measurement in Education, 132
National policy, 135–36
Negueruela, E., 189

New teacher anxiety, 293–94, 296
Nguyen, H., 216, 232–33
Nguyen, T., 257–58
Noah, J. B., 271
Noijons, J., 57, 135
Non accredited programs, 56
Northcote, M., 257
Norton, B., 189
Nunan, D., 13

O'Donnell, M. B., 189
Odd jobs, 273–74
Office of Teaching and Learning, University of Guelph, 255
Ollerhead, S., 37
Online classrooms, 252; asynchronous, 252, 257; flipped class, 252; synchronous, 252, 257
Online presence, 276–77
Opening of a lesson, 86–88, 91; agenda, 86, 90, 99; background knowledge, 87; homework review, 76; lesson objectives, 85–86; review, 86, 90; warmup, 86, 90
Operating without set curriculum, 48–51; CEFR alignment, 57–58; diagnostic tests, 57; student placement, 57; teacher collaboration, 56; textbooks as curriculum, 56–57
Ortega, L., 189

Pacing of a lesson, 83, 92–94
Paige, D. D., 146
Pallotti, G., 180
Paran, A., 300
Participation, 104, 106–9; cultural differences, 15; translanguaging, 13, 26, 246; wait time, 13, 26, 117–18, 256
Pawan, F., 254
Peer initiated feedback, 181
Peirce, B. N., 14, 114
Pentón Herrera, L. J., 12
Pérez-Paredes, P., 192
Performance, 146–49, 152
Phonological features, 206
Phraseology, 189, 205–6, 211

Pica, T., 181
Pivoting, 75, 78, 80
Placement tests, 129, 134
Plagiarism, 28, 30–33, 148, 152–53, 157, 231
Platt, M. B., 40
Plonsky, L., 271
Poehner, M. E., 146
Policy interpretation, 33–34, 36–38
Policy levels, 29–33; classroom policy, 33;
    hierarchy of policy, 29; institutional
    policy, 31; national policy, 30–31;
    personal policy, 40–41; programmatic
    policy, 30–32
Polly, D., 252
Poole, D., 110
Practicality in assessment, 130–32, 134;
    materials, 132, 134; grading, 132, 134;
    timing, 132, 134
Prades, A., 205
Presentations at professional
    conferences, 302–5
Professional communities for support, 293
Professional conferences, 59, 136, 268,
    273, 277, 280, 293, 302
Professional development opportunities,
    280, 298–301, 303, 305–7
Professional organizations, 273, 277, 280
Professional qualifications, 271;
    CELTA, 272; certificates, 270–72;
    degrees, 270–72, 281; endorsements,
    271; licensure, 271; practicum
    courses, 272–73
Programmatic policy, 30–31; curriculum,
    30–21; learning outcomes,
    30–31; prerequisite courses, 30–31;
    standards, 30–31
Prompt engineering, 228–30, 234
Puentedura, R. R., 218–19
Punitive feedback, 174
Purgason, K. B., 67, 85, 90, 94, 245
Purpose of assessment, 135, 138

Quenk, N. L., 100

Raffo, D., 245
Rao, H. K. L., 47
Rao, K. S., 47

Rasekh, A. E., 2
Referencing, 78
Reframing, 78
Rehn, N., 254
Reinders, H., 232
Reinholz, D. L., 257, 260
Reliability in assessment, 131, 134;
    environmental conditions, 131;
    interrater reliability, 131; intrarater
    reliability, 131; test reliability, 131
Renshaw, T., 10
Replacing, 78
Resume, 267, 274–76, 281, 301–2
Reynolds, B. L., 60
Richard-Amato, P. A., 11–12
Richards, J. C., 9, 12, 85–88,
    90–92, 217
Richardson, D., 189, 216, 232–33
Richardson, P. W., 270
Rimm-Kaufman, S., 14
Rimmer, W., 273
Ritzhaupt, A., 252
Robinson, P., 88
Römer, U., 189
Ross, G., 245
Rubrics, 146–48; analytic, 147;
    assignment tailoring, 147; complexity,
    148; descriptors, 147; holistic, 147;
    trait focused, 147
Rulon, K. A., 181

Sadeghi, K., 78
Safe spaces, 112
Sammephet, B., 293
SAMR framework, 218; augmentation,
    218–19; enhancement, 219; formation,
    219; modification, 219; redefinition,
    219; substitution, 218–19
Sandilos, L., 14
Sarem, S. N., 115
Sayers, D., 218
Saying no, 289
Sazdovska, J., 272
Scharff, L. F. V., 149
Schuemann, C., 52
Schumann, J., 189
Schussler, E., 257, 260

Selecting an LMS, 236, 241–42; needs analysis, 241; student interactions, 242; equitability, 242–43; cost of use, 239, 243

Self-care, 293, 296

Selvi, A. F., 300

Sequencing of a lesson, 83, 85, 87–88, 96; coherence, 89–91; guided to independent, 84–85, 88; instructional stages, 84–85, 88–89; transitions, 89, 90

Setting boundaries, 284, 286, 288–90

Shaffer, C., 68

Shah, N., 257, 260

Shakespeare, W., 289

Shaping forces, 27, 30–33

Shaw, C., 220–21

Shieh, J., 60

Shindler, J., 14–15, 91–92

Shishavan, H. B., 78

Shoghi, R., 138

Shugurova, O., 36

Shulman, L. S., 24

Sianez, L. M., 257, 260

Siepmann, P., 138

Siwi, M. K., 121

Slemrod, T., 10

Smagorinsky, P., 108

SMC Academic Senate Distance Education Committee, 255

Smith, G. S., 146

Smith, L., 13

Snow, M. A., 164, 192

Social climate, 7–8, 13

Social constructs, 113–14; age, 113, 204, 225, 242, 269; cultural group, 15, 54, 113, 278; ethnic group, 15–16, 54, 113, 278; faith, 114; familial relationships, 114; gender, 113–14; sex, 113–14; sexuality, 113; socioeconomic status, 114

Social media, 108, 216, 276–78, 281, 299, 305–7, 310

Soft skills, 271

Sokolik, M., 252, 257

Soproni, Z., 272

Souza, G. F., 110

Spoken (oral) feedback, 175–76, 179–81, 184; accuracy, 180; comprehensibility, 183; fluency, 180

Standardized language proficiency tests, 127

Steinman, L., 89

Stevens, P., 292

Stoller, F. L., 89–90

Stone-Johnstone, A., 257, 260

Strategies to promote engagement, 254–60; chat box participation, 255, 259; chunking lessons, 254; closing activities, 256; encouragement for camera sharing, 255, 258; engagement in diverse activities, 255, 259; student physical engagement, 256, 258; warmups, 256, 259; wider view of presenter on camera, 258

Stuart, C., 2

Student anxiety, 109, 112; debilitative anxiety, 112; facilitative anxiety, 112; microaggressions, 112; second language anxiety, 109

Student engagement, 104–8, 113

Student grouping, 109–10; learning styles, 110–11; personality types, 109–10; Myers-Brigg model, 110; personality characteristics, 104, 109–10, 113

Student progression, 127–28; grade point average (GPA), 128; holistic grades, 35, 128, 147, 157, 168, 176, 178, 180; letter grades, 128, 148; numerical grades, 128; pass/non-pass, 128

Student-teacher trust, 8, 14–17; accepting student feedback, 16; constructive and supportive spaces, 11; contract of inclusion and acceptance, 15; favoritism, 14; teacher empathy, 17

Students as individuals, 20, 40, 118, 184; teacher-student investment, 8, 10, 14, 17; cultural biases, 15, 54, 113, 278

Summative assessment, 136–38l; capstone projects, 138; performance assessment, 138; portfolios, 138; quizzes, 138; tests, 138

Swain, M., 189
Swales, J. M., 85
Syofyan, R., 110
Szabó, G., 57, 135

Takimoto, M., 68
Tarone, E., 189
Tavakoli, M., 2
Teacher material selection, 50–55;
    desk copy textbooks, 59; materials
    development, 59; open access materials,
    59; positive cost return, 49, 51, 55, 59;
    teacher reflection and decisions, 52
Teacher socialization, 298, 300, 309
Teaching assistantships, 268, 273, 306, 307
Teaching philosophy, 29, 40, 42, 50–52,
    153, 267, 276, 281
Technology resources in materials
    selection, 53; projectors, 53; online tools,
    59; learning management systems,
    53, 59; Open Access materials, 59;
    copyright and crediting authors, 54, 59
Technology tool access, 53
TESOL International Association, 136,
    271, 273–74, 280, 298–99, 30
Test bias, 131–33; cultural bias, 131–32;
    teacher bias, 133
Test design, 130, 135
Test equity, 132–33
Test fairness, 130, 132–34
Textbook selection, 50–55; constraints
    in selection and adoption, 50–51;
    cost, 53; cultural awareness, 54;
    curriculum deviation, 52; electronic
    versus print texts, 53; instructor
    comfort, 49; student needs, 54;
    supplementation, 49, 53
Thank-you notes, 279
Thayer, A. J., 10
The International Research Foundation
    for English Language Education
    (TIRF), 306–7, 311
Thornbury, S., 54
Tindell, D. R., 30
Tobin, T. J., 257
Tofel-Grehl, C., 216, 232–33

Total Physical Response (TPR), 22, 258
Transparency in Learning and Teaching
    (TILT), 246
Trautwein, U., 270
Trial and error, 66, 72, 80, 88, 290, 295
Turner, M., 136
Tyler, A. E., 189

Universal Design for Learning (UDL),
    242, 259–60
U.S. Copyright Office, 54
U.S. Department of State, 305–7
Ushioda, E., 102
Utting, I., 292

Valentim, R. A. M., 110
Validity, 130–31, 134; consequential
    validity, 132; content validity, 131
Van Houten, K., 301
Varied proficiency, 111–12, 117; mixed
    level classes, 117; placement, 117
Videoconferencing, 238–39, 250–54, 256,
    260; Google Meet, 239, 253; Microsoft
    Teams, 238, 253; Skype, 238, 253;
    Webex, 238, 253; Zoom, 238–39,
    250–56, 258, 260–62
Virtual classroom(s), 252; asynchronous,
    252, 257; synchronous, 252–59;
    tours, 258
Vogel, S., 13
Volunteering, 268, 273, 279, 301
Vuogan, A., 149
Vyatkina, N., 191

Walsh, S., 253–54, 257
Wanphet, P., 293
Warren, M., 205
Warschauer, M., 205, 216, 232–33
Washback, 130, 132, 134; negative
    washback, 132; positive washback,
    132; promotion and inhibition of
    learning, 132
Wasley, P., 34
Waterfall technique, 255–56
Watt, H. M. G., 270
Webb, S., 206

Wergin, J. F., 30
Westbury, I., 29
White, I., 257, 260
Wiles, J., 47
Williamson, M., 254
Willingness to Communicate (WTC),
    109, 111–12
Windle, J., 136
Winkelmes, M.-A., 246
Wong, S. D., 54
Wood, D., 245
Work-life balance, 284, 287
Written feedback, 172

Yang, J., 75
Yeganehpour, P., 11
Yip, J. W. C., 37
Yu, C., 181
Yu, L., 146

Zarifi, A., 290
Zeegers, Y., 59
Zhang, T., 111
Zimmerman, C. B., 75
Zonoubi, R., 2
Zoom fatigue, 254